Steffen Hantke

Conspiracy and Paranoia in Contemporary American Fiction

The Works of Don DeLillo and Joseph McElroy

PETER LANG
Europäischer Verlag der Wissenschaften

Die Deutsche Bibliothek - CIP-Einheitsaufnahme

Hantke, Steffen:

Conspiracy and paranoia in contemporary American fiction :
the works of Don DeLillo and Joseph McElroy / Steffen
Hantke. - Frankfurt am Main ; Berlin ; Bern ; New York ; Paris ;
Wien : Lang, 1994
    (European university studies : Series 14, Anglo-Saxon
    Language and Literature ; Vol. 280)
    Zugl.: Marburg, Univ., Diss., 1993
    ISBN 3-631-47641-8

NE: Europäische Hochschulschriften / 14

D 4
ISSN 0721-3387
ISBN 3-631-47641-8
© Peter Lang GmbH
Europäischer Verlag der Wissenschaften
Frankfurt am Main 1994
All rights reserved.

Printed in Germany 1 2 3 4   6 7

Acknowledgements

I would like to express my gratitude to the Studienstiftung des Deutschen Volkes for supporting the writing of this thesis.
For their encouragement, advice, and support, I would like to thank Volker Bischoff, Eric Rabkin, Charles Caramello, Mark Koch, Mike Sell, Rafael Ezekiel, Katrin Lambertz, Mary Lacey, Samuel Delaney, Neil Isaacs, Robert Levine, Carla Peterson, Joyce Kornblatt, Lora Wildenthal, and the members of the Fantasy & Science Fiction/Theory Reading Group at the English Department of the University of Michigan, Ann Arbor. And for being patient and generous in many ways that truly count, my family and my wife.

With special thanks to Joseph McElroy.

For my father.

Conspiracy and Paranoia in Contemporary American Fiction
The Works of Don DeLillo and Joseph McElroy

European University Studies

Europäische Hochschulschriften
Publications Universitaires Européennes

Series XIV
Anglo-Saxon Language and Literature

Reihe XIV   Série XIV
Angelsächsische Sprache und Literatur
Langue et littérature anglo-saxonnes

Vol./Bd. 280

PETER LANG

Frankfurt am Main · Berlin · Bern · New York · Paris · Wien

Contents

I. Introduction

II. The Works of Don DeLillo and Joseph McElroy

I. Introduction
1. *Toward a Morphology of Conspiracy Fiction*

Culture needs to stage spectacles in which it recreates its own practices and conventions, to enter into dialogue with itself, interrogate itself, and understand itself better. These spectacles are reflections of conscious and unconscious knowledge; their size and relative accessibility make this knowledge visible and tangible. Cultural anthropologists like Clifford Geertz have elaborated on the fact that these spectacles are necessary because they resolve conflicts within the culture, at least on the level of their conceptual intricacies, without recourse to open aggression. Addressing the sophisticated and mystifying network of metaphoric correspondences surrounding the cockfight in Bali, Geertz remarks that,

> like any art form . . . the cockfight renders ordinary, everyday experience comprehensible by presenting it in terms of acts and objects which have had their practical consequences removed and been reduced (or, if you prefer, raised) to the level of sheer appearances.[1]

In this sense, a spectacle like the cockfight, which remains morally reprehensible or culturally mystifying for most outsiders to Balinese society, fulfills a function that Western society has largely focused upon all those elements within culture that are clearly identified as representations. Geertz himself, however, who is mostly concerned with cultures other than his own, is hardly aware of the possibilities of his approach. Elsewhere, he asserts that

> the whole point of a semiotic approach to culture is, as I have said, to aid us in gaining access to the conceptual world in which our subjects live so that we can, in some extended sense of the term, converse with them.[2]

Conversation with one's own culture, to adopt Geertz's imagery for a moment, is a clean-cut metaphor for the process of creating and understand spectacles of this kind. As long as there is a dialogic format that includes anthropologists as representatives of their culture and, opposite them, the "subjects" of the study or investigation, which betray themselves through their customs and practices, Geertz's metaphor is sufficient. To adopt this image for anthropologists studying their own culture, creating a situation in which they are both object and subject, adds a dimension that Geertz's safe distance through the dichotomy between inside and outside has successfully avoided. Would this mean that scholars are talking to themselves--an unhealthy habit if there ever was one, clearly associated with the early stages of creeping schizophrenia?

That self-analysis is not suspicious has been demonstrated by cultural critics like Roland Barthes, who, in his *Mythologies*, has taken on the "spectacles" within his own culture. "The starting point of these reflections," Barthes explains in the introduction to his work,

> was usually a feeling of impatience at the sight of the 'naturalness' with which newspapers, art and common sense constantly dress up a reality which, even though it is the one we live in, is undoubtedly determined by history.[3]

From Geertz to Barthes, the leap from one ideological position to another becomes most conspicuous when Barthes goes on to declare that his goal was to "track down" the "ideological abuse" that was commonly concealed behind the consensus about what is generally considered natural and what isn't. While the anthropologist is concerned with the mediation of data through research parameters, which would necessarily include prejudice, intuitive thought, unconscious responses, etc. the cultural critic like Barthes, who is equally aware of the existence of these influences, is concerned not so much with screening them out, but with integrating them into the data he has already collected and the observations he has already made. Judgement is as imminent as it is inevitable for one, while the other takes great caution to come across as objective or sufficiently self-conscious about the limits of his methods and approaches. Most of all, however, Barthes differs from Geertz in his assumption that culture conceals, mystifies, and "dresses up" what must remain invisible.

It is this element of deceit that creates the dramatic subtext and makes self-analysis into the "spectacle of excess" that makes Barthes' argument so compelling.[4] Unlike the anthropologist who reports back from somewhere else, the cultural critic acts as a detective in our midst, uncovering the secrets we have been keeping mostly from ourselves and confronting us with unpleasant truths; most likely, these truths are unpleasant since Barthes uses the term "ideological abuse" with the intention of unmasking (and perhaps unmaking) an element of manipulation for the specific culture his investigation has targeted. The everyday use of the term "myth," which Barthes decides to apply to the individual semiological element in the language of truth projected by "newspapers, art and common sense," has itself come to imply a falsehood or falsification. It does not refer to a language, the same way as the term "mythology" does, which articulates truth in a register different from the literal, heuristic truth of everyday language. Like any good detective, from Philip Marlowe to Oedipa Maas, Barthes' detective must uncover as many myths about himself as about the object of the investigation; after all, he himself is partly that object as well. Disillusionment or demystification are therefore always close at hand.

The curious lack of distance also means that Barthes' kind of investigation is less "safe" than that of Geertz, who is much less likely to have to face potentially unpleasant truths about himself. Yet, the leap from Geertz's image of dialogue to Barthes' image of detection becomes curiously significant if we choose to combine both critics' arguments for a moment and see how they interact as mutually illuminating theories. In this context, we would have to regard Barthes' metaphor of detection--apart from its even more insidious effect of criminalizing cultural production--as an act of mystification in itself. Since all metaphor is necessarily tied to the cultural sphere in which it is produced and validated, detection itself must become ideologically suspect; an image, a metaphor, to cover up the tautological truth about bringing about something we have already accomplished; about the process of entering "the conceptual world in which our subjects live;" this time, however, not as natives, but as tourists who are still not sufficiently naturalized to overlook the obvious.

Most likely, to return to Geertz, Barthes' detection metaphor covers up the rivalling image of dialogue. How can something enter into dialogue with itself if dialogue necessarily implies two participants, opposites, complementary forces conversing? Is it conceivable that Barthes covers up the dialogue image because it takes on pathological, insane connotations as soon as it is being applied to a distinct entity conversing with itself? Only if the entity is internally diversified, i.e. sufficiently heterogeneous, can it enter into dialogue with itself because then, properly speaking, the essential precondition of opposing or complementary agents is being fulfilled. This is why Barthes' detective is so morally outraged about the "ideological abuse" he must witness, again a curious reminder of hardboiled detectives; he is superior to all those whom he will educate about their true condition, a loner, a force of late retribution.

His enemy, "newspapers, art and common sense," is not an individual or a force emanating from a distinct origin. Corresponding to Geertz's account of the production of culture, false consciousness does not emanate any more; it permeates, and effectively so. In fact, it is so disseminated and untenable that the only arena in which it can be properly pinpointed and described is the "spectacle" of the cultural representation where it is at its most curtailed, precisely defined, and rigidly structured by consistent rules and regulations. Barthes' detective would be ill advised to think that this is where he will get his man; Barthes himself probably doesn't think so either. But he knows that he can take on the enemy here, where it makes itself vulnerable to appear so physically; where it has taken on bodily form, where word has become flesh. As a representation of the detective, he can interact with the representation of who he is after. As interacting representations, both have had "their practical consequences removed and been reduced (or, if you prefer, raised) to the level of sheer appearances," to quote Geertz again.

Obviously, it must be significant that Barthes is the one who is talking about the culture he himself is living in, while Geertz is addressing foreign cultures. Between the two, it is also Barthes who dramatizes the encounter with one's own culture in terms of the detective story, complete with its conventional agents--one of them individual, the other ominously collective. Whether this happens to conceal the dialogue metaphor, which works so well for any encounter with a foreign culture and takes on the unpleasant and undesired connotations of pathological disturbance, or whether one critic eschews the metaphor that is essential for the other because of personal, generational, cultural, or political preferences, remains largely a matter of speculation. Also, what is at stake here could very well be the problematic addition Geertz makes; how much does a virtual conflict between virtual agents count if both of the agents have had "their practical consequences removed?" Will the reso-lution of a conflict have fewer or less grave consequences for the investigator, given that investigator and investigated are technically identical? However, what remains an undeni-able fact of both critics' arguments is the correlation between the object of investigation and the conceptual organization of the approach. This suggests that, for asking questions about one's own culture, one must pay the prize of being either ostracized by others (rather than integrated into an ongoing dialogue) or deliberately isolate oneself from them.

Considering that the investigation of one's own culture is such a dangerous enter-prise, fraught with risk and sacrifice, Barthes' argument is quite revealing about the status of cultural criticism and its metaphorical apparatus. Unlike Geertz, who must have had similar metaphors available for describing his activities as an anthropologist, Barthes' dis-cussion of cultural analysis turns into an apotheosis of self-empowerment. It is a narrative about making the internal workings of the culture visible to its indigenous subjects, about revealing a manipulated and prefabricated version of the truth as the simulacrum that it is, and about reinstating the world to a degree of greater clarity and understanding. Through all of these previous acts, power is redistributed among the members of society in order to es-tablish the proper dialogue that Geertz was referring to. In establishing this oscillating movement between defamiliarization and familiarization, Barthes decides on a trope that could hardly be more indicative of the culture it derives from: that of conspiracy and para-noia.

The curious combination of anxiety and insight, which Barthes' figurative language shares with the complex of themes surrounding conspiracy and paranoia, is indicative of both the qualities of Barthes' very own analysis and of the metaphorical language he uses to this end. Barthes' language and its subtext mark the intersection of epistemology with politics, of the social with the psychological. It is characterized, unlike Geertz' dialogic metaphor, by a confrontational element, even to the degree of a much harsher enmity than simple structural opposition. And it manages to endow the cultural anthropologist's act with an element of danger and risk, which testifies, even in the purely metaphorical and therefore not "really" effective arena of representations, of the grave consequences that his/her actions can, and should, have. Conspiracy, moreover, marks the spot where Western cultural analysis becomes self-conscious. This is not a sign of cultural analysis in general, of all critical thinking about one's own culture. It characterizes a conceptual operation performed under specific circumstances, with specific goals, and by specific agents.

Barthes' analysis gives an insight into how deeply the conspiratorial metaphor is rooted in Western society's political unconscious. To investigate and analyze such deeply rooted narratives in order to expose the homogeneity underneath the heterogeneity--in critical discourse as I have done here or in artistic production as I am about to do--opens up the cultural production at a point where it appears most seamless and most inconspicuous. As Barthes has argued, it is what is being passed off as "natural" that is most revealing when challenged as to its historical and cultural origins, when questioned as to 'how it is made.'

Conspiracy and paranoia have been quite successful in establishing a place for themselves in Western culture which makes them appear as part of human nature or the human condition. It takes some effort to restore them to the status of a convenient fiction or an ideological construct and view them within their constitutive contexts. Critics from different disciplines have, in fact, argued that conspiracy and paranoia constitute fundamental narratives that go much deeper than the specific cultures in which they can be found and that are determined by them to to one extent or another. Sociologist Dieter Groh, for example, makes the case that conspiracy theory transcends a wide variety of ideological borderlines. According to Groh,

> it is obvious to anyone with even a superficial knowledge of the historical multiplicity of conspiracy theories, to just what extent they spread universally through time, social structures of some duration, and through classes.[5]

This wide distribution, according to Groh, can be observed not only across lines separating high cultures from so-called primitive cultures. It also permeates both elite and folk culture within more highly differentiated and hierarchic cultures. Just as it penetrates the barriers between progressive and conservative politics, it encompasses foreign and domestic policies in one grand reconciling gesture. The only major transition it has undergone itself takes place during the Enlightenment when its emphasis shifts "from metaphysical to worldly conspiracy theories."[6] Otherwise, the conspiracy theme has proven stable, yet malleable. It has remained identical with itself while showing virtually endless flexibility under new circumstances and adaptability to different demands. If we are willing to ignore for the moment the disturbing ethnocentric implications of such an interpretation, conspiracy theory's ubiquity could very well be seen as an indication that it answers to some human need which exceeds the limitations of any one culture; that it constitutes one of a number of basic narratives, a kind of ideologeme, embedded deeply within the human psyche. This interpretation, however, calls for two crucial amendments. On the one hand, the case of Barthes and Geertz seems to suggest that the persistent recurrence of the conspiracy theme is dependent on a particular subject--in this case the anthropologists' gaze inward at their own culture--which provides a meaningful context for conspiracy to function in. This context could hardly be any *less* universal or transcultural, considering that Barthes' exemplary anthropologist is not the 19th century male, imperialist, positivist explorer, but clearly a self-conscious and ideologically self-aware late-twentieth century academic. William Bywater has noted that it is this latter type of scholar, whose methods of scientific inquiry and notions of erudition are grounded in epistemological practices we commonly refer to as "postmodern," who is most prone to develop theories displaying alarming affinities to conspiratorial themes and narratives.[7] The anthropologist whom Geertz has in mind is still the one reporting back; the expert who attempts to establish a dialogue with the foreigner who constitutes the object of his studies. For Geertz, object and subject of scientific inquiry are separate, just as the goals and methods to that effect are still largely unproblematic. Since postmodernism is a phenomenon of some historical, social, political, and economic specificity, and since this specificity applies exactly to one of the two cultural critics discussed and not the other, the idea of conspiracy as a transcultural, ahistorical human fundamental becomes difficult, if not impossible to uphold.

On the other hand, historians like Richard Hofstadter have argued convincingly that, for whatever reasons, it is primarily American culture in which conspiracy theories have flourished unlike anywhere else.[8] Despite the fact that Barthes, as a Frenchman, is talking about his own culture, the similarities between French and American culture (at roughly the same point in history and in terms of economics, politics, and culture) are sufficiently obvious to allow reading both writers as if they elaborate upon the same point. Hofstadter's narrowing down of conspiracy's universality is even more significant in this context because, like Barthes, Hofstadter is one of those critics who look at their own rather than a foreign culture. Although it must remain arguable if this coincidence does indeed suggest that cultural self-examination is conducive to conspiratorial imagery, Hofstadter's argument is more useful than Barthes' because it combines an aspect of pragmatic universality with the idea of cultural specificity. While it remains impossible to argue convincingly that conspiracy is a fundamental human concept, it would not only be conceivable to argue that it is a local phenomenon that successfully passes itself off as a fundamental one, but also that this self-aggrandizing gesture itself carries enough significance to give access to a deeper understanding of the cultures which allow it to conceal itself in this manner.

Having laid the theoretical groundwork for the following remarks about conspiracy as an epistemological and ideological narrative, it is now possible to outline and discuss briefly the morphology and genealogy of conspiracy fiction in order to position the writings of two authors in a context that has been narrowed down in a number of successive steps: from Geertz (cultural critique) to Barthes (critical self-examination), to Bywater (postmodernism), to Hofstadter (the "American scene"). Following this series of specifications, I will attempt to narrow the focus of the discussion down even further. Analyzing a series of novels by two significant American writers, Don DeLillo and Joseph McElroy, the argument will return repeatedly to these consecutively larger contexts. It will view the results with regards to the contrast between specific and abstract observations. In order to do this, however, it is necessary to discuss what constitutes and characterizes conspiracy fiction, and then to question the genre as to its historical roots and its most crucial historical transformations; in other words, to write the story of conspiracy fiction up to the arrival of Don DeLillo and Joseph McElroy upon the scene.

As one of the two constitutive agents of conspiracy fiction, the detective functions as the figure of individuality. He is not defined by his profession but by the fact that he is the one to investigate, to analyze, to construct comprehensive theses, and to expose the conspiracy responsible for what he has witnessed. This agency has often been taken literally so that the detective appears as a professional in the line of law enforcement; the private eye in hard-boiled detective fiction or the inspector in the classic detective story. In other cases, he works as a reporter, a scientist, or in any other profession that concerns itself with problems of knowledge and knowing.

Individuality may be a somewhat problematic mark to carry for the detective, considering that many cases of conspiracy fiction involve a group of detectives, such as the team of experts in Phil Alden Robinson's film *Sneakers* or the ragtag assemblies of outcasts that populate William Gibson's *Neuromancer* or *Count Zero*. In the same context, one is also reminded of detective figures who are accompanied by a sidekick, such as the Holmes/Watson pairing of detectives in Michael Crichton's recent *Rising Sun*. The convention of interpolating a companion between the inscrutable mastermind and the reader also appears to undercut the individuality of the agency opposite the conspiracy. At first glance, these cases seem to contradict the notion that the detective invariably represents individuality within the tightly structured dichotomy between individual and collective. Is it convincing that conspiracy generally tends to represents collectivity if numerous stories that are synonymous with conspiracy fiction present the detective's antagonist as one single in-dividual, who has managed to gather others around him, but always maintains a firm posi-tion of superiority over them, such as, for instance, the master-mind behind the plots in Lawrence Norfolk's *Lempriére's Dictionary*?

In order to answer to both supposedly complementary inversions of the pattern, one must keep in mind that the distribution of characteristics is based on dichotomy. While, for example, *Sneakers* confronts a team of experts with several government and business con-spiracies, it is exclusively the group of "sneakers" that is characterized as hierarchically structured, its members as individualized and fully-rounded characters, and its internal workings as governed by psychological verisimilitude. The conspiracy they face, however, is anonymous, decentralized and shapeless, governed by a logic determined by the imper-sonal interests of politics and economics. As the reader is introduced to what appears at first as two collectives trying to outsmart each other, the sharp and systematic contrast be-tween every single definitive feature of each group pretty soon amounts to a clear picture about their significance. While the conspiracy stands for collectivity in its most negative connotations (anonymity, ruthlessness, impersonality, etc.), the group of "sneakers" repre-sents the opposite of its opponent; shelter, privacy, friendship, etc. In the language of stark contrasts that rules conspiracy fiction, non-conspiracy is synonymous with being fully in-dividualized. Dichotomy asserts itself as the generative principle for maintaining the oppo-sition between individual and collective.

Moreover, individuality and collectivity are qualities that can very well be repre-sented by signifiers that do not literally correspond to their signifieds. While, for example, William Gibson's teams of detectives are dependent on each others' skills for solving their tasks, the group is almost always dominated by one member whose skills make him irre-placeable, even if he is not literally the leader of the group. He tends to be the one character who is most strongly individuated, such as Case in *Neuromancer*, and whose actions and motivations become the mark of the entire group, such as Turner in *Count Zero*. Similarly, conspiracies tend to retain the crucial element of collectivity, even though they may be cen-tered around some mastermind criminal like Babo, the leader of the slave revolt in Melville's *Benito Cereno*. Whenever texts foreground qualities that are associated with collectivity, conspiracy is established as inimical to individuality. The fact that, for exam-ple, collectivity has been identified with alien infiltration at one time and with the govern-ment's vast bureaucratic apparatus at another is evidence that the associations about what constitutes collectivity are subject to historical, political, and social changes. The leap from one form of Cold-War paranoia in Jack Finney's *Invasion of the Body Snatchers* to another form in E.L. Doctorow's *The Book of Daniel* demonstrates how the negative associations of collectivity migrate from subversive to official power, from the alien invader to the State.[9] Yet, despite this crucial difference, the particularly American dichotomy of collectivity versus individuality remains in stable opposition and for the most part retains its ethical connotations.

All these cases that appear to refute the notion of a strictly sustained, symmetrical dichotomy between individuality and collectivity are simply metaphorical transformations of the two essential qualities contained within it. Addressing this "radical dualism" of conspiratorial thinking, sociologist Serge Moscovici has noted that "the conspiracy mentality does not recognize the individual, except to the extent that he is bound into the conspiracy . . . each individual is merely a different shape containing the same "substance.""[10] This predisposition toward an essentialist model of thought places conspiracy fiction and theory in one category with other forms of allegorical speech.

Besides being the representative of individuality, the detective does not necessarily enter the narrative by being professionally involved in bringing conspiracies out into the open. Being a professional investigator in one form or another may very well be a genealogical remnant from the close link between conspiracy and detective fiction. In the latter, detectives do what they do because they are privileged, by virtue of their skills or position, to complete the task at hand successfully. They are exceptional, eccentric, sometimes even superhuman, like Holmes or Poirot. In conspiracy fiction, however, it is inevitably the innocent bystander who becomes, mostly against his will or by mere accident, the agent to bring about the disclosure of the conspiracy. In John Crowley's or James Blaylock's fiction, for example, amateurs and idlers are most susceptible to notice the concealed clues trailing behind conspiracies because they are most like Baudelairian *flaneurs*. By allowing their attention to wander aimlessly, their view is least clouded by goals and ambitions. In Thomas Pynchon's work, the idea of the innocent bystander is being expanded into a more encompassing system of thought. Borrowing from Calvinist dogma, Pynchon selects his detective figures among those that are left out salvation history, overlooked, and cast aside--the Preterite. In *The Crying of Lot 49*, for example, Oedipa Maas is only a housewife who is being appointed executor of a friend's will and becomes involved in The Tristero only by small incremental doses of paranoid curiosity. As her own degree of engagement increases, the novel carefully sustains the possibility that, if the conspiracy does exists, she is being systematically ignored by it.

These complex marginal positions in the grand scheme of things, whether they lead to salvation or damnation, tie in with another significant feature of Crowley's or Pynchon's hesitant detectives. Usually, they are not the primary targets of the conspiracies they uncover. Although their lives are affected to one degree or another by conspiracies, they are hardly ever at the center of all of the secretive conspiratorial activities. As innocent by-standers, they may eventually shift closer and closer to this center because they themselves attract attention with their inquiries, but with few exceptions their position is at the periphery of the plot. To suspect themselves at the conspiracy's center is often more congenial to their psychological nature than it is to the truth.

As innocent bystanders, the protagonists of conspiracy fiction represent the legal, licit, and legitimate side of the conflict between individual and collective. They bring into focus questions of power by phrasing them in terms of the law and/or ethics. Having few or none corroborating sources to support their suspicions, they nevertheless find themselves in the position of carrying society's values against a society which has already been undermined and infiltrated by the alien plot. Unlike detective fiction, in which detective and criminal share a marginal position in the society they oppose or protect, conspiracy fiction construes a conflict that is based on the dichotomy between society as an ideal and society as a reality. While one is pure and just, the other is fundamentally compromised and co-opted, a mere shadow of its own values and possibilities. Outsiders to society and eccentrics like Chandler's Marlowe or Doyle's Sherlock Holmes reinstate society's values without being their most ardent defenders. Marlowe just wants to return to his office, which is perpetually empty of clients and from which he permits himself to be coaxed only by the occasional exceptional case. Holmes is looking for an opportunity to prove his intellectual superiority, which alienates him from the society that profits legally from his intellectual accomplishment.

In discussing the history of the evidential paradigm with which Western traditions have commonly provided a select number of professions, historian Carlo Ginzburg has suggested that what art historians, detectives, and psychoanalysts all have in common, and what links them to the reluctant detectives of conspiracy fiction, is that they are readers in the widest sense of the word. The paradigm itself, in which they all figure as central agents and which, "depending on the context," Ginzburg himself calls "venatic, divinatory, conjectural, or semiotic,"[11] describes the "ability to forecast retrospectively." The detective subscribes to, "the idea of a method of interpretation based on discarded information, on marginal data, considered in some way significant."[12] It is this unique ability to make sense of the world out of what remains hidden to most others that defines the detective in conspiracy fiction.

Opposite the detective is the conspiracy itself, most of its characteristic features already prescribed and defined by its position within the symmetrical pattern of dichotomy mentioned before. Besides representing collectivity and all its accompanying features (illegality, mystery, secrecy, etc.), conspiracy constitutes a form of organization that, on the surface, concerns itself with communication. It is concerned with any aspect of human affairs that goes beyond the limits of the individual. Readers must, however, approach conspiracy as a representation of collectivity with some degree of caution because of its inherent predisposition toward allegory. Within a code of non-mimetic speech, such as allegory, conspiracy could conceivably come to stand for any kind of agent who is individualized enough to pass itself off as a coherent, unique, and seamless figure; in other words, as an agency that signals individuality. Related to this possible source of ambiguity is the consideration that collective processes and practices have often been individualized, not so much as a rhetorical operation, but as part of a well-founded, systematic scientific approach based on the hypothesis that, fundamentally, collectives do indeed act and behave like individuals. Aptly named with a certain degree of oxymoronic vagueness, the discipline of mass psychology is an example of such a scientific theory. However, the assumption that collectives are subject to the same behavioral patterns as individuals is based on so many unchallenged presuppositions that it would require a sophisticated theoretical apparatus to support. It would also depend on a set of additional assumptions to break away from the inevitable reductionism that occurs when one discipline, i.e. psychology, is being superimposed upon a number of others, i.e. political science, sociology, historiography, and so on. As in the case of allegorical speech, most models that are worthwhile considering aim for a more dialectic relationships between the forces of interiority and exteriority, rather than remain caught in the reductionist rhetoric of binary or linear models of collective behavior. Such intelligent discussions of conspiratorial collectives and the influence they exercise as Elias Canetti's "Herrschaft und Paranoia" in *Masse und Macht*, for example, have proven that it is possible to accommodate psychoanalytical theories in the background of political and historical analysis without oversimplifying or compromising either one of the methods involved.[13] Similarly, fictional texts of great complexity, such as Oliver Stone's film *JFK*, are not only self-consciously placing themselves on the borderline between allegorical and mimetic representation, but are deriving their great emotional and ideological impact from this rhetorical ambivalence.

With these concessions to ambiguity in mind, conspiracy can be read much less problematically as a figure of collectivity. Unlike the body of social values represented by the detective, conspiracy is illicit and pragmatic. Its workings challenge or invalidate the social, political, legal, and historical order by placing a second, secret narrative alongside the story that consensus declares as the one and only truth. Instead of breaking openly with the official order, conspiracies infiltrate and subvert it by inscribing their own narratives into its text, inconspicuously defamiliarizing its essence while maintaining the cover of its familiar appearance.

In this particular sense, every conspiracy poses a dilemma for the detective in his function as the representative of society's values. If power lies in consensus and the common effort of the collective, then what distinguishes the conspiracy from the official order? Obviously, both legitimize their power through the assumption that the collective constitutes the joined knowledge and skills of its members and that it is therefore superior to the individual. Of course, there are other features that allow to make a distinction between one form of collectivity and the other, but it is this specific structural correspondence between legitimate and illegitimate, licit and illicit, that generates the two basic variants of conspiracy. In one of these variants, conspiracy is identified as the illicit, secretive collective working against official, institutionalized power. Most of the memorable examples for this case belong to the genre of the thriller, such as Richard Condon's *The Manchurian Candidate* or Finney's Invasion of the Body Snatchers, but also classic literary texts like Melville's *Benito Cereno* incorporate this model.

In the other variant, conspiracy is associated with the collectives that constitute official power itself, such as the government in Bob Woodward's and Carl Bernstein's *All the President's Men* or the labyrinthine bureaucratic apparatus in Joseph Heller's *Catch 22*. The destabilizing effect of this conflation of official power with conspiratorial activities can be felt not only in the center but also in the more peripheral manifestations of this power. By logical extension, the conspiratorial defamiliarization of official power leads to suspicions about the Orwellian fabrication and falsification of history, the truth and reliability of scientific theory, or the integrity of moral and ethical systems of belief. In such novels as Sinclair Lewis' *It Can't Happen Here*, conspiracy undermines society's master-narratives by casting doubts upon the objectivity and integrity of those in power, as well as defamiliarizing the ideological agenda they administer and the political system that has given them access to their privileged positions; an effect that recreates exactly the ambiguous position of conspiratorial collectives suspended between allegorical and mimetic rhetorical codes.

Besides splitting up into two distinct strains--"us versus them" on the one hand, and "the enemy within" on the other--the collective in conspiracy fiction is commonly staged in terms of Oedipal conflict. Although Pynchon takes the precaution of making the detective of *The Crying of Lot 49* a woman, a name like Oedipa Maas points clearly at the psychoanalytical implications of the individual's struggle for empowerment, identity, and authenticity against the collective. As a strong collective voice whose power is legitimized through consensus, the conspiracy functions as superego, transmitting society's values and providing an ultimate frame of reference for anyone whose perceptions differ significantly from those of the others. Since conspiratorial fears and paranoia are stigmatized as pathological, even if they eventually prove to be accurate and realistic, the detective stands alone

13

and must mediate between the sheer persuasiveness of his experience and the categoric laws of the community; an impossible situation which puts him inevitably at odds with either himself or those around him.

In most conspiracy fiction, however, the Oedipal struggle is being denied altogether, as the conspiracy sidetracks, diverts, and evades the detective's efforts to bring the latent antagonism to a stage of open conflict. To no avail, the detective figure in Jack Finney's *Invasion of the Body Snatchers* tries to convince others, for instance, that their community is being invaded and subverted. The invaders' avoidance of all confrontation is an all-the-more maddening strategy since threatening the detective's life openly would mean providing the corroboration of his suspicions that he craves so urgently.[14] Unlike Finney's novel, there are, of course, plenty of texts that stage the conflict between individual and collective in terms of open, mostly physical terms. Most of these texts belong to the genre of the thriller and therefore thrive on physical action, which appears as a kind of literal interpretation of the plot's internal logic. In novels such as Robert Heinlein's Cold-War fantasy *The Puppet Masters*, it is literally the detective's father who threatens to annihilate the son's individuality.

The Freudian family romance, which serves as he backdrop for conspiracy fiction's central conflict, occupies such a central role in the genre because it functions so conveniently as a pattern for formulating questions about the nature of knowledge in a society that places great emphasis on scientific method. The requirement that experimental data need to be replicable under identical circumstances, i.e. the notion that repetition provides corroboration, is at the root of conspiracy fiction's insistence on distinguishing between appearance and reality. Since conspiracies falsify appearances only within the parameters of plausibility, the detective needs to assert an individually formulated statement against a consensus that does not seem to require the same amount of evidence to pass muster. Finney's Miles needs to accumulate a significant number of occasions, at which the truth about the ongoing alien invasion is beginning to shine through in order to convince others, but mostly to convince himself, that he is not insane, i.e. a victim of clinical paranoia. The temptation to recreate harmony between individual perception and communal consensus by switching sides and joining the conspiracy is strongly tied to the possibility of acting out his Oedipal rebellion against the collective superego. Weighing his options, Finney's hero decides to persist in his resistance because joining the anonymous collective would mean accepting the fact that there will never be an Oedipal transfer of power from one generation to the next. The ultimate goal of defining his identity against the power of the conspiracy is therefore only possible because of the nature of this specific kind of conspiracy. As individuality is coupled with knowledge, the conspiracy can represent both the origin of Oedipal self-definition and the obstacle on the way there.

At this point, it has become clear that the two complementary agents of conspiracy stories with their characteristic features and interlocking functions determine the course of the narrative. The "plot," in both senses of the word, that the two agents enact is highly reminiscent of what Poe has called the "tale of ratiocination;" i.e. a structurally specific narrative and conceptual formation that is geared toward the conflation of two types of hermeneutic activities. On the one hand, the reader must engage in a process of interpretation in order to make sense of the text, and on the other hand, the text itself depicts the hermeneutic activities that characters engage in to make sense of the mystery. The tale of ratiocination, which Robert Champigny in his study of the classic detective story has called "the investigative sequence," is common to both conspiracy fiction and the detective story. The inevitable differences between the two genres arise from the fact that the detective story plots two individuals against one another, whereas conspiracy fiction plots an individual against a collective. The ideological consequences of this fundamental difference aside, both genres are concerned with the act of assigning proper names (to the murderer, the co-conspirators, the renegades, etc.) and establishing an anterior truth that, unbeknownst to themselves, they have been operating under all along.

> A narrative is to be called a mystery story to the extent that the goal and result of the narrated process is the determination of some events anterior to the ending of the process . . . Mystery stories . . . radicalize the tension, or complementarity, between progressive and regressive determinations . . . The narrated process is oriented toward a retroactive denouement that should transfigure the whole sequence.[15]

Champigny's definition is derived from the more rigidly constructed and formulaic "classic" detective stories of the genre's most consolidated phase. It therefore does not include stories that perform more or less radical experiments with the generic prototype, if some such thing does, in fact, exist. Postmodernist fiction like that of Pynchon, Gaddis, or Paul Auster, which tends to deny the reader the satisfaction of providing a solution to the mystery, is therefore excluded although it would reaffirm Champigny's groundwork of rules through their systematic reversal. Of course, all storytelling depends on the hermeneutical interplay of mutually corresponding interpretive horizons if it wants to be able to articulate more than simply "and then. . . and then. . . and then. . . " Carlo Ginzburg has made the connection between the evidential paradigms that determine the detective's "ability to forecast retrospectively" and the rise of the novel as a narrative form which is fundamentally rooted in these paradigms as the basis of its narration. But the mystery story, and with it conspiracy fiction, does more than simply employ Gadamer's hermeneutic circle as a figure of narrative; it thematizes, even reifies the process, injecting a crucial element of self-reflexivity into every text it dominates. By increasing the degree of visibility of the artifice involved in the act of reading and writing, all narrative based on the "investigative sequence" is "baring its devices," to use a phrase popularized by the Russian Formalists.

Intimately involved in the unfolding of investigative sequences is the issue of secrecy. Its creation and preservation are essential sources of any conspiracy's power, as the detective attempts to uncover, expose, and make public what secrecy conceals. Through its significance as a technology of power, secrecy functions as the narrative's object of contention, as the goal whose permanent status needs to be defined by either one of the competing forces. The power struggle for the status of secrecy--intact/defunct, complete/deficient, total/partial, etc.--is also the source of narrative suspense. In the course of the narrative, secrecy is always portrayed as potentially in danger. To be perpetually on the verge of determining "what will have happened" is the promise that more conventional narratives will infallibly deliver after they have sustained its latency for as long as possible.

By indulging extensively in the hermeneutical alternation between concealing/revealing, covering/uncovering, dismantling/recuperating, etc, conspiracy fiction places great emphasis upon the moment of revelation or denouement. Since the moment when the conspirators can finally be named is one in which the world is reconstituted to its proper state, the act itself carries great ontological and even metaphysical weight. As the narrative process makes good on the promise of culminating in a revelatory moment, which itself had been sustaining the reader's interest all along, the world of the narrative is brought to a moment of ontological closure. The act of naming is a gesture that points toward a more mythical than historical view of the world;. Once the conspiracy is uncovered, the world is permanently set right and history stops at this particular point in the *discours*. The strategy is not unlike that used in fairy-tales and other forms of representation that are not strictly mimetic. The moment of revelation serves as *telos* for the narrative universe; a preordained point of ultimate reference that retrospectively legitimizes the existence of every single prior narrative move, not to mention the existence of the text itself. The metaphysics of conspiracy fiction are therefore fundamentally eschatological.

The eschatological fantasy to be in on the grand plan of history, or to suspect that there is such a plan which is being jealously guarded by a small power-elite, is obviously a form of paranoia. The same delusion of grandeur, which Freud observes in combing Schreber's autobiographical sketches for clues to the psychoanalytic nature of his condition, manifests itself in almost all forms of millennialism, both religious and secular. Conspiracy fiction has provided its readers with a wide variety of such eschatological narratives. Novels such as John Crowley's *Little, Big* and *Aegypt* do not all conform to the rule of thumb that wants to lump all varieties of conspiracies in with a grossly oversimplified notion of paranoia.[16] *Aegypt*, for example, sketches a bird's eye view of history in which moments of eschatological fulfillment have come and gone so frequently and inconspicuously that nobody who has lived through them has the slightest idea that the world has ended and begun anew. Accordingly, the chosen few who are "in the know" see no reason to be alarmed, as they continue their conspiratorial preservation of the secret knowledge. A clinical concept of paranoia and its symptoms would thus do very little to aid in understanding a novel like *Aegypt*.

Despite the popularity of the term "paranoia" and a kind of public intuition that it constitutes a basic element of contemporary American life,[17] clinical psychologists seem to agree by and large that "currently there exists no reigning theory of paranoia."[18] Instead of a comprehensive theory, psychologists have delivered a detailed description of paranoia as a syndrome; that is to say, as a pattern of pervasive features which tend to recur together with some degree of consistency and are therefore considered to mark the presence of a particular pathological condition. The symptoms emerging from this somewhat provisional approach are usually grouped and arranged to form a coherent perspective which helps to distinguish the disease from other, similar pathological conditions. The coherence of the paranoid view itself insinuates a more systematic and comprehensive epistemological model than the description of a "syndrome" would seem to account for. In fact, its systematic rigidity even suggests structural similarities to other cognitive processes which are not considered pathological at all, such as scientific thought or artistic creation. Sociologist Dieter Groh, for example, notes that

> conspiracy theories are not only logically consistent, they can also be equipped with everything normally associated with a scientific paradigm as understood by modern history of science --a statement that Thomas S. Kuhn (1970) would reject but Paul Feyerabend (1975) accept.[19]

This emphasis on the paranoiac as a creator of significant patterns, an avid interpreter of seemingly random events, may very well be one explanation why paranoia appears so congenial to the pattern-making of narrative, be it in the creation of scientific theory or the fabrication of literary artifacts. Like the storyteller, the paranoiac follows Champigny's "investigative sequence."

Groh's discussion of collective forms of paranoia brings the argument back to the earlier question of the paranoiac's individual frame of mind. How does the individual's condition extend itself into larger social and political entities? How does it bridge the gap between psychology and sociology? Since it is unlikely that this happens by the sheer plausibility and ideological convenience of the paranoid delusion, all those patterns deserve a closer look whose power is not based on the individual's helplessness when faced with the disease, but rather on the pragmatic value that they acquire when transferred to the public sphere.

Although the medical field is divided about the conceptualization and causes of paranoia as a psychopathological condition, the following symptoms are generally considered indicative of an individual's paranoid disposition:

1. Projective Thinking
2. Hostility
3. Suspiciousness
4. Centrality
5. Delusions
6. Fear of loss of autonomy
7. Grandiosity.[20]

Since the Freudian account of the two case studies, which outline Schreber's transfer of latent homosexuality onto his immediate environment, attempts mainly to describe the generative principle behind the patient's condition, it provides few answers as to the effect that the affected individual can have on society or vice versa.[21] Clinical studies, like the one by Swanson, Bohnert and Smith, place stronger emphasis on the paranoiac's conceptual framework, which then gives more immediate access to the conceptual link between psychology and ideology that is at the core of conspiracy fiction.

Although Freud himself has not explicitly made the connection between paranoia and what he calls "the illusion of central position," the list of symptoms compiled by clinicians strongly suggests that the paranoid frame of mind is an atavism or regression in the individual's development. Caught in the center of a rigidly structured universe, the paranoiac indulges in the same fantasy of omnipotence that infants leave behind as soon as they recognize and accept the relativity of their position toward others. The paranoiac, at any age or point in his development, is permanently arrested at this stage. Assuming that his environment reciprocates his attention, he is "in a state of perpetual crisis,"[22] searching for clues revealing his place in the designs that the world has upon him.

Grounded in this ironclad intrinsic logic, perpetual suspiciousness begins to emerge as the one crucial characteristic of the paranoid frame of mind. It constitutes a kind of interpretive frenzy where pathological loss of control joins sane and sound epistemological method to create "the hermeneutic circle, arguably, the philosopher's trope for paranoia."[23] As there is no self-evident boundary to the number of potentially relevant phenomena, the paranoiac constantly moves in an environment that is concealing its true meaning. Being suspicious means being alert to these potential meanings; being suspended in a pose of interpretive readiness, in a delicate balance between knowing intuitively and not being able (yet) to substantiate this knowledge through solid proof. In systemic terms, paranoia is a runaway system, which, instead of feeding both corroborating and conflicting data back into the loop, can only reaffirm its findings. As its spinning away from reality accelerates, it becomes increasingly incapable of realizing its own errors and correcting them. From the linguistic point of view, this behavior constitutes a discourse without a recourse to a meta-discourse, closed in the contemplation of its object but incapable in seeing itself as yet another object in need of interpretation. Conspiracy conflates all hermeneutical horizons into the one relevant to the paranoiac.

Conspiracy always leaves a certain degree of residual indeterminacy. Unlike the detective story, in which all crucial ambiguities can be resolved by naming the murderer, conspiracy fiction tends to leave a vague impression with the reader that only part of the plot has been--or perhaps even *can be*--exposed. Secrecy, the conflation of paranoia and conspiracy, and the element of hyperbole all contribute to the sense of unease that accompanies even the most perfect solution. For that reason, most conspiracy fiction provides a more pragmatic than categoric closure, accepting the fact that a plot which is potentially limitless can of course never be exposed in its totality. Complete resolution can only be hinted at if the text wants to avoid belittling the size and threat of the conspiracy it depicts.

The problem of evaluating the extent of their potential paranoid delusions is part of the problem-solving that all detectives in conspiracy fiction are involved in. To distinguish what is real from what is imagined, i.e. to trust that one's own sense of reality provides an accurate representation of the way things really are, becomes more difficult if it appears reasonable to assume that conspiracies *are* at work everywhere; even paranoiacs do, after all, have enemies. Not only does the detective in such novels as, for example, Philip K. Dick's *A Scanner Darkly* have to make decisions about "reading" the conspiracy correctly. But he must also distrust himself and heed his own instincts of self-preservation. Going too far in his suspicions, he will entrap himself and erase all options how to proceed. Accordingly, the cognitive process for the reader, whose access to information is entirely dependent on the protagonist's impressions, is suspended between wanting to include more and more data into the "dis-covery" of the plot, and wanting to discredit as many assumptions and inferences as possible to arrive at a clear picture of what the protagonist is up against. The conspiracy conceals itself, therefore, not only through deliberate cover-ups, but also through its individual opponent's inability to determine accurately the demarcation line between appropriate and inappropriate inference, between correct interpretation and overinterpretation. Emanating from the detective, paranoia communicates itself to the reader.

With the arrival of postmodernism, the dialectic relation between paranoia as a cultural phenomenon and paranoia as an aesthetic strategy has come more to the forefront than ever before in the theme's history. Paranoia has almost exclusively come to be regarded as a complex metaphor in which epistemological, political, and cultural concerns intersect; a trope of knowledge and power. In this situation, the increased interest in the previously discussed hermeneutical paradigm, which permits the transfer from individual to collective, psychological to political, and allegorical to mimetic discourse, has contributed further to the almost explosive proliferation of conspiracy fiction, particularly in postwar American fiction. Postmodernist discourse in film, television, and literature has explored paranoia alternatingly as an ideologically somewhat precarious scare tactics, which first conjures up and then publicly laments the fragmentation of contemporary life, and as the metaphysical panacea against the existential emptiness and political powerlessness resulting from this fragmentation.

2. Toward a Genealogy of Postmodern Conspiracy Fiction

In order to understand how conspiracy in theory and fiction has become such an integral part of contemporary American culture, any critique must focus on Althusserian "welcome structures" that exist within this culture, at a specific point in history and in the development of its social, economic, and cultural practices and institutions; in other words, it must investigate how a complex of themes, which is not the original property of this or any other single culture, can insinuate itself upon complex social systems and inconspicuously work alongside with them. What is it about conspiracy that makes it so intrinsically American? What are the circumstances that have aided it in finding its way into and taking a firm hold on American culture so that, by the 1960s, it appears as a thoroughly indigenous phenomenon?

Regarding the integration of conspiracy into the American popular imagination, Robert Levine has presented the argument that conspiratorial fears help constitute, legitimize, and consolidate collective identity at the moment when this identity is in a state of crisis. The precarious historical conditions under which American national identity was initially being formulated explain why it is particularly the American imagination that conceives of itself as being in a state of perpetual crisis. In the introduction to *Conspiracy and Romance*, which itself focuses exclusively on antebellum literature, Levine comes to the following conclusion.

> A rhetoric of extremity, conspiratorial discourse more often than not manifests at its least
> flexible and most repressive a culture's dominant ideology--the network of beliefs, values,
> and, especially, fears and prejudices that help social groups to construct and make sense of
> their social identity and reality.[24]

As a recurring discursive pattern that contributes to the formulation and consolidation of a political entity in the making, conspiratorial discourses, fiction among them, have been a crucial theme in American culture. Historians like David Brion Davis or Richard Hofstadter have, in fact, suggested numerous contexts in which what Hofstadter calls "the paranoid style" functions as a hallmark of American imagination and rhetoric.[25] The cases are numerous; they range from early Republican concerns about foreign political subversion, to the anxieties leading up to the witchtrials in Puritan New England, all the way to such twentieth century examples as the internment of Japanese Americans during WWII, McCarthyism or other Cold War manifestations of global conflict. Contemporary American experience has predictably carried on the tradition; from anxieties about the loss of American economic power to Southeast Asia, to the distrust of government bureaucracy after the series of assassinations in the early 60s, to Watergate and the Iran-Contra Affair, or the confrontation with the massive rearrangements of power on a global level with the collapse of the Eastern Bloc from the mid-1980s on.

Sociologists and historians have argued quite persuasively that, instead of freezing the state of affairs at one stage and preserving them indefinitely, conspiracy fears instigate a dynamic and possibly recursive process which runs its course through successive stages of integration and fragmentation. As the formation of a collective identity progresses beyond its pragmatic goals, paranoid fears continue determining the individual's perception of the social environment. Locked in from all sides, a society initially strengthened by conspiracy fears turns its power to create structure and significance inwards. Suddenly everybody is a potential outsider. Suspicions turn from foreigners to neighbors. Alliances can incorporate fewer and fewer individuals until, finally, nobody is worthy of anybody else's trust. The phase of consolidation through conspiracy is followed by a phase of disintegration through conspiracy. Since every step along this route is already haunted by the inevitable decline to follow, it is easy to see how the entire process could be perceived as an uninterrupted series of crises.[26]

Of course, it remains arguable whether the "New World Order" has forced more serious crises upon the collective imagination than any previous historical moment. The wide variety of historical test cases, however, indicates that the original historical thinking has persisted throughout. American history is believed to consist of a series of consecutive moments of crisis--to democracy, the free enterprise system, military dominance in a particular region, etc. Only in retrospect are lacunae in this frenzied process even discernable. Collective identity is incessantly challenged and therefore requires constant reinforcement through a rhetoric conjuring up the specter of conspiracy.

Another reason why conspiracy discourse has proven so persistent is linked to the fact that conspiracy defamiliarizes and ambiguates what is generally considered known and predictable. Unlike other rhetorical tropes which would help to conceptualize the encounter with foreign cultures, conspiracy is suited to accommodate all ideologies geared toward the intrinsic homogenization of American society. In a culture that is trying to replace a multitude of cultural narratives with one authoritative national ideology (the melting pot, manifest destiny, etc.), conspiracy expresses the lingering unease about the barely concealed heterogeneity underneath the willed unity. In this sense, American culture is always latently, secretly alien to those at its very center because it always and inevitably incorporates the Other into the fabric of the allegedly homogeneous community. The distribution of real political and economic power notwithstanding, conspiracy provides the means to express the discomfort with this flipside of the ideological map.

Thus, an intuitive sense of the uncanny as a social phenomenon is part of the American experience. Ideologies of homogeneity abound within this culture to repress the knowledge about its fundamental heterogeneity. Postmodernism has been accused of celebrating this condition through its radical fragmentations and disruptions, but it appears reasonable to assume that the clash between these conflicting ideologies and not the intent to instigate political unrest is at the root of postmodern aesthetic strategy. At the end of a historical period characterized by American global hegemony, the repressed heterogeneity returns in the guise of complaints about cultural fragmentation. In order to verbalize this sense of the uncanny explicitly, conspiracy fiction conceptualizes conflict as interplay between competing readers/authors. The preceding discussion of Robert Champigny's *What Will Have Happened?* has already introduced a model for all hermeneutic fiction in which the narrative must be contested for, revised, and reconstituted, depending on the degree to which current knowledge and future prediction can be brought into alignment. However, Champigny's model derives from detective fiction and is therefore geared toward a binary model of competition: criminal against detective, one on one. Yet conspiracy fiction requires a model that can deal with a greater degree of heterogeneity in the facing off between antagonistic forces; a model that critic Peter Hühn has provided in his article "The Detective as Reader: Narrativity and Reading Concepts in Detective Fiction." Hühn's accomplishment lies in his rephrasing of Champigny's hermeneutic as a communicative model. By shattering the constraining binary pairing, Hühn emphasizes the social relevance of hermeneutic fiction. According to Hühn,

> stories that are narrated in detective novels can profitably be described as stories of writing and reading insofar as they are concerned with authoring and deciphering "plots."[27]

With the increasing popularity of all forms of semiotics based on Saussurian structuralist linguistics, language itself becomes the dominant paradigm for the analysis of any complex system of signification. After one agency "authors" the crime, taking all necessary precautions to conceal its actions, the other agency must "read" the clues and reconstitute the concealed text, discarding irrelevant or deliberately misleading data and correcting the competing reconstituted narratives along the way. Other agencies participate in the process and increase the number of interpretive options. Since the reading activity of one agency creates a new, revised text for its antagonist to decipher, both agencies constantly alternate between being readers and being authors. By metaphorical extension, this process is being projected upon the relationship between the author of the text and its reader. At the moment the detective and the reader solve the puzzle, the proliferation of competing narratives is being halted and all options are narrowed down to one. Retrospectively, this gesture of closure establishes a hierarchical order among the now closed narratives.

Casting the movements of the plot in terms of narrativity, Hühn's argument does more than simply apply a new metaphor for something that is already well-known. His argument invalidates the most common criticism against hermeneutic fiction; that it generates self-consuming artefacts that lose all relevance once the reading process is over. Relevance, however, does not reside in the moment of closure. If that were so, the *telos* of the story would justify the apprehensions felt by readers of classic detective stories who complain that simply re-establishing law and order is a solution reminiscent of the worst kinds of reactionary politics. Instead of concentrating on the moment of closure, Hühn directs the reader's attention to the process of detection itself. Who gets to tell the story? Whose voice is being listened to? Whose story survives and emerges as the one passed on to posterity? Whose voice is being silenced and by what means?

Hühn's model aids in understanding the distribution and facilitation of power within a society that is geared primarily toward the preservation of the status quo. Conventional hermeneutic fiction is less reactionary for its desire to see justice triumph than for its refusal to see justice as subject to history. Hühn's model historizes the hermeneutic process by asking specific questions about the agents involved. Authorship must be questioned as to its motivations, its will to knowledge/power.

More significant for the development of conspiracy fiction than these specific political contexts, however, is the intrinsic history of the genre, its affiliations to other tropes, and its changing position within a broader history of ideas. For this purpose, Robert Levine's argument lays the groundwork by pointing out that some of the great canonical conspiracy fictions in American literature--Brockden Brown's *Ormond*, Cooper's *The Bravo*, Hawthorne's *The Blithedale Romance*, and Melville's *Benito Cereno*, to mention only the cases Levine himself has selected--tend to fall into the category of Romance rather than Realism. While any single correspondence between conspiracy and Romance may be coincidental, Levine's list provides more than accidental cross-references between the two to suggest that both forms display a unique affinity for each other.

Starting from the commonsensical observation that the conspiracy trope has a strong tendency toward exaggeration, melodrama, adventure, suspense, or even propaganda, Levine suggests that these features correspond to the separation of Realism and Romance in American fiction that was originally suggested by Hawthorne and has come to establish itself as a kind of common truth in the discussion of these traditions. Quoting such seminal studies of American Romance as Richard Chase's *The American Novel and Its Tradition* or F.O. Matthiessen's *American Renaissance*, Levine traces the binary model of Romanticism/Classicism through its historical transformations. Unlike Romanticism, which deals in metaphysical abstractions and allegory, Classicism and/or Realism is concerned with historical specificity and metonymic representation. The "concern about the experimental provisionality of creation,"[28] as reflected in both romance fiction and the discursive formations surrounding American national experience, is easily mistaken for the author's willingness to replace social concern with metaphysical abstraction, mimesis with fabulation, the citizen's responsibility with the subversive's rejection of integration, and so on. Obviously, all the elements that are commonplace to conspiracy are already in place.

Certain select examples of conspiracy fiction have preserved features that belong closely to the kind of Romance that Levine has in mind. Ranging from such diverse cases as, for instance, G.K. Chesterton's *The Man Who Was Thursday* to William Gibson's and Bruce Sterling's *The Difference Engine*, the Romance tradition has generated texts in which the genuinely transcendental has not yet yielded to the sensational. Despite the time, space, and sensibility separating their respective authors, the two novels share a concern for conspiracy as a cosmic metaphor that will reveal itself as a source of spiritual salvation if approached through a process of catharsis. In the grand scheme of things, however, this variation on the joint recuperation of conspiracy and Romance remains but an oddity; a rare atavism that is greatly outnumbered by the main course of progression in the historical development.

Obviously, the affinity between conspiracy and Romance has historically more pertinent reasons than these intrinsic correspondences. As mentioned earlier, the argument that conspiracy creates and consolidates community ceases to be convincing as America enters the twentieth century and the height of its global political, cultural, and economic power. As crucial as conspiracy may have been in the formative phases of the body politic, it is safe to say that community must have been firmly established at this point in time. Power is safely implemented in institutions and practices. Nearly all concepts of national identity are undergoing changes within parameters which safely exclude subversion to the degree of total annihilation. To these historical changes critics like Tony Tanner have responded by pointing out how conspiracy migrates from the political arena to the politics of representation. As the fears connected with problems of self-determination continue, slightly disguised, to haunt American literature up to the present day, the act of writing itself becomes an act of self-assertion. As a representative man, the writer must struggle for identity. This struggle is necessarily exacerbated to the degree that society moves toward modernity. The allegory it produces then becomes the arena in which national identity is being defined. In *City of Words*, his seminal study of postmodernist American fiction, Tanner suggests that "the possible nightmare of being totally controlled by unseen agencies and powers is never far away in contemporary American fiction."[29] The sheer exuberance, iconoclasm, and idiosyncrasy of American writers are expressions of their troubled relationship with language as a form of communal discourse.[30] Through language, collective norms and conventions, as well as fears and prejudices, are communicated and enforced, so that the writer as an individual, supreme consciousness can only resist the pull of conventionality by asserting himself through the unconventional use of language. While "the specter of a pre-existing and pre-signified social whole maintains its presence"[31] as a threatening vision of anonymity, the American writer is willing to accept "the paranoia of a humanism that wishes to maintain its rights on a reality which it will yet not recognize as its own offspring or construction."[32] This struggle between freedom and self-determination permeates all of American literature and, according to Tanner, manifests itself most obviously in postmodernism's preoccupation with conspiracy and paranoia. Thus, Tanner's accomplishment is to connect the two critical perspectives outlined so far by adding a historical element to the morphological description and vice versa. Conspiracy remains linked to the conventions of Romance, yet its relevance is extended beyond the historical periods in which Romance happened to constitute the dominant form of literary expression.

This is not to say that Romance has vanished from the scene without a trace, though. Its influence can be felt in a substantial number of genres, which all constitute a wide variety of historical descendants of Romance as a form of high culture. Most of these descendants, however, indicate a shift away from the literary mainstream to forms of lowbrow or popular fiction, if not extraliterary or subliterary genres altogether. Romantic paradigms associated with domestic fiction, for example, have found their way into the more lurid versions of the so-called "historical romance" or the soap opera; a correspondence that even recreates the relationship between the predominantly female readership and their almost exclusively female authors. Similarly, Romantic subgenres like the Gothic have developed into contemporary genres like horror or science fiction, which are, despite all recent developments toward generic crossovers, still markedly geared toward mass-market audiences and their tastes.

One major transformation in this context is the shift from conspiracy as a literary theme to the medium of film as a popular genre. The functions that mass-market fiction still fulfills to some extent have been largely taken over by the one form that can claim to be the dominant cultural discourse for the time period before television takes over. Film has largely preserved the genre distinctions typical of popular fiction and, by the same token, the close tie between the conspiracy theme and popular genres. Hollywood's production of conspiracy narratives has been too prolific to even start listing specific examples.[33] From the generic thriller, to the 1950s *film noir*, to science fiction, film has participated in the preservation and dissemination of conspiracy as a theme associated with post-Romantic discourses. With similar adherence to genre distinctions, television has taken over where film has left off from the 1950s on. These are, as a general rule, the spaces that conspiracy has occupied after its disappearance from mainstream and "literary" culture. From there it has made its return into the mainstream with the onset of postmodernism.

Aided by the industrialization of publishing and distribution, as well as the application of sophisticated methods of consumer research and prediction, the demarcation lines separating the genres in today's publishing market are more precise, more numerous, and more jealously guarded than ever before. Set down into this hierarchical landscape, postmodernism's predilection for transgression helps define the place that the conspiracy theme can occupy today, as its affinity to the demoted forms of Romance alone does not define it clearly enough any more. Notions of transgression, eclecticism, and fragmentation, which are so essential to the popular understanding of postmodernism, help to understand the work of such authors as William Gaddis, Thomas Pynchon, or Robert Coover, whose writing has become the showcase for conspiracy's return to mainstream "literary" fiction. As the writing of this group of authors defies easy classification, especially in its crossing of lines separating high from low culture, themes and strategies from one side of the sociological divide could be moved to the other. Novels like Pynchon's *Gravity's Rainbow*, which will serve as a kind of exemplary fiction for most of the argument to follow, are hybrids that play out their own sense of generic dislocation with sheer bravado, turning themselves into a kind of "democratic" fiction that appears to be genuinely American.

Refuting the Habermasian notion of postmodernity as a strategy of radical delimitation and increased communication, these fictions tend to reaffirm the borderlines they transgress. Critics like Brian McHale have pointed out that the recent critical recognition of writers like William Gibson or Bruce Sterling, who are working and publishing within the confines of genre fiction, have tended to remind readers of the distinction between highbrow and lowbrow, rather than make this distinction invisible.[34] Since cyberpunk constitutes a subgenre of science fiction, and science fiction constitutes a historical and generic descendant of the Romance, attention and appreciation from academic criticism is required to trace these historical and sociological transformations back to their origins and recreate the contexts that restore validity to what must appear as mere formula. The argument commonly used to restore these contexts, however, generates its critical insights out of the friction between incompatible social categories which writers like Gibson or critics like Larry McCaffery play against each other for aesthetic effect. The postmodern gesture of transgression remains oxymoronic as long as these interpenetrations play an important role in the aesthetic vocabulary.

To a lesser but still noticeable extent, these transformations are also taking place in the visual media. Directors like Oliver Stone, whose *JFK* is deeply enmeshed in strategies of delimitations between factual and fictional, have taken the conspiracy theme from the thriller and transplanted it into such forms as the documentary or agitprop.[35] With such films as Robert Altmann's *The Player* or Joel and Ethan Cohen's *Barton Fink*, postmodern autoreferentiality is channelled into conspiratorial narratives about Hollywood and the process of filmmaking. And in television, which obviously tends to think of itself as a demotic medium, such programs as the ABC miniseries *The Wild Palms*, written by Bruce Wagner, push the limits of what any popular genre can still accommodate without alienating the viewer.

Any analysis of conspiracy fiction that tries to focus on phenomena from its theme's cutting edge, however, must inevitably return to the literary form. It is here, where commercial success dictates, relatively speaking, the least degree of conformity and formulaic predictability, that new developments are taking place as the genre adapts to the changing conditions around it. Popular genres have established a version of conspiracy narratives that is relatively consistent across the board. Film, television, and formula fiction elaborate on a limited set of narrative premises, which are formulated to allow discussions of contemporary issues without drastic alterations of the aesthetic format. As critical opinion regroups to make room for fiction that, following McHale's observations, self-consciously and strategically cuts across the conventional segmentations of the canon, a set of writers begins to emerge that has come to provide the basis for formulating a canonical postmodern conspiracy fiction.

First and foremost among these writers is Thomas Pynchon. Time and again, his work has been cited as evidence for the alleged paranoid nature of contemporary American culture; as the concrete manifestation of a broad-based cultural condition, a *zeitgeist* or *weltanschauung* for postwar America. As a founding father or icon, Pynchon's reputation and presence, his influence on others, and the nature of his work are, of course, a convenient fiction. He provides an ideology in the service of those whose interest, in one way or another, is to categorize and canonize conspiracy fiction as a structurally consistent, authentic, and culturally relevant statement about and within the American experience in the late twentieth century. Under close scrutiny, Pynchon's work, as any other's or even more so, displays inconsistencies and ambiguities that are difficult to resolve into authoritative statements about the category it is supposed to represent, whether it is "meta-fiction," the "anti-novel," "Menippean Satire," "carnevalesque," or "systems novel." It is equally problematic to resort to such ploys as to state that its unique unclassifiability is the category into which it properly belongs. However, Pynchon's resistance to classification and the strategic choices he forces his critics to make are ideal conditions to investigate the communal consensus about his writing, rather than clutching at straws to define some unattainable essence it is supposed to possess.

Pynchon's significance can be measured by the reception his work has received from the academic establishment. Only few others, among them John Barth, Donald Barthelme, and Robert Coover, were accepted into college syllabi with such rapid speed. Pynchon's own influences, most notably William Gaddis, had to wait much longer to gain the same recognition. Though reviewers were divided on the question how influential this type of writing would be for future American authors, academic critics were generally so enthralled with Pynchon's "literariness" that they tended to elevate him to the status of representative figure of postmodernism; a showcase in which most of the troublesome, but also the brilliant and critically celebrated features of the newly emerging, iconoclastic writing coincided. Jerome Klinkowitz, for example, celebrates Pynchon as one of the writers responsible for the "radical disruptions" that need to occur at a time when the "death of the novel" is imminent and can only be averted by experimentation and subversion. Even though "thematically it may suggest chaos and disorder,"[36] Pynchon's preoccupation with entropy suggests that his fiction is addressing the notion of a state of exhaustion or equilibrium that applies not only to theoretical physics but also to the fiction written by most of his contemporaries; a kind of fiction that, according to Klinkowitz, is still rooted deeply in conventions, themes, and strategies appropriate to 19th century experience. Together with writers like Philip Roth or John Barth, Klinkowitz agrees that the world has changed to a degree that requires a new, different definition of mimesis.

> If the world is absurd, if what passes for reality is distressingly unreal, why spend time representing it? . . . so when everything else has changed, including the very ways we experience our world, should not the novel change too?[37]

Contrary to Klinkowitz, whose model of legitimization is grounded in the notion of historical gaps, disruptions, and leaps, Ihab Hassan has tried to determine the nature of postmodernist fiction from the perspective of historical continuity. In *The Dismemberment of Orpheus*, Hassan outlines a generic history that connects postmodernist fiction with traditions of Romantic experimentation.[38] His model undercuts fashionable notions of exhaustion or fatigue like those of Klinkovitz or Barth and thus provides a corrective to an aesthetic based on the uncritical adoration of the new. The resulting historical gap is instead bridged by the oscillation between silence on the one hand and withdrawal on the other. Despite Hassan's reluctance to support the newly emerging paradigm of literary expression, the emphasis on historical continuity and the "good company" of postmodernist fiction clearly indicates that the ground is being prepared for something that is aesthetically different, yet culturally valid. Though Hassan is not concerned with Pynchon specifically, his goal is to define the term "postmodernism" in terms of a historical model of periodic recurrence that favors a mode of writing similar to Pynchon's. Stating that "we cannot simply rest . . . on the assumption that postmodernism is anti-formal, anarchic, or decreative,"[39] Hassan simultaneously acts as arbiter of the new and defender of the canon. His reservations against postmodernism listed in the previous quote, however, reflect exactly the judgement of critics like Gerald Graff, whose main critique of Pynchon is that his work is anti-mimetic and therefore escapist.[40]

Graff argues that what Klinkovitz, and to some extent Hassan, accept as a historically new but generically consistent form of mimesis is, in fact, an indication of further cultural fragmentation.

> The realistic perspective that gives shape and point to works of tragicomic postmodernism, permitting them to present distortion *as* distortion, gives way to a celebration of *energy*--the vitalism of a world that cannot be understood or controlled.[41]

Although Graff avoids dealing with Hassan's notion of historical continuity by postulating two diametrically opposed kinds of postmodernism--one realistic, the other animistic--he implicitly concedes that postmodernism is capable of making valuable contributions to contemporary culture as long as it curbs its extravagance and fabulative vitalism. The non-mimetic "celebration of energy" associated with Pynchon troubles Graff mostly for its political implications. Hovering "somewhere between revolutionary politics and sophisticated acquiescence to the agreeably meaningless surfaces of mass culture,"[42] Pynchonesque postmodernism fails in Graff's eyes. The absence of verisimilitude, which Graff reads as a failure to represent accurately, prevents it from taking a politically constructive stand. While most critics grant Pynchon the status of having captured both the contemporary historical moment and the psychological response it elicits, Graff points out that a response like paranoia refuses to take on history on its own terms and instead permits aesthetic and political escapism.

Trying to establish postmodern fiction as a mimetic discourse, Tony Tanner's argument in *City of Words* answers to Graff's critique by reestablishing the link between history and psychology. Instead of insisting on the autonomy of art, Tanner reverts to the allegorical reading that both Graff and Klinkovitz have ignored for obvious reasons, one being concerned with formal innovation, the other with mimetic accuracy. Tanner suggests that it is, first and foremost, Pynchon who has captured

> that new anxiety in fiction which reveals itself as a nervous compulsion to undermine the fiction in the act of erecting it--the verbal equivalent of auto-destructive art."[43]

Tanner pinpoints the element of fear that his peers have overlooked; the nameless, indistinct dread that motivates autoreferentiality. Unlike other forms of self-referential art in

Modernism or Romanticism, postmodern fiction construes the skepticism at the root of all autoreferentiality as grounds for insecurity and fear. It is his skepticism which opens the door for Pynchon's obsession with paranoia as both the condition of, and the response to the trappings of contemporary life.

The discussion about mimesis and its relevance to the postmodern fascination with conspiracy, which I have sketched rather roughly here, is more or less openly a struggle for the formulation of the canon. To declare Pynchon as the personification of American postmodernist writing silences the dissent from all those sources that insist on a more heterogeneous canon, which creates a place for all those whom Pynchon's paradigmatic position forces into the margins. The fact that not only Pynchon himself is a white male, but also that the other writers associated with the paradigm he represents fall into this unpopular category--William Gaddis, Robert Coover, Don DeLillo, or Joseph McElroy--suggests that what is being passed off as "American literature" is, in fact, only a small segment of the literary production that happens to command enough cultural clout to remain at center stage. Whether justified or not, the critique of Pynchon's predominance from the perspective of social power has provided a background against which the alleged homogeneity of postmodern fiction must be reconsidered. Why has a genre "belonging" to a social group, whose power is increasingly being challenged, been able to maintain its hold on the dominant cultural paradigm? How does this restructuring of the canon affect the texts themselves, as a new wave of postmodern writers, male and female, encounters and responds to the traditions and the image of homogeneity they present?

The decision to discuss the breakup of the dominant paradigm of postmodern conspiracy fiction through critical analysis of the works of Don DeLillo and Joseph McElroy has been motivated by several strategic advantages, most of them already alluded to in the preceding pages. First of all, both writers have produced early works that clearly indicate their adherence to the traditions represented by Pynchon and others like him. DeLillo's *Americana*, a reworking of themes developed by Joseph Heller in *Something Happened*, and McElroy's *A Smuggler's Bible*, are both concerned with cultural fragmentation and the paranoid response it elicits. Though sufficiently unique and original to establish both writers as major new voices in contemporary American fiction, the novels demonstrate the overwhelming presence of Pynchon and the influence he has had on a whole generation of writers.

Secondly, the fact that DeLillo and McElroy are both white males places their work in the tradition associated with Romance by Levine and Hassan and anti-mimetic discourse by Graff and Tanner. Accordingly, they are in the position from which conspiracy has been used as a tool of defamiliarizing American culture "from the inside," so to speak. Although writers like Marge Piercy, Diane Johnson, Kathy Acker, or Ishmael Reed have also made use of the conspiracy genre, their efforts are often directed toward describing the encounter with America, almost by definition, as a foreign culture. For them, American culture is self-evidently conspiratorial so that the whole notion of detection/ratiocination/investigative sequence, etc. is completely irrelevant to begin with. The author's social "marginality" seems to predispose the narrative toward another conceptual paradigm altogether; most likely toward something reminiscent of the contrast between Clifford Geertz's and Roland Barthes' ideas of the cultural anthropologist. The "Plight of the White Male Writer," to paraphrase John Kucich, takes the reader into a social space that conceives of itself as homogeneous and unambiguous and is therefore most susceptible to conspiratorial subversion.

Thirdly, DeLillo and McElroy are seriously concerned with generic hybridization. This interest in all forms of popular fiction, from the thriller to science fiction, places their writing at the busiest interface between socially, aesthetically, and ideologically differentiated sources of discourse today. At the same time, neither one merely reproduces an already deeply entrenched formula, which at this point refers not only to popular or mass-market fiction, but also to the academic canon that includes Gaddis, Pynchon, and Coover. Staying in touch with genre fiction, DeLillo and McElroy are nevertheless writers on the cutting edge. Their work is demanding and at times deliberately difficult. Occasionally it is daunting, maybe even intimidating, though never obscure. And, while it is entertaining, funny, and humane, it manages to be also cerebral and abstract. This complexity, which has endeared them more to academic criticism than rewarded them with the widespread popularity they deserve, demonstrates that they are sufficiently separate from the inherent conservativism of popular genres. Predictably, it is this kind of fiction where new developments in the development of ideas and generic conventions announce themselves first before they trickle down into the broad cultural base.

Once DeLillo and McElroy have put behind them the transitional phase of *Americana* and *A Smuggler's Bible*, their writing begins to employ a new set of concepts. Their work begins to differ in a number of significant ways from the paradigm out of which it had originally developed. To the present day, DeLillo and McElroy have consistently elaborated on these distinctive features. In fact, they themselves are beginning to define a paradigm by which younger writers, most notably among them Richard Powers, are perceiving the traditions of postmodern conspiracy fiction. Since these features have not yet begun to solidify into a prescriptive poetics, a guidebook on how to write the new postmodern American fiction, they are harder to pinpoint and synthesize into a comprehensive body of thought.

The best way, therefore, to approach these experimental fluctuations is to launch a series of investigations into themes and concepts that have proven crucial to the old paradigm and have been carried over into the new: the preoccupation with the trope of hyperbole, encyclopedism, the close association between conspiracy and paranoia, the construction of genre and genealogy, the representations of history and space, and the politics of power. In each of these themes, a change in attitude and thought, strategy and ideology is taking place, so that an overall sense of what the paradigm shift entails will begin to emerge from the sum of all individual close readings. Since this analysis is concerned with a massive shift, involving a wide variety of texts, genres, and writers, no one single text can of course embody the new paradigm in its prototypical form. For that reason, the relationship between the two central texts, discussed in each of the following analyses, varies from one essay to the other; at times, both novels are read as complementary halves, then they are being explored for the contrast between them, then one provides the critical focus through which the other is being approached, and so forth. Also, one analysis of individual texts attempts to link up with the one in the following chapter so that, for instance, one reading will discuss the breakdown of a paradigmatic feature while the next will try to determine what is taking its place; or one chapter will sketch a feature of the newly emerging paradigm and the next will try to fill this outline with concrete content. This way, the argument can alternate between abstract theoretical thought and close reading, as well as between describing absence, decline, and fragmentation on the one hand and continuity, coherence, and presence on the other.

Notes

[1] Clifford Geertz, "Deep Play: Notes on the Balinese Cockfight," *The Interpretation of Cultures: Selected Essays* (New York: Basic Books, 1973), 443.

[2] Geertz 24.

[3] Roland Barthes, *Mythologies* (New York: The Noonday Press, 1972), 11.

[4] Barthes 15.

[5] Dieter Groh, "The Temptation of Conspiracy Theory, or: Why Do Bad Things Happen to Good People? Part I: Preliminary Draft of a Theory of Conspiracy Theories," *Changing Conceptions of Conspiracy,* Carl Graumann and Serge Moscovici, eds. (New York: Springer, 1987) 11.

[6] Groh 11-12. A second shift of similar significance occurs at the point in history when bureaucracies grow into such baroque labyrinths that conspiracy theories shift the locus of conspiratorial threat from one's foreign enemy to one's own social, economic, and political organizations. See also Leo Braudy, "Providence, Paranoia, and the Novel," *Native Informant* (Baltimore: Johns Hopkins UP, 1981) 619-637.

[7] William Bywater, "The Paranoia of Postmodernism," *Philosophy and Literature* 14.1 (April 1990) 79-84.

[8] Richard Hofstadter, *The Paranoid Style in American Politics* (Chicago: University of Chicago Press, 1979).

[9] Finney's text, translated into film, has proven more resilient than anyone expected, considering that, after Don Siegel's 1956 version, two more remakes were made of *Invasion of the Body Snatchers*; one by Philip Kaufman in 1978, another by Abel Ferrara in 1992. Since the historical circumstances surrounding each remake could hardly be any more different from one another, the material must somehow lend itself to multiple reinscription.

[10] Serge Moscovici, "The Conspiracy Mentality," *Changing Conceptions of Conspiracy* (New York: Springer, 1978) 155.

[11] Carlo Ginzburg, "Clues: Roots of an Evidential Paradigm" *Clues, Myths, and the Historical Method* (Baltimore: Johns Hopkins UP, 1989) 117.

[12] Ginzburg 101.

[13] Elias Canetti, "Herrschaft und Paranoia: Der Fall Schreber, Erster Teil," *Masse und Macht,* vol. 2 (Regensburg: Hanser, 1960) 179-213.

[14] This characteristic feature constitutes a generic link between conspiracy and horror fiction. In both genres, the threat to the community goes largely unnoticed because nobody listens to the detective figure.

[15] Robert Champigny, *What Will Have Happened: A Philosophical and Technical Essay on Mystery Stories* (Bloomington: Indiana UP, 1977) 13-14.

[16] John Crowley, *Little Big* (New York: Bantam, 1983), and *Aegypt* (New York: Bantam, 1987).

[17] see Hendrik Hertzberg and David C.K. Mc Clelland, "Paranoia," *Harper's Magazine* (June 1974) 51-60.

[18] Kenneth Colby, *Artificial Paranoia: A Computer Simulation of Paranoid Processes* (New York: Pergamon Press, 1975) 13.

[19] Groh 4.

[20] David Swanson, Philip Bohnert, and Jackson A. Smith, *The Paranoid* (Boston: Little Brown & Company, 1970) 8.

[21] for further reference, see Sigmund Freud's seminal studies, "Psycho-Analytic Notes on an Autobiographical Account of a Case of Paranoia," *The Standard Edition of the Complete Psychological Works of Sigmund Freud* vol.12 (London: The Hogarth Press, 1958) 9-85; and "A Case of Paranoia Running Counter to the Psycho-Analytic Theory of the Disease," *The Standard Edition of the Complete Psychological Works of Sigmund Freud* vol.14 (London: The Hogarth Press, 1958) 261-273.

[22] Hertzberg and Mc Clelland 56.

[23] Patrick O'Donnell, "Engendering Paranoia in Contemporary Literature," *boundary 2: An International Journal Of Literature and Culture* 19.1 (Spring 1992) 191.

[24] Robert Levine, *Conspiracy and Romance: Studies in Brockden Brown, Cooper, Hawthorne, and Melville* (Cambridge: Cambridge UP, 1989) 12.

[25] see David Brion Davis, ed., *The Fear of Conspiracy* (Ithaca: Cornell UP, 1971), and George Johnson, *Architects of Fear: Conspiracy Theories and Paranoia in American Politics* (Los Angeles: J.P. Tarcher, and Boston: Houghton Mifflin, 1983).

[26] see Serge Moscovici, "The Conspiracy Mentality," Changing Conceptions of Conspiracy (New York: Springer, 1978).

[27] Peter Hühn, "The Detective as Reader; Narrativity and Reading Concepts in Detective Fiction," *Modern Fiction Studies* 33.3 (Autumn 1987) 451.

[28] Levine 3.

[29] Tony Tanner, *City of Words: American Fiction 1950-1970* (New York: Harper & Row, 1971) 16.

[30] Pynchon's notorious reclusiveness is just one example of how the image of the Romantic "original genius" has preserved itself all through the twentieth century. The modernist strategy of rewriting the position of the postmodern artist is being explored most poignantly by Don DeLillo in his novel *Mao II*.

[31] Paul Smith, "Paranoia," *Discerning the Subject* (Minneapolis: University of Minnesota Press, 1988) 87.

[32] Smith 91.

[33] For an overview of conspiracy in film, see James Palmer and Michael Riley, "America's Conspiracy Syndrome: From Capra to Pakula," *Studies in the Humanities* 8.2 (March 1981) 21-27; or Dana Polen, *Power and Paranoia: History, Narrative, and the American Cinema: 1940-50* (New York: Columbia UP, 1986).

[34] see, for instance, Paula Bryant, "Extending the Fabulative Continuum: DeLillo, Mooney, Federman," *Extrapolations* 30.2 (1989) 156-165; or Brian McHale, "POSTcyberMODERNpunkISM," *Storming the Reality Studio: A Casebook of Cyberpunk and Postmodern Science Fiction*. Larry McCaffery, ed. (Durham & London: Duke UP, 1991) 309-323. Despite the argument about postmodern predilections for transgression, McCaffery's entire anthology itself constitutes an effort to establish cyberpunk as a "literary" form and integrate it into an emerging canon of contemporary American fiction.

[35] *JFK*. Writ. and Dir. Oliver Stone. With Kevin Costner, Tommy Lee Jones, and Donald Sutherland. 1991. Stone's recent, highly publicized and ultimately successful attempts to use the film to promote the opening of restricted FBI files on the Kennedy assassination is part of the film's text and constitutes another gesture of delimitation. They extend the film's own montage of fact and fiction into the realm of politics. Geared toward opening access to another text--the FBI files and the text of history--*JFK*'s representational politics remains conspicuously anchored, however, in the traditions of melodrama.

[36] Jerome Klinkowitz, *Literary Disruptions: The Making of a Post-Contemporary American Fiction* (Urbana: University of Illinois Press, 1980) 15.

[37] Klinkowitz 32.

[38] Ihab Hassan, *The Dismemberment of Orpheus: Toward a Postmodern Literature* (New York: Oxford UP, 1971); also *The Right Promethean Fire: Imagination, Science, and Cultural Change* (Urbana: University of Illinois Press, 1980).

[39] Hassan, *Dismemberment of Orpheus*, 265.

[40] An opinion shared by a number of critics and often carried into the discussion of Don DeLillo's earlier writings; see, for example, John Aldridge, *The American Novel and the Way We Live Now* (New York: Oxford UP, 1983) 53-59.

[41] Gerald Graff, *Literature Against Itself: Literary Ideas in Modern Society* (Chicago: University of Chicago Press, 1979) 58.

[42] Graff 58.

[43] Tanner, *City of Words*, 180. Tanner's evaluation has initiated a critical tradition that has altogether ceased discussing postmodernism in terms of mimesis and has focused instead on the Romantic traditions that persevere as part of its wide discursive options; see, for instance, Charles Caramello,

Silverless Mirrors: Book, Self, and Postmodern American Fiction (Tallahassee: University of Florida Press, 1983. Whereas the discussion of Pynchon has moved away from the question of mimesis in recent years, DeLillo's and McElroy's writing is, to the present day, still going through that same phase; see, for example, Robert Nadeau, "Don DeLillo," *Readings from the New Book On Nature: Physics and Metaphysics in the Modern Novel* (Amherst: University of Massachussetts Press, 1981), or, phrased in a more contemporary rhetoric, Thomas Schaub, "What is now Natural: DeLillo's Systems," *Contemporary Literature* 30.1 (1989) 128-132.

II. *The Writing of Don DeLillo and Joseph McElroy*
1.White Noise *and* The Letter Left To Me*: The Trope of Hyperbole*

Conservative political wisdom has it that the family is one of the cornerstones in any citizen's sentimental education. It is supposed to be a force that will preserve moral integrity in the most corrupt of societies and guarantee historical continuity and stability, particularly amidst the evils of what is often referred to as "the postmodern condition." Also, the family can provide the individual with a sense of community in an environment built on rugged individualism--an expectation that is especially valid for American society. Underlying these optimistic views is the assumption that the family is a strong unit, held together by reliable ties, and that it therefore manages to withstand all kinds of pressure, from the outside as well as from within.

The observation that the family in American society may, in reality, not conform to these claims at particular moments in history has brought critics, particularly on the conservative side of the political spectrum, face to face with the embarrassing problem that their theories seem more prescriptive than descriptive. How is it possible that this basic unit of society, whose strength and resistance to outside forces was considered vital for survival in a hostile world, was found in a state of dissolution after the 1950s, a period immortalized as the quiet before the storm in the popular imagination? Explanations vary with the individual political leanings of whatever critic hazards a guess at the sorry state of the contemporary American family.[1]

Common to almost all theories, however, is a tendency to conceptualize the relationship between the family and its environment in conspiratorial terms. This does not imply that there are, in fact, conspiracies in the legal sense of the term, and that they are working towards a deliberate dissolution of society and its foundations. Rather, it points to a vocabulary of conspiracy which figures prominently whenever the issue of this interrelation is being addressed. In its prototypic appearance, this form of discourse has been characterized best by Richard Hofstadter as "the paranoid style."[2]

Addressing itself to the issue of family, the discourse of conspiracy functions as a conceptual framework that holds together both parts of a rigid dichotomy in describing its object as an abstract term. A simple binary opposition distinguishes between individuals according to their status as members or non-members of a family. In the process, it creates mutually exclusive categories, such as inside/outside, relative/stranger, friend/enemy, and so on.[3] The system allows for all kinds of permutations; someone may, for instance, be related to a person whom one has never met and who is, therefore, a stranger; just as somebody may have close and intimate friends outside the immediate family. Like any binary pairing, it establishes standards of normality according to which all of these permutations are perceived as derivative or even inferior. The title of a book like Christopher Lasch's *Haven in a Heartless World*[4] indicates, for example, that the dichotomy determines even the rhetoric of sociological arguments whose authors appear least susceptible to the "paranoid style" because of their liberal political stance.

Unlike Allan Bloom, who argues in *The Closing of the American Mind* that the family has only temporarily ceased to occupy center stage in the social fabric of American society and will return in due time, Lasch is concerned about what will happen in the meantime. Lasch worries about processes, transformations, and developments, whereas Bloom, positing a conservative ideal, ignores history in favor of a myth or nostalgia for a better time. Besieged from all sides and weakened to the point of collapse, Lasch's family at its worst can either turn out altogether ineffective, or it can overcompensate for its loss of coherence by becoming overprotective, stifling, and confining. In both cases, the "heartless" outside world has managed to exert enough pressure to collapse the previously--or ideally--stable family unit, but in the case of overcompensation, the pressures are internalized and work from the inside out.

The scenario evolving from this dichotomy and its consequences is rich in paranoid and conspirative suspicions. If, on the one hand, the family is intrinsically stable, then it is unlikely that the forces leading to its demise could have been random and unorganized, no matter if they come from without or within the group. If, on the other hand, the family responds to outside forces by withdrawing its beneficiary effects and reversing its protective function, it turns into a conspiracy itself. Instead of nourishing its members, it begins to imprison them and stifles their development and growth.[5] Between these two extremes, there is only a minuscule normative middle-ground where a family actually qualifies as "functional." The variety of deviations suggests, however, that temporary imbalance is the state an organizational system like the family seeks.

Both Don DeLillo's *White Noise* and Joseph McElroy's *The Letter Left To Me* present families that are far from being intact "nuclear" families and thus appear to reflect the state that corresponds to Lasch's or Bloom's sombre diagnosis.[6] In accord with increasing divorce rates, the Gladney household in *White Noise* consist of adults and children from both partners' consecutive marriages so that, in Thomas Ferraro's words, "not a single child that Babette has born or Jack has fathered, whether in their custody or not, is living with both parents or even with a full brother or sister."[7] Unlike this almost farcical reaffirmation of what Ferraro calls "bonds of blood and marriage," the narrator's family in McElroy's novel is characterized by interrupted lineage and the silent harm it causes. In a reversal of Marx's famous dictum, the crucial death of the narrator's father represents a kind of tragic repetition of his grandfather's death, which the family, over a period of years, has transformed into a rather harmless and merry, almost lighthearted episode in its fund of anecdotes.

Harboring the seed of disintegration from the very beginning, both families experience a crisis, which leads the respective narrators to re-examine their own position in the group, as well as the interrelation between the group and the world around it. The paranoid and conspiratorial fears, which both narrators superimpose on the circumstances around them, hark back to the earlier distinction between the possible responses to crisis available to the family. In *The Letter,* the narrator's paranoid fears focus on the possibility that his family's overprotectiveness will lead to an implosion of community, whereas Jack Gladney's anxieties in *White Noise* are concerned with a fragmentation of his family due to the massive onslaught of corrosive influences from the outside. Both texts allow for an ambiguous coexistence of paranoia as the mental condition of the narrator, and the possibility that some conspiracies do, in fact exist, even if they are not necessarily identical with the narrators' specific suspicions.

Although the two novels are primarily concerned with personal interaction on the level of domestic and family life, they both, conspicuously enough, choose to start with a scenario in which not people, but objects occupy center stage. Joseph McElroy's *The Letter Left to Me* opens with a scene in which the narrator's mother hands him the crucial letter from his dead father.

> The woman holding, then handing over the letter to this poised, dumbfounded fifteen-year-old:
>
> is the letter also *hers* ?[8]

The son's response, given its complexity and ambivalence, characterizes him as an inquiring mind with a certain degree of self-irony. "Stupidly sleuthing just where the letter was when,"[9] his method and his general approach to the world make him a manifestation of the classical detective figure for whom the presence of the letter primarily constitutes a mystery that needs to be solved. His devotion to solving the mystery of what the letter means to him and to others by applying rational methods is accompanied by an attitude that discerns design, intention, and significance in the smallest detail and suspects hidden meaning behind actions that appear clear-cut on the surface; a mixture of characteristics that clinical psychology associates with symptoms of paranoia. Yet it is not certain if the mysterious letter will have any significance at all; or whether he will be the one to profit from its contents.

The precocious accuracy of the description signals the narrator's assumption that every move may be significant. The letter itself serves as a clue that helps him to decipher his mother's intentions. She is holding the letter first, signaling ownership and control, which are both key-issues in the novel. Then, almost hesitantly, she relinquishes it as if she would prefer to keep it to herself. Since her behavior alone, however, is inconclusive as a physically tangible manifestation of her present intentions, the narrator can only narrow his interpretive choices down by concentrating on the letter itself. Objects remain stable and reliable, even if people do not. If he only knew more about the letter, he would be capable of gaining more information about his mother. A process of logical deduction, of "building backwards naturally,"[10] that synthesizes all diverging pieces of information into one coherent narrative, will later help him make the leap back from the world of objects to that of human beings.

Since the question about the ownership of the letter will remain unasked, the passage introduces the narrator more as a detached observer than as a participant. He is caught up in the "busy solitude" of his analytic processes instead of being an active force influencing the events revolving around the letter. For him, his mother has the status of a clue, not that of a witness. Like any good detective, he trusts objects more than human beings. Objects, like unconscious human behavior, provides clues. It is free from the potentially misleading interference of hidden motivations. The epistemological status of both objects and the signature of the unconscious makes them self-sufficient and therefore reliable traces of what really happened.

The narrator's idiosyncratic detachment determines the narrative perspective of the novel. It recurs as a thematic concern whenever the narrator refers to his mother as "the woman" and himself as "this fifteen-year-old." Being alert and highly attentive to the most subtle nuances of the letter, he nevertheless establishes an objective stance toward others; an attitude that primarily denies family relationships whenever family members are involved. His insistence on introducing characters through their functional relationship to himself (e.g. "my father's church friends," "a girl who had known of my father's death before I did," or "a woman friend of my mother's") becomes a gesture of pathetic futility since it is exactly the father's death that has upset relationships in this one respect. Al of a sudden familiar characters have, in fact, acquired a life separate from their functional position to the narrator. The mother's male friends, for example, take on a new, unsettling meaning for her son. His grandfather, who is really his step-grandfather, becomes more of a stranger, as the father's absence echoes the premature disappearance of the physical father in his own father's life, and so forth.

As the narrative spirals out and includes more and more characters, which are "precisely, yet ambiguously, created through their responses to the letter,"[11] the narrator continues using the letter as a kind of triangulation device to determine his own position in a confusing network of familial and, to a lesser degree, extrafamilial interactions. Instead of

relying on actual family relations, he creates his own bonds by following rhetorical correspondences like the ones between fathers and sons in successive generations.

Apart from the narrator's obsession with the letter as the organizing principle of his
perception, which the text itself reflects through its own preoccupation with the letter as its
central metaphor, the novel leaves little doubt that his quest for knowledge is legitimate and
that vital issues are at stake for both the narrator and the reader. Since the letter contains
words which, "by the giver's real absence," have gained even more weight, the Oedipal
struggle for an authoritative reading of the text is up against an even more unmovable opponent. To penetrate the text and, in one way or another, achieve closure to the challenging
questions that its presence raises means to establish oneself as master over its maker. The
son's interpretation must replace the father's letter--the letter of the law he has to live by--if
he wants to come into his own and determine his own identity, which, in turn, determines
his relationship to others.[12]

Obviously, McElroy does not consider this rivalry between father's and son's text
to be resolved simply by the capacity of the son's narrative to incorporate the father's letter-
-a kind of access that, in reverse, is denied to the letter itself. Although both texts address
their issues retrospectively--the father's with a sense of leisurely nostalgia, the son's with a
sense of urgency that forbids the luxury of such sentiment--the letter becomes mere material
for the narrator's rewriting. It can be quoted, rephrased, taken out of context, or commented on. Although it will be exactly the physical manipulation of the letter which will
lead to a sense of resolution toward the end of the novel, the narrator's sense of coming to
terms with the burden of his father's message is constituted by a deeper sense of disorien-
tation than any act of physical appropriation alone can resolve.

Yet to be preoccupied with the essential question of true understanding does not
necessarily mean that the narrator is on the verge of paranoia. Obsessiveness is, after all,
relative to the vital importance of the issue in question, and McElroy leaves little doubt that
a guiding word from the absent father would be welcome at this point in the son's life.
However, there is a paranoid tendency in the narrator's deliberations that finds opportunity
to develop its full impact in the space that opens up with the displacement of this struggle
from real life into the text of the letter.

The letter itself is full of good intentions, ""regular" in form and style,"[13] as Tom
LeClair puts it, but ultimately of a blandness and superficiality that frustrates all efforts of
penetration. What is one to make of a remark like this,

Laziness consists primarily of not doing what one ought to do when one ought to do it . . .
14

if everybody seems to agree that it was the writer's command of language that made him excel in his life? The cliché-ridden passage itself does not offer the depth that would invite an act of interpretation, and the background information provided by family folklore does not measure up against what is incontrovertibly on the page. The narrator's only refuge seems to be an interpretation that tries to achieve coherence by reading the letter as a signifier that is identical with its signified and then measuring it against the history of its physical medium.

Focusing on the letter as a physical object, which can be manipulated, altered, falsified, and so on, the meaning of the text now does not only depend on the writer's intentions any more but on the intentions of anybody who, at one time or another, was in possession of the letter; in this case, several family members and close friends.

Since the exact circumstances under which the letter was written are only partly known and must be painstakingly pieced together, the narrator's insecurity establishes a narrative and psychological structure which invites paranoid explanation. The crucial "leap into paranoia,"[15] occurs at precisely the moment when the narrator superimposes his own strategy of relating to others onto their behavior toward himself. Since, by his own choice, the letter constitutes his link to these others, their manipulation of the letter becomes necessarily a manipulation of himself. In one passage, that, in its wording, is deliberately reminiscent of the novel's title, he literally takes the place of the letter by stating that "my father was "survived by me," he left *me* to *them* [i.e. his family]."

Establishing an authoritative reading of the letter now constitutes the prerogative for dealing with the world itself. A collective has taken over the significance of the individual opponent; "the "family" is like one person alone--or unit, I see--after my father's death."[16] Based on the paranoid assumption that this collective acts out one collective will, which goes against the narrator''s interest of liberating himself from its grasp, his search for identity is now contingent on interpreting a text which, in addition to defying any effort of penetration in itself, has acquired multiple authors and therefore produces an even higher degree of ambiguity. The intersection of these three texts--the cliché-ridden letter itself, the history of its physical manipulations, and the history of human intentions behind its dissemination--suggests the close proximity of rational, scientific method and paranoid superimposition.[17]

This proliferation of meaning is accompanied by a process in which an increasing number of actual copies of the letter is being produced and distributed. The decisions that eventually lead up to the decision to print and hand out copies of the letter exclude the narrator. Even though he is the official addressee, he is informed after the fact. Given his psychological profile, what could very well be sheer indifference on behalf of his relatives thus appears as conspiratorial secrecy, purpose, and design.

With an ever-increasing number of copies, the central issue of possession, which already surfaces in the second sentence of the previously cited passage ("is the letter also *hers?*"), takes a different turn. With the existence of only the original, the issue of possession is tied more strongly to the letter as a physical object. It becomes precious for its status as an original, for its aura, to use Walter Benjamin's term. Having and holding it--"manipulating," in the original sense of the word--define ownership without regard to the letter's quality as a message or signifier. Serving the purpose of the traditional MacGuffin in a mystery, the letter is reduced to its sheer physicality. Physical presence becomes everything when there is only one unique object. Only with the dissemination of an increasing number of copies, the narrator becomes aware that he is not so much singled out by his family, and therefore susceptible to their manipulations of the letter's physicality, but rather by the father's "attention" to him. Acknowledging the implicit shift from object to performance, or from finality to inexhaustibility, is an essential prerequisite for opening the first breach in the narrator's paranoid perception.

Moreover, the process of proliferation endows the letter with a history of its own. Its expansive development proceeds from one distinct point of origin. New circumstances produce new intrinsic meanings and subsequent generations of reproduction are hierarchically structured in their relative position to the original. The characteristics of this history are curiously reminiscent of the history that used to be the exclusive privilege of human beings--a history that is based on an ideology of blood and family relations, binary pairings, and metaphysical alliances.

It would, of course, be problematic to suggest that in *The Letter Left To Me* the connotations of human beings and inanimate objects are reversed on the basis of their ideological properties. Just as Tom LeClair suggests, readers do, after all, feel the familiar tug of all those ""regular" and "sensitive" American novels"[18] that *The Letter* is designed to resemble. There is still a strong presence of the Freudian notion of family interaction to be felt, though. Characters manage to evoke genuine and heartfelt concern in the reader for their conflicts and desires; not to mention the impression of being a "well-made novel" that the text successfully communicates. Still McElroy's writing does "teem with options,"[19] as Sandra Schor has pointed out, and it is this sense of ambiguity that not only applies to characters in the novel, but also determines the significance of objects in McElroy's revised notion of family paranoia.

In a brief reconsideration of the opening passage quoted earlier on, it becomes obvious that the function of the letter is not exclusively to establish distance between the two characters. Although the narrator emphasizes their lack of involvement by cancelling possible pathways of communication, his description might just as well be read the opposite way. The mother is after all "handing over" the letter, and the boy himself is "poised", expectant, attentive, or open to whatever he is in for. Spatially, the letter is in between both characters, and even though they themselves do not touch, it establishes the link between them. Boths' desires, however diverse they may be at this moment, are focused on the letter and, through it, toward each other.

Like a mask that simultaneously conceals and reveals something about its wearer, the letter not only separates but also connects the characters. Once, however, the shift from physicality to performance has lead the narrator to reconsider his original notion of ownership, the letter is free to assume this new function. In contrast to a Freudian scenario, father and son are not competing for sexual access to the mother, but rather for control over the space unto which these conflicting desires are projected in the absence of the father and, with it, the absence of unmediated struggle. To a certain degree, it is exactly the shock of this absence that causes the narrator's sense of dislocation and compels him to substitute the individual competitor with the collective, conspiratorial one. Scenes of Oedipal conflict, such as the father's intervention between the son and his girlfriend, are confined to memory. Reality after the father's death sets familiar figures free to abandon their confining positions, much to the narrator's disturbance and envy. Talking about family "as other people. . . [as] famous and infamous careers of habit, made up" in a college classroom constitutes a scandal or disruption as long as one maintains what Freud calls "the illusion of central position." Releasing others from their conceptual dependency upon oneself may, at this point, be a wild and reckless experiment for the narrator, but eventually he will come to accept the lack of family coherence that comes with a lack of conflict.

In order to come to an understanding of what motivates the narrator and drives the narrative towards this crucial insight, the reader needs to be reminded of the novelistic subgenre that McElroy's novel operates in. Although the novels of Raymond Chandler, Dashiel Hammet, or Ross McDonald may, at first glance, not have all that much in common with the refinement and sensibility of McElroy's writing, Geoffrey Hartmann's interpretation of classic American hard-boiled detective fiction points out what their crucial structural correspondences might be.[20] Common to both is the detective figure, who, in the end, temporarily manages to replace the absent father within a family in crisis and thus fulfills the enactment of the Oedipal struggle; the paranoid fear that manipulation or transgression is not committed by "an outsider but someone there all the time, someone we know only too well--perhaps a blood-relation;"[21] and, most of all, what Hartmann, in accordance with Aristotle's *to pathos*, calls "the scene of suffering" which the narrative "seeks to evoke . . . as strongly and visually as possible" and therefore returns to time and again."[22]

Although *The Letter Left To Me* leaves no doubt that, unlike the mystery story, the trauma behind the narrative is not violent death (even though the death in *The Letter* is no less traumatic for that matter), the parallels are obvious. Hartmann himself even accounts for a type of mystery that, by deliberately excluding the scene of suffering, undercuts the basic premises of the genre it utilizes. To his examples--Alain Resnais' *Last Year at Marienbad* and Antonioni's *Blow Up*--one could easily add such by now canonical post-modernist texts as Pynchon's *The Crying of Lot 49* or Paul Auster's *New York Trilogy*. In fact, one could argue that Hartmann's description pinpoints exactly the most crucial feature of fiction attempting to undermine the classic detective story. However, as accurate as this approach may be to certain forms of postmodernist writing, McElroy's novel does not quite fulfill the requirements for this category, since it provides the reader with a kind of *to pathos* that ultimately refuses to serve as the "highly condensed, supersemantic event"[23] that Hartmann suspects at the center of these texts.

As long as there is only one letter, the narrator experiences its dissemination as a betrayal of its original purpose and a lessening of its integrity. About his family, he complains that "they're showing and *sharing* the letter, letting it be seen."[my emphasis][24] As soon as the letter, however, is being "handsomely printed" and sent out in 100 copies, the narrator's initial attitude starts to change. He discovers, for example, that in "its new copies the letter seemed to belong to my mother,"[25] and that "each letter's becoming different, it's the person who's laid eyes on it."[26] McElroy's peculiar preoccupation with sharing, which plays an even more important role in his preceding novel *Women and Men*, goes against the secrecy that is so typical of all conspiracy fiction. Sharing opens the object to a more generous collective appropriation. Sharing defies secrecy. Unlike Pynchon's monolithic and mysterious Lot 49, in which all ratiocination is supposed to culminate and all potential meanings are focused and anticipated, the letter undergoes a process to the opposite effect. In the "corporate act"[27] of mass-printing--McElroy's play on the notion of embodiment is deliberate--Hartmann's "supersemantic event" is being multiplied until it loses its mysterious, metaphysical depth which the narrator had projected onto it as long as there was only the original.[28]

As copies of the letter are being distributed to the narrator's classmates, he wanders through the corridors of the dorm that are now littered with the remnants of what used to be the metaphorical embodiment of his father. He must admit that "the letter is everywhere and I can't answer for it."[29] Significantly enough, this wasteful ubiquity of the letter provides a backdrop for the first scene in which the letter, in its physical as well as its signifying capacity, functions as an unambiguous means of establishing social contact outside the family. Talking to Nina, his roommate's friend, the narrator discovers with a sense of surprise and relief that "the letter stood well and truly between us for us to talk about."[30] To the extent that this scene replays the opening scene between mother and son, it not only suggests that the son's sexual desires have been rerouted to an "object" outside the family, but also that the letter has been stripped of its basic ambiguity. If it does, in fact, constitute a link, then this one quality exists separately from its other functional appropriations. When the narrator is finally alone with Nina he even feels liberated enough to ask her,

Would you like to go to bed with me?" . . .

"No," she said with attention to me and to herself all at once," certainly not."[31]

The emphasis on "attention," a quality previously associated with the father and the paranoid interpretive pattern revolving around the letter, indicates that the narrator has distanced himself from his own conceptual assumptions to a degree that allows him to invest the ideologically charged words with new, positive meaning. Even though his effort fails to a certain extent, the success of his gesture lies in making contact without reference to the letter.[32]

As the family pulls together to repair the fissures that the father's death has opened up in its foundations, its efforts of maintaining coherence ultimately prove to be self-defeating. The proliferation--or, in the narrator's understanding, multiple divisions--of the letter has not increased its impact, but rather lessened it by thinning it out. If the narrator's paranoia has relied on the presence of what Hartmann calls the Freudian "supersemantic event," then the act of printing has transformed depth into surface. It has also virtually erased all legitimacy for the question of ownership, and it has stripped to pathos, and with it the supreme significance of Oedipal conflict, of its privileged position. There is no single place to act out this conflict, and even the father's permanent absence does not stand in the way of the son's growth. If the logical extrapolation of family conspiracy, achieved by technological means, erases all foundations it is grounded in, then conspiratorial activity ceases to be threatening and things can be once again "blessedly incomplete."[33]

Don DeLillo's White Noise follows a similar pattern as The Letter Left To Me, confronting one family member who already displays a predisposition toward paranoia with traumatic events that force him to re-evaluate the internal coherence of his family and his own position in it. Again, the narrator is characterized by an obsessive preoccupation with one subject, but, unlike McElroy's displacement of his narrator's struggle from real life into the mediated ambiguities of a text, Jack Gladney's concerns are of an almost brutal immediacy.

I found myself saying to the assembled heads, "All plots tend to move deathward. This is the
nature of plots. Political plots, terrorist plots, lovers' plots, narrative plots, plots that are part
of children's games. We edge nearer death every time we plot . . .[34]

This monologue that Gladney delivers to his students does not express so much a critical
academic insight--after all, he wonders immediately afterwards "Is this true? Why did I say
it? What does it mean?"--but rather his personal obsession with death and the finality of his
own life. His view of the world tends strongly toward hyperbole and an almost hysterical
insistence on the omnipresence of death as its primary ordering principle and *telos*. The
logical extension of this perhaps defensible assumption leads to the paradox that death
reigns supreme particularly in those activities that, on the surface, are constructive, ordering, and creative. Clearly, the narrator's psychological disposition is reminiscent of that of
The Letter Left To Me: an obsessive preoccupation is projected onto the world, which supposedly reciprocates the individual's attention.

For that reason the world of *White Noise* is teeming with events that do, in fact,
seem to testify to the omnipresence of death. Children need to be evacuated since building
materials used in the construction of their school turn out to be poisonous; Jack's son
Wilder miraculously survives crossing the interstate on his tricycle; an elderly couple dis-
appears and is found, days later, on the verge of starvation; Jack's ex-wives and their new
spouses are involved in clandestine activities that are never fully revealed, and so on. As
the narrator, Jack is of course preselecting these events for the reader according to his own
peculiar list of priorities, but the pervasive sense of imminent danger appears to be larger
than the degree of Jack's obsession. There are, in fact, real dangers out there, but, being
caught up in matters of representation as DeLillo's characters tend to be, it is difficult to tell
which ones are real enough to justify Jack's existential fear and trembling.

Jack's paranoid frame of mind is not the only basis for his preoccupation with death
in all its varieties. He also assumes that his being so attentive to death will cause a recipro-
cal response, which will, in turn, legitimize the attitude he held all along. The kind of death
by which he feels persecuted is the result of a planned, premeditated, and deliberate action
that singles out its target and pursues it with a fateful sense of purpose and inevitable mechanistic inevitability. With the paranoiac's typical reassurance, Jack produces the evidence to
sustain his fears and expects his own personal vision of the world to be reciprocated.
Accordingly, the narrative follows him and his family through a number of situations in
which his life is, in fact, endangered. These events culminate in the so-called "Airborne
Toxic Event," an ominous environmental disaster caused by an industrial accident close to
the Gladneys' suburban neighborhood. In every case, Jack's status as a predestined victim
testifies not so much to his individuality as to his status as a member in an entire group or

class of victims.[35] Applying a logic similar to that of the protagonist of his own *Americana* or that of Yossarian in Joseph Heller's *Catch 22*, Jack is correct in assuming that there is somebody out there who is trying to kill him, and incorrect in assuming that this attempt on his life is targeting him as a specific individual. Circumstances rather than villains seem to be conspiring, so that, in order to regain the sense of personal persecution and the "illusion of central position," the paranoiac must individualize the anonymous historical process.

Piece by piece, however, the narrative reveals that there is a second, more pervasive plot, which is geared not toward Jack's life but the integrity and coherence of his family. In order to participate in the testing of an experimental drug called Dylar, which supposedly eliminates the fear of death, his wife Babette has agreed to exchange sexual favors with a renegade company executive, Mr. Gray; or, as Jack himself puts it, "to join in a sexual conspiracy at [his] expense."[36] Both actions--taking the drug and being unfaithful to her husband--are construed by Jack, and accordingly by other family members, as acts of betrayal and indications of intrafamilial estrangement which compromise the family's capacity to function as a "haven in a heartless world;" an interpretation which Babette's own insistent denials and efforts of concealment only seem to corroborate. Not even Jack's attempt to form a counter-conspiracy together with his daughter Denise manages to erase these effects. In fact, Denise's at times ambiguous behavior creates further suspicion that the dissolution of the family may have progressed even beyond the point where one conspiracy can counter another.

The alleged episodic structure of the novel, which some critics have taken as its deliberate "formlessness," therefore reveals itself as an account of the silent infiltration of the family from the outside as witnessed by one of its members.[37] Even at the early stages of the narrative, when the story seems to amble on at its own sweet pace, something else is going on. Together with the narrator, who assumes the function of the detective, the reader has to sort the relevant from the irrelevant, the essential from the marginal, and the real from the imaginary. While the daily concerns and activities of the family dominate the surface narrative, the text supplies hints and clues that, at second reading, tie together seemingly disparate events. As early as in Chapter 2, the effects of Dylar are being announced clearly for any reader who is willing to go back and look for confirmation.

"You should have been there," I said to [Babette].

"Where?"

"It's the day of the station wagons."

"Did I miss it again? You're supposed to remind me.[38]

Memory loss being one of Dylar's more modest effects, the drug nevertheless succeeds in separating husband and wife as they fail to perform one of the small rituals by which the family commonly reaffirms its integrity. The duplicity of Babette's behavior is underscored by Jack's unwittingly ironic assertion that she "lacks the guile for conspiracies" because she conforms to a certain physical type. Physicality, it turns out, is exactly the object of chemical manipulation that she, with the conspiratorial assistance of Mr. Gray and his associates, keeps a secret from everybody else.[39]

In fact, the strategies of invasion that Dylar employs in its effect on the human body serve as a metonymy that also represents the infiltration of the family, its being "compromised by something unnatural, some small and nasty intrusion."[40] Winnie Richards' description of the drug emphasizes the massiveness of the alleged attack on Jack's family, which, for the paranoid frame of mind, follows logically from its secrecy masquerading as inconspicuousness.

> "It's not a tablet in the old sense...It's a drug delivery system... It self-destructs. It implodes minutely of its own massive gravitation. We've entered the realm of physics..."
>
> "Fantastic. Now tell me what the medication is designed to do? What is Dylar? What are the chemical components?"
>
> "I don't know," she said.[41]

Obviously, the description juxtaposes the organic with the artificial and, in showing how both systems interact, sets up a kind of rivalry between them. The notion of the designer drug that utilizes not one but several strategies of invasion (chemical, physical, biological, technological, etc.), in turn, reduces the human body to an equivalent conceptual abstract--a drug delivery system presupposes a drug receiving system. This act of conceptual intrusion on the level of language indicates the relative status of dominance that the intruder has achieved over its "host." The representation of reality following from this intrusion may be valid for the scientist, but does not help Jack to understand the predicament he is in if he accepts the expert's hollow and alarmingly euphemistic terminology.

The second and rather unsettling effect of this description is its juxtaposition of precision and vagueness. If the objectives of the drug can be reconstructed from the complexity of its physical shape and design then it is unlikely that the drug targets the trivial, the banal, or the merely marginal. Something so complex presupposes grand objectives. Complementary to this relative density of information about surfaces and appearances, the text refuses to answer immediate questions, Jack's or the reader's, about the depth or reality underneath. The passage describing Dylar introduces an element of defamiliarization by reconceptualizing the human body in terms of surface or systemic abstract. By doing so, it reminds the reader of other instances in the novel where structure, shape, process, or form are emphasized in order to distract from certain characters' curious ignorance of or indifference toward content (the efforts of SIMUVAC, Jack's learning German, Babette's seminars in which she teaches sitting or breathing, etc.). By dominating the representational systems it infiltrates, Dylar extends the sphere of its own austere vision.

On the level of novelistic discourse, this would mean the slow atrophying of Bakhtinian "heteroglossia," of social and political conflict and competition as reflected in artistic language--a state that *White Noise*, at least in its novelistic versatility and inventiveness, manages to avoid. To ask the question what kind if intrusion Dylar represents, therefore, makes it necessary to suppose an ideological statement where none is suspected.

One of Dylar's most obvious characteristics, particularly in contrast to the sphere it invades and subverts, is the fact that it is mass-produced and technologically advanced. Dylar is a commodity designed for economic exchange between manufacturer and consumer. The paths of its economic circulation are reminiscent of its physical progress through the body and its complex systems. In this respect it is the perfect representation of the kind of object that the Gladneys are constantly surrounded with. Unlike the ontological distinction between, and historical coexistence of, original and copy that the reader encounters in *The Letter Left To Me*, *White Noise* is filled with objects that are copies without originals or simulacra, a term that has acquired currency in the debate on postmodernism with its refinement through Jean Baudrillard.[42]

In the opening scene of the novel, which is reminiscent of *The Letter Left To Me* in its tableau-like configuration, the isolated narrator is faced with a multitude of objects and the challenge that they pose in their indifference and superficiality.

> The roofs of the station wagons were loaded down with carefully secured suitcases full of light and heavy clothing: with boxes of blankets, boots and shoes, stationary and books, sheets, pillows, quilts; with rolled-up rugs and sleeping bags; with bicycles, skis, rucksacks, English and Western saddles, inflated rafts.[43]

While in McElroy's novel the content of the letter lacks the sense of depth or density corresponding to the mystery that its mere existence creates, *White Noise* achieves a similar effect by drowning potential meaning in an undifferentiated quantitative richness--something that its title already alludes to. The question what every single one of these objects in itself means is obliterated by their confusing multiplicity.

As the list continues, it describes indirectly, but none the less precisely, the students and their parents as a community that is defined by its position within a consumer society and its relative access to the goods it produces. John Frow has pointed out how problematic the act of individual and collective self-definition turns out to when it is accomplished through acts of concumption; in other words, when identity is contingent on a notion of style rather then historical necessity. For the novelist "the opposition between the general and the singular collapses as they merge into a singular, undialectical unity,"[44] while for characters in the novel authenticity is not a matter of essence any more but of surface, appearance, shape, etc.--obviously all qualities that the reader has already come to associate with Dylar.

Curiously enough, however, Jack's attitude toward the world of commodities and consumerism in general differs from his attitude toward Dylar in particular. While he associates the latter closely with his paranoid anxieties about the imminent dissolution of his family, he looks upon the former as a space in which family can be reaffirmed. As Thomas Ferraro points out, the Gladneys celebrate their sense of familial togetherness and solidarity repeatedly in elaborate meals and shopping sprees of almost epic proportions, in communal rites of consumption and acquisition. Jack himself seems to affirm the integrity of his family by rejoicing in the temporary suspensions, reversals, and refigurations of traditional roles that these carnivalesque excursions allow for. But the strategy is caught up in paradox from the very beginning.[45]

Like Dylar, consumerism ultimately isolates family members from one another. As the Gladneys scatter in different directions during their trips to the mall, or fall into silence during their binges around the kitchen table or in the car, what used to be a collective separates into several individuals with desires that are being served individually. However, the aura of connectedness between individual consumers, if compared to the family, is non-hierarchical. Individuals are not organized according to their relationship with each other any more, or in relation to one privileged point of origin, but according to their relationship to the commodity, which is infinitely reproducible and therefore lacks an intrinsic sense of value. Whereas the relative degree of access to the commodity differs from one consumer to the next, every consumer is equal to the other in relation to the commodity.

Dylar creates bonds that are incompatible with the family hierarchy because it creates outside communities. Babette's link with Mr. Gray, for example, constitutes an act of marital infidelity. It also creates a new, small community between the two and all those in Mr. Gray's company who silently condone his behavior. Thus, it endangers the coherence of the Gladney family. Babette's submission to Dylar's conceptual aggressiveness, which turns her into a commodity or, at best, into a guinea pig in a pharmaceutical experiment that requires large numbers of subjects, and series testing, undercuts the notions of organicism that Jack's understanding of family is based on.

With the revelation that Dylar does not fulfill its promise of liberating human beings from their fear of death, *White Noise* qualifies as much as an anti-mystery as *The Letter Left To Me*. The anticlimactic moment of denouement hardly qualifies as a solution to the plots' mysteries. As Jack decides to take significant action and act out his part in what he perceives in terms of conventional conspiracy stories, the novel even goes on to collapse systematically the key elements of its genre. The motel room where Babette and Mr. Gray met in conspiratorial secrecy is in reality shabby and bleak. Mr. Gray himself, whom Babette described as a composite and whom Jack builds up to be literally the "gray" eminence behind the corporate conspiracy against his family, is not the more powerful for the conceptual multiplication of his identities. Instead he turns out to be a "weary pulse of a man, a common pusher now, spiky-haired, going mad in a dead motel."[46] The final disclosure of his name, Willie Mink, adds to this overall anticlimactic effect, as melodrama slides into farce and mystery into insignificance.

Similarly to the omnipresence of the father's letter in McElroy's novel, Dylar itself has lost its powerful, mysterious aura at the moment when it is present in great quantities. As Jack "watch[es] Mink ingest more pills," what used to be one single bottle behind the radiator cover or a few rare specimen sacrificed for Winnie Richard's chemical analysis is now suddenly everywhere. Dylar is spilling out of Mink's mouth, scattering on the floor, and caught in the folds of his clothes. With this moment of demystification, Dylar is reconciled with the sphere of commodities where it originally belongs and from which it had only temporarily been elevated by Jack's paranoid projection.

Since Dylar represents simply one particular case within the arena of commodities in *White Noise*, DeLillo's characterization suggests that the two sides of the same phenomenon are inextricably intertwined. While certain facets of consumer capitalism herald the forming of new hierarchies, chains of command, and collectives competing with social institutions such as the family, others merely lead to a fragmentation of the old institutions, a splitting up of collectives into large numbers of less powerful individuals that relate to each other through mediation of what ultimately separates them. As Thomas Ferraro puts it, "Consumer capitalism brilliantly exploits the need for strengthening family bonds that it has itself, in part, destroyed."[47]

Since neither the narrator of *The Letter Left To Me* nor the one of *White Noise* comes to realize the conceptual leap between the real and the imagined dangers, between paranoia and conspiracy, it seems rather unlikely that DeLillo or McElroy are primarily interested in testing conspiracy theories for their validity when measured against the real world. Both their narrators remain caught up in an understanding of the world that does not significantly differ from the one they started out with, even when they both, at the end of their stories, have managed to work out some of their problems. Unlike the narrators, the reader may be left with an uneasy sense of compromise, which Katherine Hayles would probably attribute to the commitment of both texts to what she calls "postmodern parataxis."

For DeLillo, there is no progression toward a recuperated embodiment that does not end in
death. To achieve the one is to be subject to the other. Although this is scarcely a novel
conclusion, the transformations that constitute it are distinctly postmodern, marking the
construction of consciousness in an information age.[48]

Similarly, McElroy's novel ends on a Beckettian note of irreconcilable opposites that the
narrator finally comes to embrace.

I am wild, in my haste, and I will live a new life. The letter is everywhere and I can't answer
for it. I'll answer the letter. I can't. But I will.[49]

If the validity of conspiracy theories in itself is not a matter of interest for the novelist any
more, then what must be at stake is more likely to be the transformations they undergo, as
Katherine Hayles calls it. How can the twists and turns of conspiracy fiction be re-de-
ployed and what can they accomplish when implemented within familiar territory? What
exactly constitutes this familiar territory may be arguable given the fact that both novels operate within a crossover of different genres--by my count, one could at least argue convincingly for the presence of elements from the domestic novel, the mystery, and the
Bildungsroman.[50] This kind of hybrid, or rather, this gesture of postmodern hybridization,
may have already lost its innovative freshness for the contemporary reader, who has come
to associate its characteristics with what Stefano Tani calls "the anti-mystery" or what
Geoffrey Hartmann calls "the whodunut, a story with a hole in it."[51] Through such
canonical texts as, for example, Pynchon's *The Crying of Lot 49* or Alain Resnais' *Last
Year At Marienbad*, the notion that deferred closure denotes subversion of the convention
seems already firmly established. DeLillo's and McElroy's demonstrable lack of interest in
the concerns of these postmodern anti-mysteries suggests, however, that they already perceive them as a solidified trope, complete with its own set of traditions and conventions.

Considering how narrowly circumscribed both authors' treatment of conspiracy and
paranoia is and how precisely measurable their effects and ramifications in a "small" environment like the family are, the question arises what kind of parataxis is achieved or preserved by the novels' paranoid vision. The answer to this question appears to be simple if
one considers all those elements in the texts that appear paradoxical or contradictory. On the
one hand, both novels present families that are already deeply compromised by the contemporary condition of society; lineage is inconsecutive and discontinuous, "bonds of blood
and marriage" are fragmented. Given their options, both families are even more compromised by their respective responses to these symptoms of fragmentation. One, in turning
inward, becomes a potential threat to its members; the other embraces its state of imminent
collapse so lightheartedly that one critic suspects repression or denial on a grand scale.[52]

On the other hand, however, these families are still capable of fulfilling their functions as if they were intact and fully functional. The narrator of *The Letter Left To Me* does live out the struggle with his father and eventually overcomes the restrictions placed upon him. Jack Gladney in *White Noise* manages to create moments in which the family pulls together and achieves the quality of a "haven in a heartless world" after all.

Among the essential characteristics of the paranoid vision that Richard Hofstadter describes is the speaker's assumption that there is "a vast, insidious, preternaturally effective international conspiratorial network designed to perpetrate acts of the most fiendish character."[53] Contrary to this description, both *The Letter Left To Me* and *White Noise* demonstrate that conspiracy becomes weaker and eventually dissolves completely when it reaches the culmination Hofstadter describes. When the father's letter is reproduced in sufficient numbers to approach the quality of DeLillo's "white noise"--a shapeless, overabundant, emptied out commodity--it loses its power and grasp on the narrator. Similarly, Dylar changes its metaphorical properties at the moment its physical ubiquity is being revealed. At the moment both narratives reach a juncture where they could easily adopt what Hofstadter describes as a disproportionately and dramatically hyperbolic, highly charged style, they reverse direction and reaffirm conspiracy as personal, focused, and precise.

This allows the narrators to experience, with a sense of authenticity, what they long for from the safe distance of nostalgia. Jack Gladney knows quite well that the ideological machinery that enables him to construct his particular notion of family in a postmodern environment is contingent on exactly the same forces by which he sees this construction jeopardized. Equally, the narrator in *The Letter Left To Me* has succeeded in creating a scenario in which his family is barely threatening and "conspiratorial" enough to allow him the enactment of the conflict which, as his culture tells him, is essential for achieving maturity and growth. It is, however, a scenario equipped with the vital safety device of self-destruction in case of unforeseen acceleration and momentum.

The particular sense of conspiracy that arises from these transformations is free of both condemnation and glorification. Neither are conspiracies delusional mystifications, nor are they expressions of the mind's ordering instinct that creates meaning in a fragmented and chaotic world. Instead, they are pragmatically accepted as ideologies which allow for the necessary recuperation and the creative and critical recombination of certain elements within a given culture. If, for example, conspiracy tends to deny the detective the conflict with his father-figure, another conspiracy, this one mediated through technology and textuality, can make it happen after all. The achievement of the novels discussed here consists in their extrication of the paranoid style from the trope of hyperbole and its assignment to one proper place in the imagination of the reader of postmodern fiction.

Significant is, however, that for whatever purpose, a newly emerging type of writing insists that conspiracy must lose its tendency toward hyperbole. It will require the example of other texts to determine how radical this reformulation is and how it affects the ideological fabric of postmodern conspiracy fiction.

Notes

[1] The most influential of these recent discussions about the condition of social institutions in America has been Allan Bloom's *The Closing of the American Mind: How Higher Education Has Failed Democracy and Impoverished the Soul of Today's Students* (New York: Simon & Schuster, 1987). As for the general direction of the argument and the political persuasion of its author, the book's title speaks for itself.

[2] Richard Hofstadter, *The Paranoid Style in American Politics* (New York: Alfred A. Knopf, 1967).

[3] see particularly the discussion on blood as a normative category for establishing systems of kinship in the transition from feudal to bourgeois societies in Michel Foucault's *The History of Sexuality: An Introduction* (New York: Random House, 1978) 147-50.

[4] Christopher Lasch, *Haven in a Heartless World: The Family Besieged* (New York: Basic Books, 1977).

[5] The pattern evolving from these choices is clearly related, in its simplicity and the richness of its mythical resonances, to certain elements in the fairy-tale. The temporary or final absence of the family produces the orphan, who must either recover his/her identity by finding the lost parents and thus re-establish the temporarily suspended order, or establish a family-scenario of his/her own. The overprotective family, consequently, generates the reversal of familiar roles; mothers are replaced by evil stepmothers, etc.

[6] Don DeLillo, *White Noise* (New York: Viking, 1985), and Joseph McElroy, *The Letter Left To Me* (New York: Alfred A. Knopf, 1988).

[7] Thomas Ferraro, "Whole Families Shopping at Night," *New Essays on* White Noise (Cambridge: Cambridge UP, 1991) 17. I am also indebted to Thomas Ferraro for pointing out Lasch and Bloom as two of the foremost examples of cultural criticism addressing the decline of the American family.

[8] *Letter* 3.

[9] *Letter* 35.

[10] *Letter* 3.

[11] Tom LeClair, "Opening Up Joseph McElroy's *The Letter Left To Me*," *Review of Contemporary Literature* 10.1 (Spring 1990) 261.

[12] McElroy actually goes so far as to extend the letter's sphere of influence within the narrator's consciousness to the realm of inanimate objects. Everything the letter may have touched upon in its erratic course seems transformed into "luminous detail": "a drop-leaf desk. . . a china vase. . . that open lower drawer. . ." (3-4). The loving, yet precise evocation of these objects endows them with the potential meaningfulness that comes easy to the narrator given his psychological disposition.

[13] LeClair, "Opening Up Joseph McElroy's *The Letter Left To Me*," 261.

[14] *Letter* 121.

[15] see the discussion on the necessity of "welcoming structures" for the formation of the paranoid frame of mind in Dieter Groh, "The Temptation of Conspiracy Theory, or: Why Do Bad Things Happen to Good People? Part I: Preliminary Draft of a Theory of Conspiracy Theories," *Changing Conceptions of Conspiracy*, Eds. Carl Graumann and Serge Moscovici (New York: Springer, 1987) 3. Similar observations can also be found in Hofstadter.

[16] *Letter* 38.

[17] In reference to Max Weber, Dieter Groh points out that human intentions and historical events are hardly ever identical. Therefore, the assumption that events can be reliable traces by which schemes and plots can retrospectively be reconstructed and exposed is false and may lead the historian into acceptance of conspiracy as the only viable explanation derived from this faulty assumption.

[18] LeClair, "Opening Up Joseph McElroy's *The Letter Left To Me*," 260.

[19] Sandra Schor, "*The Letter Left To Me*," *Review of Contemporary Literature* 10.1 (Spring 1990) 268.

[20] Geoffrey Hartmann, "Literature High and Low: The Case of the Mystery Story," *The Fate of Reading and Other Essays* (Chicago: University of Chicago Press, 1975).

[21] Hartmann 221.

[22] Hartmann 204.

[23] Hartmann 207.

[24] *Letter* 33.

[25] *Letter* 50.

[26] *Letter* 65.

[27] *Letter* 65.

[28] It is significant that the family member mostly responsible for and instrumental in the printing of the letter is the step-grandfather, who, after losing his job with the Underwood typewriter company, opens a business as a printer. Carefully, McElroy develops the contrast between the handwritten letter (the father's handwriting, his personal style are frequently commented on) and the printed copies. One represents Western notions of logocentric integrity while the other is associated with the uncontrollable, free play of the signifier. The narrator's paranoid anxieties are focused on the original which is still endowed with the "aura" of originality. Curiously enough, however, the novel's specific genealogy suggests a reversal of generations between father and (step-)grandfather, just as it does between modernism and postmodernism. What is the reader to make of the fact that the historical antecedent survives its offspring and takes on the responsibility as curator of its heritage? Most likely, McElroy suggest that the relationship between both is based on choice rather than historical sequence or necessity since father and grandfather are not related by blood.

58

29 *Letter* 152.

30 *Letter* 148.

31 *Letter* 150.

32 In an interview with Tom LeClair, McElroy himself has pointed out that other people are often taken aback by him because of the intense degree of attention he devotes to them; an attention often mistaken for apprehension or even aggression. In this sense, the novel also reinterprets paranoid concepts like "surveillance" or "persecution" as forms of loving attention. See Tom LeClair, "An Interview with Joseph McElroy," *Anything Can Happen: Interviews with Contemporary American Novelists,* Eds. Tom LeClair and Larry McCaffery (Champaign: University of Illinois Press, 1983) 235-251.

33 *Letter* 151.

34 *White Noise* 26.

35 The activities of SIMUVAC, therefore, represent the reification of these fears and, with it, the curious overlap between Jack's paranoia and events in reality that seem to reaffirm his worst fears. "The trajectory of the novel," as Katherine Hayles suggests, "then arcs from fetishized embodiment to a dissipation of materiality into information, onward to a recuperation of embodiment through violence." In this alternation between concrete embodiment and abstract dissipation, DeLillo's characters enact the surface narrative of consumerism; information and violence are, after all, commodities in their own right. The conspiracy story they conceal, however, points toward the possibility that power can be seized from this surface and dissipated to a degree that its effects become virtually nil in certain spots. See Katherine Hayles, "Postmodern Parataxis: Embodied Texts, Weightless Information," *American Literary History* 2.3 (Winter 1990) 411.

36 *White Noise* 199.

37 For the most comprehensive overview of critical opinions on *White Noise,* see Frank Lentricchia, ed., *New Essays on* White Noise (Cambridge: Cambridge UP, 1991).

38 *White Noise* 5.

39 Undeniably, there is an element of Oedipal struggle in the relationships between Jack and Babette, and Mr. Gray and Babette. While the whole text indulges freely in depicting characters reverting to atavistic behavior, Jack repeatedly describes his wife as a particularly maternal presence, calling her "ample" and praising her "girth and heft"(5). Their lovemaking is strongly reminiscent of mother-son relationships. Jack's nickname for her is "Baba" and his physical longings are primarily directed toward her breasts. At the same time, Jack imagines Mr. Gray as "his bleak hands enfolded a rose-white breast. . . I felt his mastery and control. The dominance of his position." (241) Similar to McElroy's novel, the Oedipal rival for sexual access to the mother is associated with a collective rather than an individual. Mr. Gray is first described as a "composite," as one of "four or more figures engaged in a pioneering work" (241). In this respect, the paranoid tendencies of both narrators create the same conflation of Oedipal conflict and paranoid anxieties,

just as their indulging in Oedipal fantasies is both made possible by the intervention of technology and textuality (the letter/Dylar).

[40] *White Noise* 240.

[41] *White Noise* 188.

[42] Important in this regard are two studies that focus primarily on this particular aspect of the novel: John Frow, "The Last Things before the Last: Notes on *White Noise*," and Frank Lentricchia, "Tales of the Electronic Tribe," both in *New Essays on* White Noise (Cambridge: Cambridge UP, 1991). Frow and Lentricchia focus on the fact that the world of the novel is dominated by representations that only refer back to other representations rather than nature itself. For usage of the term "simulacra" as one of the central concepts of the discussion on postmodernism, see Jean Baudrillard, *Simulations* (New York: Semiotext(e), 1983).

[43] *White Noise* 3.

[44] Frow, "The Last Things Before the Last," 173.

[45] Ferraro, "Whole Families Shopping at Night," .15-38.

[46] *White Noise* 307.

[47] Ferraro, "Whole Families Shopping at Night," 36.

[48] Katherine Hayles, "Postmodern Parataxis," 412.

[49] *Letter* 153.

[50] see John Johnston, "Generic Difficulties in the Novels of Don DeLillo," *Critique* 30 (Summer 1989) 261-75.

[51] Stefano Tani, "The Dismemberment of the Detective," *Diogenes* 120 (Winter 1982), and Hartmann, "Literature High and Low," 206.

[52] Ferraro, "Whole Families Shopping At Night," 18.

[53] Hofstadter, "The Paranoid Style," 14.

2. Ratner's Star *and* Women and Men: *Encyclopedic Fictions*

In a chapter of Joseph McElroy's *Women and Men* simply entitled "Larry," a young man does his homework.[1] In front of him, the paper is filled with graphs and other abstract representations. As he struggles to understand economic theories in their confusing vocabulary and bewildering multiplicity, he must try to ignore his parents' constant fighting, which at that moment is inevitably leading them into a divorce. He is also distracted because his girlfriend Amy is seeing an older man, who also happens to be a good friend and mentor to Larry himself. And then there is of course the world around him, unfolding with all its brutality and beauty, splendor and squalor. How does Adam Smith's "Invisible Hand," Keynesianism, or Pareto's theory about the equal distribution of property relate to Larry's life? What does the abstract language of economic theory contribute to his efforts to establish a sense of identity; as an consumer in a global economy, an individual in a mass-society, a man confronted with women, a child dealing with his parents, a citizen dealing with state authority, an intelligent person, a reader, coping with information?

In addition to these distracting circumstances, which themselves deserve careful study and consideration, Larry knows that whenever human beings are concerned one must look beyond the material world and things as they are and instead determine their intentions. Human beings who are motivated by intentions have invented the theories Larry is studying, just as they are facilitating the knowledge he is absorbing and processing. One of them has given birth to him and two of them have raised him. Then there are others who are after his money or are interested in his sexuality; who want to share with him or take from him. Just as objects are only theoretically separate from intentions, Larry has learned, abstract theories are only theoretically separate from concrete experience. Torn between conflicting and shifting alliances and loyalties, Larry finally manages to take the step away from the impersonal "one," the convenient positivistic fiction by which he used to refer to himself, and accept the personal "I," mostly for the sake of Amy. Eventually, he will come to realize that this personal breakthrough, which allows him to create a stable entity in the continuous flow around him, also connects him with others in unforeseen ways. To be connected means sympathetically or vicariously participating in somebody else's experience, and to be unreservedly engaged in somebody else means giving up the stable separate identity Larry has just achieved. What then is the lesson for Larry, what the use in trying, successfully or not, to halt the chaotic flow of experience?

Like so many of the characters in his fiction and like McElroy himself, Larry is capable of "passionate attendance to the full particulars of our daily lives and the plural worlds we inhabit."[2] Keeping an open mind, Larry creates a relationship to the world that is determined by curiosity and an insatiable appetite for information and sensation. He pays scrupulous attention, which makes him a paranoiac, albeit a curiously composed one. Discerning hardly visible patterns and finding himself surrounded by other peoples' intentions and designs, Larry lacks the sense of anxiety which is typical for the paranoid frame of mind; the protagonists of *White Noise* and *The Letter Left To Me* were prime examples. But Larry knows that even the most precious and strongly developed sense of identity does not place him at the center of the universe. In most cases, the recognition of his own relative (in-)significance teaches him to distinguish between the plots that are directed against him and only him, and the plots that may affect him but are not directed against him personally; a distinction that would carry little weight for the true paranoiac. The things that trouble Larry are closer to home: the breakup of his parents' marriage, the lack of commitment from Amy, getting good grades, making sense of his readings.

In his economics class, Larry discovers that the market in a global free--market economy can be imagined as a grand conspiracy. At the hands of a "Chief Executive"[3] the "Big Board . . . transactivates its parts to plot a collaborative global act by which both Gravity and Government are divided by both Agency and Anarchy."[4] As a result, peoples' lives in some remote places of the world like Chile or New Mexico are destroyed, while others have the opportunity to devote themselves to classes in which they are taught the basics of economic theory. On a very personal level, Larry was already aware of these hidden correspondences. He understands how one experience can explain another through their shared properties, similarities, and contrasts. As Larry's parents are growing apart because they have allowed themselves to become intimate with others outside of their marriage, Larry himself is worried about the friendship between Amy and James Mayn, both of them good friends. Is their friendship a threat to Larry's and Amy's friendship, the same way the strangers, who used to be close friends to either his mother or his father, have come between his parents as a couple? With James Mayn becoming a surrogate for Larry's estranged biological father, does Amy's relationship to Mayn alienate her from Larry in the way Larry's mother is alienated from him? As correspondences proliferate, Larry learns about either one situation by comparing it to the other. The latent meanings about the sum total of their interactions create a kind of emotional marketplace. It would be equally fair to say that their shifting alliances and schemes constitute a tangle of conspiracies that continuously lurk in the background of all that politeness. After all, economics already suggested that the market was a grand conspiracy. Could a graph represent and explain this emotional and personal, yet fundamentally political tangle?

In summarizing this part of Larry's story, it becomes clear that McElroy expects the reader to consider the possibility of applying abstract theory to concrete experience. If we consider this suggestion as an instruction on how to read the almost 1200 pages of *Women and Men*, Larry's individual experience could serve as a test case for any number of abstract theories, or as their metaphoric representation. Since McElroy keeps subject and object of abstractions indistinguishable, he also suggests that two abstractions could interact with each other in that manner. Instead of, for example, Larry being simultaneously the creator of an economic theory, its object, and the metaphor representing it, economics itself could be seen as a conspiracy, and the interaction between economics and conspiracy could then be reapplied to Larry's personal experience. The paranoid possibility that everything is merely Larry's creation never comes up; the world is simply too real to indulge in paranoid power-fantasies like that.

More engaging than endlessly cross-referencing between private and public or abstract and concrete, however, is the semantic field in which this proliferation takes place, such as, for example, the one surrounding the term "economics" itself. Its etymology can be traced back to the notion of "housekeeping," or, as McElroy himself has suggested, to "homework." The image of managing a household or doing homework reintegrates the daunting abstraction immediately into the sphere of the personal, the domestic, the concrete. Looking back to Larry's parents and friends, it is clear that their shared emotional, maybe even sexual economy--the give and take, supply and demand, production and consumption--must have been disturbed for things to get out of hand that dramatically. If equilibrium is the state that a system like a household strives for, then nothing would be further from it than these intersecting lives. The family's house, which Larry is about to lose through "the changed equation between one's married parents,"[5] is also the home where Larry does his "home-work," which these days may consist of an effort to "keep it together." The shelter that this home provides, its peace and seclusion, and the sense of belonging and identity are the prerequisites for doing good work. Part of this work on problems of economics then is to ask questions about value: how does one determine the value of something that is both object and abstraction and therefore charged with many conflicting interpretations? Is its value dependent on the potential user's interpretation? And what if the user changes his mind; after all, like Larry himself, others are only a temporary manifestation of a permanently fluctuating identity? What is needed is a modulus: "a constant factor--a multiplier! for the conversion of units from one system to another!"[6]

If it was true that any abstract could function as metaphor for other abstracts, then the idea of the modulus can be read both as a valuable contribution to economic theory and as, among other things, a pointer for the reader to follow expanding metaphors beyond the limitations of this one chapter. In other words, the modulus could serve as a metaphor for metaphor. Tracing the idea of "economics" in all its variety, readers will realize that the small chapter devoted to Larry suddenly grows in all directions. There is, for instance, the apartment building Larry and his parents live in and which Larry's friend and one half of the novel's protagonist-pair, James Mayn, is trying to convert into rent-controlled housing. If the New York brownstone were rent-controlled, the novel further suggests, it would resemble the abandoned Anasazi Cliff Dwellings, which Jim Mayn happens to visit on his travels in the Southwest. Jim is haunted by these ruins and the mystery of their vanished inhabitants. At home in New York, Jim is someone who keeps returning to his old apartment; as he haunts the new tenants with his inexplicable appearances, he himself is haunted in turn by this space he is so reluctant to leave behind, his imagination a space occupied, in turn, by the the space like an absentee landlord. In order to get home, one must abandon another house sometimes. Foley, one of Mayn's numerous connections, is in a correctional facility: a house of a different kind, which is not a home, yet still an ultimate destination, as he jokingly points out to Mayn: "In my keeper's multiple dwelling there are many Mansons."[7]

Then there are houses in *Women and Men* that are not quite literally houses. As a house that circles the earth, the Skylab station stretches the metaphor to its furthest extreme on the macroscopic end of the spectrum. Similarly, the house loaded on a trailer and moved across the continent as a Wide Load poses serious questions about the nature of houses: are they homes whenever they are reliably confined to one place? Or when they are "havens in a heartless world," surrounded by a hostile environment? Or when they contain "functioning" communities, like scientific research teams, or a prison population, or a family? On the other end of the spectrum is the small, physical, and intimate; the Chilean diva's body, for example, as it plays host and home to a tapeworm. From the largest to the smallest scale, readers need to reconsider and economize what they think they know about houses and, by implication, housekeeping, homework, economics. Once the connotations of individual metaphors begin interacting in the way I have tried to demonstrate, new metaphors are being generated, and these new, composite tropes are more daring, dazzling, and far-reaching than anything a first reading can reasonably recognize. In the combination of extremes, the economy brings together inside (the diva's) and outside (the planet), far (Skylab) and near (the apartment), familiar (the brownstone) and exotic (the cliff dwellings). Does *Women and Men* suggest to its readers to consider one extreme as a concealed manifestation of its opposite?

If *Women and Men* were any less unique in its rhetorical strategies, it would be content to expose metaphors as means of concealing the truth about the world. Ultimately, they would aim for a sense of apprehension and dislocation. Of course, the facility Foley is confined to is no "mansion," although the reference to a certain kind of house by that particular term has an acute political implication about property, the law, architectural space and jargon, or social class. Yet McElroy goes beyond solely dismantling the metaphor; he reinvests it with new meaning after it has been dismantled, endowing the deconstructive turn with a reconstructive connotation. The ideological gesture is not one of dramatic revelation, typical of conventional conspiracy fiction and, if delayed or subverted, of postmodernist fiction as well. Instead, the text indulges in a kind of thoughtful, "economic" recycling of something that has intrinsic value and must therefore not be discarded. This is also one of the reasons why *Women and Men* "has magnitude rather than final shape."[8] A novel that begins again and again and is hesitant to let go of anything has, of course, no strong sense of climactic resolution. It is in this sense that the novel also exceeds the limits of the metaphor of "economics." When seen as a capitalist market, economics falsely implies a sense of restraint, competition, and scarcity--concepts on which our notions of value are based to a large extent. Although economics describes quite accurately the processes of exchange and circulation by which literal and metaphorical information is being created and facilitated, it remains mired in a way of thinking that relies heavily on an inappropriately sequential and linear logic. Instead of the term "economical," the term "ecological" may be more suitable for a work of fiction in which nothing is lost, abandoned, or ever completely exhausted. *Women and Men* defies the notion of consumption as the "using up" and destruction of a resource and favors instead repeated circulation, recuperation, and recapitulation.[9]

Contrary to the economic metaphor, the proliferation of information also contributes significantly to its own increase in value. Explicitly phrased in the title of one chapter, "still life: sisters sharing information," the idea of shared information is coupled with the notion of the "division of labor," which is itself integrated into the title of the novel's opening chapter. According to this complex of ideas, information is not a commodity that can be capitalized upon by artificially increasing its scarcity. The politics of anti-ecology, closely associated with the character Spence and his stealing and hoarding of information, drains information from the networks, isolating its "owners" from their vital activities and depriving the information itself of its potential value. Since information confers certain responsibilities upon those who acquire it, its proliferation divides the labor of dealing with these responsibilities between all participants: generating it, passing it on, receiving it in turn from others, and acting upon it, all activities which themselves generate more information. An independent agent who sells his services to the highest bidder, Spence deliberately attempts to arrest this multiple circular flow. Neither does he divide the labor associated with acquiring and processing information, nor does he reciprocate his own gains by feeding information back into the systems he is exploiting.

Consequently, Spence's definitions of both "sharing" and "dividing" are geared toward a capitalist reformulation of what McElroy clearly intends to be understood as an ecology. Spence's behavior and its underlying philosophy constitutes a perversion or aberration of the novel's overall system. According to him, sharing means buying and selling for profit. Dividing labor means exploiting the work of others and separating actions from their consequences. The stability of the system according to Spence, which is not an ecosystem any more but a marketplace, does not depend on homeostatic balance but on the systemic and calculated perpetual imbalance between supply and demand. Isolated from the proliferation of informational networks, Spence becomes an object of suspicion for all other characters that come into contact with him. Ironically, this sense of paranoia is perhaps the only category in which he himself can reciprocate how the world responds to him. A potential conspirator, inscrutable in all of his goals save the greed for profit and power, Spence is a representative and agent of all the forces in *Women and Men* which try to curb informational proliferation: the political conspiracies jealously guarding their secrets, the multinational corporations concerned about maintaining a centralized hold on their global operations and resources, and all the other agents whose influence on the world around them is mainly of a coercive and manipulative nature.

Augmented by this ecological metaphor, economics can now become a metaphor for the writing and reading of a novel of the scope of *Women and Men* itself. From this perspective, the novel considers itself "the articulate structure we have gradually seen built up by partial pictures, accommodating (on faith, perhaps) a multiplicity of small-scale units."[10] One of those small-scale units contains Larry and his story, while the codes and theories he explores constitute some of the "partial pictures" he is putting together. All of them join forces to form an articulate structure by extending themselves through other characters and their stories and through the theories and codes which allow for further dissemination of knowledge from one story into another. Assuming that there is no break in the chain early on, this process of metaphorical extension could continue until, theoretically, the sum total of all possibilities is exhausted; that is, the possibilities of the world, which are technically endless, and not those of the narrative.

The resulting structure must be vast and looming, somewhat intimidating and challenging, difficult and perhaps even incomprehensible if it wants to accomplish all of these ambitious goals. It must be part cathedral and part penitentiary; part comforting retreat from the world, just like the diva's large intestine, and part global environment, home of humans and other sentient beings. It must include a gesture of grandeur and empathy by extending itself into the world the way it does. And it must necessarily admit its failure since no text can technically live up to this challenge. Every book has a first and last page, just as events follow each other through the medium of language and print in linear order. If the novel were to approach its subject from the point of view of literary realism, that is, by inscribing itself into the world in all its plenitude through metonymy, these problems would never occur. As agents in a "slice-of-life story," the novel's characters would be recognizable social types, and the novel itself would be content to imply everything that otherwise must be left unsaid through metonymy. *Women and Men* and other novels like it, however, do not restrict themselves in a manner that suggests a clear distinction between sign and referent; they want to *be* what realist novels merely point at.

All of this means that an image like the "modulus" describes the process of informational codes proliferating through a kind of cross-fertilization. What it does not account for is the way in which this process is ordered, or the structure itself which holds it together. As information is being shared, the number of hands it is passing through increases and the quantity of information increases correspondingly. As the labor of generating and distributing information is being divided, its depth, density, and specificity increases through internal differentiation. The modulus enables both processes--that of internal and external differentiation--to intersect. Again, what it does not do is provide the metaphoric means of reversing the process and superimpose an abstraction upon the information. To have such an abstraction available would allow the reader to perceive the novel as a coherent entity. It would focus attention on similarity instead of difference, on common features instead of distinguishing traits, and on unity instead of diversity. Obviously, such a counterprinciple must exist since *Women and Men* may be vast but certainly not shapeless, random, or chaotic.

In comparing *Women and Men* to other grand novels like it, it becomes obvious that the principle of unity applied by McElroy is unlikely to be what Jean-Francois Lyotard has called a "master-narrative," or the hidden ideological trope that Fredric Jameson suspects underneath every act of interpretation, be it conspiracy or encyclopedism.[11] In fiction, such all-encompassing key-metaphors come in all shapes and forms: whaling in Melville's *Moby Dick*, the digressive mind of the narrator in Lawrence Sterne's *Tristram Shandy*, or the naturalist's display case in Jean Paul's *Flegeljahre*. In the tradition of such narratives, conspiracy plays a more significant part once postmodernism enters the picture, picks up abandoned themes, and revitalizes them for its own purposes. Still, despite the fact that *Women and Men* addresses conspiracy in some detail and depth, conspiracy is not the one key-metaphor that holds the novel together. Rather, it appears as one theory among others whenever Chile and the overthrow of the Allende regime are being mentioned, the Masonic conspiracies, the economic and colonial plots, or the intrigues in the Mayn family and in other families all through history. Conspiracies, though they consider themselves the counterweight to information shared and labor divided, are just another category mediated by the modulus.

In a review of *Women and Men*, critic and writer Harry Mathews attributes the reviewer's by now all-too familiar problems with isolating individual themes and narrative strands in the work to

> the way everything is linked to everything else, [which] makes talking about separate bits of subject matter difficult: a discussion of almost any detail will lead to another and eventually involve the whole book . . . In *Women and Men* every what is turned into another what and eventually into *every* other what.[12]

In order to determine how McElroy's novel differs from other postmodernist fiction in which conspiracies provide unity and, most of all, a pervasive sense of hyperbolic delimitation, Mathew's observation can be compared to Antonio Marquez' assessment of Thomas Pynchon's work in an article entitled "Everything is Connected: Paranoia in *Gravity's Rainbow*".

> Pynchon, the exemplary writer of paranoid fiction, creates a *sense* of paranoia which is extended beyond the fictional characters and situations to the psyche of the reader. One need not be a paranoid personality to acknowledge that Pynchon's metaphorical webs, mazes, intricacies, and labyrinths capture the confusion and complexity that characterize modern life.[13]

In pointing out how the two novels correspond to or supplement each other, Mathews and Marquez describe a mode of writing that relies strongly on hyperbole as one of its central tropes--*everything* is connected. They agree that both texts operate with an epistemological principle that connects even the most disparate phenomena; in *Gravity's Rainbow* this happens because the world depicted in the novel is itself structured according to this principle, whereas *Women and Men*, in turn, superimposes this principle upon the world as an aesthetic choice. The dialogue between these two critics also echoes earlier concerns with problems of mimesis, as I have discussed by comparing Jerome Klinkowitz, Gerald Graff, and Tony Tanner with each other. By embracing a kind of universal point of view, whether mimetic or not, Pynchon's "paranoia" and "conspiracies" and McElroy's "modulus" and "ecologies" are both manifestations of the same aesthetic principle, that of encyclopedism.

At first glance, *Women and Men* seems to have little in common with classic encyclopedic novels, other than their shared concern with all forms of knowledge. By extending themselves generously into the world they set out to depict, encyclopedic novels suggest that they would prefer to replace that world rather than reflect it and thus become part of it. Novels such as *Gargantua and Pantagruel*, *Tristram Shandy*, or *Moby Dick* are all characterized by "a hyperbolic metonymizing of reality;"[14] an expression that Patrick O'Donnell uses, significantly enough, in order to describe paranoia. Their ordering principle is grounded in a bourgeois aesthetic of stability and balance, which is enacted by arresting the flow of knowledge, i.e. disambiguating and simplifying it by means of rigid, well-defined classificatory processes. Even the smallest, most insignificant detail has its place in a particular system of thought, academic discipline, vocabulary or jargon, region of the body, historical period, geographical location, etc. It takes the scientist, journalist, or amateur detective at the center of this activity to assign the name and create order out of the world's confusing abundance. Encyclopedic novels are fictions indulging the extreme. They are fictions of power, utopias of knowledge, assuring the reader that the world is transparent, intelligible, ordered, and therefore accessible to be represented in its totality. Due to their preoccupation with classificatory procedure, encyclopedic novels aim to be basically ahistorical. They favor spatial arrangement over temporal sequence, and they are strongly reliant on an epistemology establishing hierarchies through the definition of difference.

As with so many other genres, postmodernism has turned the encyclopedic novel upside down, mostly through ironic or satiric subversions of its dearest characteristics. The bourgeois hyperbolic power-fantasy has turned into the kind of fiction in which hyperbole now stands for the vastness and mystery of the world. To order the world and simultaneously withdraw from its threats, paranoia provides the only possible strategy to avoid being overwhelmed by it. Critics like Tom LeClair or Frederick Karl have attempted to pinpoint and formulate how postmodernism has turned the encyclopedic novel into a fable of powerlessness. They have coined neologisms in order to set the newly emerging phenomenon apart from its historical predecessors, discovering along the way that the genre has made an unprecedented comeback in postmodern fiction. In fact, postmodern fiction is teeming with encyclopedic novels. Canonical works such as McElroy's *Women and Men*, Pynchon's *Gravity's Rainbow* or *V.*, Gaddis' *The Recognitions* or *JR*, Joseph Heller's *Something Happened*, Robert Coover's *The Public Burning*, or Don DeLillo's *Ratner's Star* are all representative of a new form which Karl calls the "mega-novel" and LeClair refers to as the "systems novel" or the "novel of excess." These neologisms emphasize the unique complexity and lavish generosity of scope and perception, which are characteristic of encyclopedic fictions that have emerged not only from American literature or the postwar period, but are typical of all encyclopedic fictions regardless of their origin.[15]

However, the two terms also describe texts, which are uniquely different from the tradition they are grounded in because they are governed by an aesthetic program that flies in the face of any traditional poetics. To insist on conciseness, organicism, or informational economy as indicators of artistic accomplishment, as, for instance, the New Critics do, would mean missing the point in this case.[16] Besides supplying the useful distinction between encyclopedic novels and novels which are simply of great length, such as Norman Mailer's *Harlot's Ghost* or Harold Brodkey's *The Runaway Soul*, LeClair and Karl are after a type of long fiction that is "not concerned primarily with chronology; rather with lateral or horizontal as well as vertical movement," and encompasses "words, entire sentences and paragraphs [which] do not function for informational or narrative purposes."[17] To describe how this new form radically challenges traditional mimetic fiction by "employ[ing] postmodern methods to displace the priority of the individual and to deform the conventions of realism"[18] requires a critical vocabulary, which both critics derive from systems theory and its application to textual criticism. Systems theory gives access to excess, explaining the

> hypertrophy of a fictional element or technique that disturbs conventional balances and expectations, shifts the scale of selection and proportion in a novel, and forces an overloaded reader to comprehend the seemingly overgrown novel in its own, often systemic, terms.[19]

As a unique and somewhat iconoclastically methodology, systems theory furnishes a critical vocabulary that is invigorated by the reintroduction of such terms as "mastery" or "excess," which, as LeClair points out, have been regarded with some degree of suspicion by critical theorists for some time now. Exceeding Karl's more modest aspirations, LeClair goes so far as to assert that the unique nature and recent emergence of the "systems novel" indicates a shift of paradigms within contemporary fiction; a shift not unlike the one that takes place more specifically in the contemporary conspiracy novel.

Apart from being prime examples of postmodern encyclopedic fiction, however, *Women and Men* and *Gravity's Rainbow* have very little in common. Returning to the comparison between Mathews and Marquez, one could argue that Mathews pinpoints the most crucial difference between the otherwise so similar novels by reading McElroy as a kind of 'Pynchon without the fear.' Even considering the inevitable differences in artistic sensibilities between the two writers, *Women and Men* is particularly remarkable for its lack of anxiety, both in the characters as well as in the reader whenever they are faced with the possibility that "everything is connected." The possibility that the world is organized according to a vast, invisible plan does not induce paranoia; neither as an appropriate response to an insight about the nature of the world, nor as a protective impulse to seize the plot before one is being seized by it. In *Women and Men*, characters who do experience a feeling of insignificance within the conspiratorial networks usually do so with a sense of awe rather than fear. They realize simultaneously how insignificant they are, and yet how irreplaceable. Thus the moment of recognition, of realizing the ambivalent existential truth, commonly carries an element of the 'postmodern sublime;' an insight into relativity, proportion and perspective that converts fear into acceptance and aesthetic enjoyment. Since the proliferation of information is accomplished through both internal differentiation and external connection, the significance of any individual "small-scale unit," such as Larry's story, is relative to all other parts. There is no metaphysical center, where everything originates and from where all developments are being monitored and guided. McElroy's notion of multiple centers plays out the idea of encyclopedic hyperbole against conspiratorial control, singling out select features of both concepts while discarding others. Only when conspiracy and paranoia are not used as a totalitarian rhetoric can encyclopedic fiction maintain the trope of hyperbole as its key-metaphor.

In the process of steering toward this conclusion, it should have become obvious that there is an empirical correlation, which deserves critical attention, between the three areas touched upon so far: encyclopedic fiction, postmodernism, and the conspiracy novel. It does indeed appear as if the majority of all postmodern encyclopedic fictions is dealing with the subject matter of conspiracy, or is employing paranoia in the manner Antonio Marquez has pointed out for the case of *Gravity's Rainbow*. First of all, however, the significance of this triple intersection depends greatly on the particular version of the canon that readers are willing to employ as a frame of reference. According to one version of the canon, novels like *Gravity's Rainbow* or *V.*, Gaddis' *The Recognitions* or *JR*, Joseph Heller's *Something Happened*, Samuel Delaney's *Dhalgren*, or Robert Coover's *The Public Burning* suggest that the conspiracy theme constitutes a necessary feature of all postmodern encyclopedic fiction. Another version of the canon, which includes postmodern encyclopedic novels that are not primarily concerned with conspiracy, such as John Barth's *LETTERS* or *Giles Goat Boy*, Gilbert Sorrentino's *Mulligan's Stew*, or Alexander Theroux's *Darconville's Cat*, insinuates that conspiracy may be a merely marginal theme, occurring as randomly in this kind of fiction as in any other. And finally, there are texts like Paul Auster's *New York Trilogy*, Pynchon's *The Crying of Lot 49*, DeLillo's *Players*, or McElroy's own *Plus*, which suggests that even the intense preoccupation with the conspiracy theme, accompanied by a genuinely postmodern attitude, does not always generate encyclopedism as a necessary consequence.

If, among all of these options, the convenient fiction of an intersection between all three elements can be maintained, it must be because of the link between aesthetics and ideology established through the figure of hyperbole. If hyperbole does, in fact, constitute an intrinsic feature of all conspiracy fiction, including the postmodernist deconstructions of the traditional genre formula, then the theme of conspiracy would be naturally predisposed to create fictional structures in which hyperbole crosses over from the thematic to the structural aspect, as it does in the texts described by LeClair and Marquez. Moreover, encyclopedism and conspiracy share a number of structural characteristics that would allow their simultaneous incorporation into the same text: the focusing around one privileged center, the preoccupation with knowing and naming, the arresting of fluctuating meanings, the gesture of ordering or exposing the inherent order of the world, and so forth. Accordingly, all encyclopedic fiction would employ some form of hyperbolic mechanism by which it proposes that there are no outer limits to its grasp upon the world.

In order to understand the significance of *Women and Men*, it may be necessary to look briefly at *Plus*, the one novel of McElroy's that complements encyclopedic fiction much better than *The Letter Left To Me*, as Tom LeClair has suggested.[20] In *Plus*, McElroy recreates the coming-to-consciousness of a terminally-ill engineer, whose brain has been transplanted into a satellite orbiting the Earth from where it is supposed to monitor global weather patterns. The whole person is reduced to the acronym of the Interplanetary Monitoring Platform it inhabits or which it is, technically speaking, identical with--an "imp" in every sense of the word. Reminiscent of a short-story by Don DeLillo, entitled "Human Moments in World War III," the protagonist of *Plus* is an observer, his position high above the planet surface the vantage of the Baudelairian *flaneur*.[21] Both texts share the sense of awe, which is also an integral element of encyclopedic fictions, only that here this aesthetic response is created by the observer's removal from the observed totality, and not his immersion in it. But this is where the similarities end and McElroy's unique vision takes over.

Most of the themes in *Plus* are immediately recognizable as those of *Women and Men*: information shared and reciprocated, the global perspective, paranoia about information being decontextualized, the individual consciousness recognizing and classifying the world, and the integration of scientific knowledge into the reader's literary frame of perception. Yet, with its roughly 200 pages, *Plus* is a tightly woven, dense, and almost austere narrative, in which all expansive energy of the theme is being restrained in the brutally curtailed, yet touchingly lyrical language.

In his essay on *Women and Men*, Frederick Karl has remarked that contemporary fiction "for the last decade or two" has split up into what he calls the ""two bookends of "languages". . . both based on a litotes, that affirmation through denial;" one the minimalist fiction of a Paul Auster, the other the "overarching and massive" bulk of *Women and Men*. Clearly, *Plus* falls into the former category, yet it defies Karl's assertion that it, like its counterpart on the other extreme, refuses to provide "the very metaphysical basis of our perceptions,"[22] as Auster's fiction may or may not do. In fact, *Plus* is deeply inquisitive about metaphysical questions, particularly when it comes to language and how it determines one's sense of identity.

As Tom LeClair demanded of encyclopedic fiction, *Plus* "shifts the scale of selection and proportion in a novel," but to the other extreme. Rather than filling all the gaps, it invites interpretation. Instead of extending hyperbole outward, it is hyperbolically dense, reaching for a balance between "imp-losion" as this depth increases incrementally, and the expansion of the protagonist's understanding of his environment. Like Imp Plus himself, the narrative is "defective," incomplete. Only slowly does it improve and grow, mostly through accretion and repetition. Deprived of all sense of physicality, McElroy's language strives toward a degree of abstraction that makes it difficult to reverse the act of allegorization in order to arrive at the concrete facts of what is being depicted.

The paranoia of a character so excruciatingly truncated derives from the same sense of austerity that the reader is experiencing through the use of language. There is so little to hold on to, so little concreteness, that the emptiness almost automatically demands the superimposition of narrative patterns. As reader and protagonist try to establish a hold in a universe in which all elements are stripped of their significance and of the human element of intentionality, the prototypical outline of a conspiratorial fiction begins to emerge. It creates order out of endless difference, bestows character and individuality to the voices and a sense of direction to the narrative. But it also pulls this world, which is so narrow to begin with, even more tightly around the borders of our perception. Once the paranoid story has taken a hold, only what is relevant to its progress is permitted any more. Significantly enough, *Plus* then becomes a story about breaking out of confinement and surveillance, making choices and perhaps even sacrifices, and creating significance outside of the conspiratorial subtext. Like *Women and Men*, it grows into a story about self-empowerment.

In its own unique way, *Plus* is both the opposite and the equivalent of the encyclopedic novel. It is equally a text of extremes. It is concerned with the same complex of themes as encyclopedic novels, and, like them, it is structured by both conspiracy's incentive to rigidity and expansiveness. In a drastic reversal of the choices characteristic of the encyclopedic novel, however, *Plus* enacts the rigidity of conspiracy through the use of metonymy, and the expansiveness through the use of metaphor.

On the one hand, the meaning of *Plus* is determined by what it represents metaphorically. Some critics have suggested that Imp Plus represents the writer himself, isolated from the world and struggling against and with language. Others have pointed toward the parallels between child development and the growing of Imp's consciousness. And finally, there is a consistent level of religious allusiveness geared toward Christ imagery.[23] All these readings rely on the conspiracy story in order to generate these metaphoric extensions. In other words, through metaphor the novel reaches out and transforms itself into a representation of numerous other stories. On the other hand, however,

Plus means only what it means. McElroy is intensely concerned with endowing the narrative with a sense of mimesis, foregrounding the scientific accuracy of the depiction and trying to create a sense of bewilderment for the reader similar to the protagonist's. To insist on the literal-mindedness of the images in *Plus* is only possible because of the novel's impossible narrative premise; something the author has set up carefully by avoiding first-person narration. The suggestion that what is being told is, in fact, beyond words and therefore impossible to talk about rechannels the power of the language back into abstraction. Words in *Plus* do not correspond to anything other than other words because they cannot possibly refer to what they say they do. Thus, on a small scale, *Plus* recreates the epistemological and representational *mise en abyme* of the encyclopedic novel.

What seems to be at stake in these radical subversions of both the small and the large form, the two extremes of hyperbole, is the reader's ability to comprehend these complex fictions. How much is being expected of readers who are working their way through the sheer abundance of facts and details and the parallel narratives and intersecting storylines in *Women and Men*, or who are clutching at straws while trying to make sense of the experimental prose and defamiliarizing devices in *Plus*? Like its minimalist counterpart, encyclopedic fiction "shifts the scale of selection and proportion in a novel," creating effects that are counterproductive to the original purposes of the form they imply. Encyclopedism in particular is striving to render the world transparent and intelligible, establish hierarchies within all accessible fields of knowledge, and reaffirm the power of the classic positivistic scientific method to dominate the natural and cultural world. Readers who expect to be part of this enlightened enterprise through reading fiction will instead be mystified. Not only do the texts resist interpretation or comprehension, but, more significantly, they defy the "humanizing" function that literature is supposed to fulfill in regard to scientific knowledge. This means that the "redemptively dismissive encyclopedism," typical of conventional encyclopedic novels, becomes obsolete because the "annihilative absorption of . . . culture's most ambitious projects into the superior "atmosphere" of art,"[24] ceases to be of any interest to writers like McElroy, who would like to do away with the notion of any "superior atmosphere" to begin with.

A novel that discusses these paradoxic consequences in regard to the reader and then channels them back into its own aesthetics is Don DeLillo's *Ratner's Star*.[25] Less daring in its challenging of conventional limits than *Women and Men*, *Ratner's Star* examines and recapitulates the history of abstract representation, exemplified most strikingly by the language of mathematics, through the efforts of a team of scientific geniuses to decode signals supposedly originating in outer space. The mission of the research team is being co-opted from day one by economic and political interests, dividing the scientific collective and compromising its work. At the center of these intersecting conspiracies is Billy Twillig, a mathematical prodigy who is supposed to contribute to decoding the signals, as well as to the development of a mathematical meta-language called Logicon, which would be crucial to the understanding not only of Logicon but of all abstract codes. Billy's unique skills allow him to be instrumental, or at times marginally involved, in the cracking of the supposedly extraterrestrial code, the development of Logicon, and the exposure of many of the private and political cabals surrounding Field Experiment Number One.

Unlike *Women and Men* with its radical strategies of delimitation, *Ratner's Star* belongs to a more conventional type of encyclopedic fiction. Besides Billy, who functions as a central figure and is part scientist and part detective, the novel's other characters are all involved in the scientific exploration and classification of the world. Answering to the conventions of encyclopedic fiction, there is, in fact, such a bewildering number of characters, all of them introduced by name, that their discourse, which is supposed to demystify the world and render it intelligible and namable, turns into a parody of all scientific assurances. Yet, even though DeLillo satirizes the scientific "business," he stays within the limitations of a proper hyperbolic rhetoric. There are too many characters for even the most attentive reader to remember; scientific discussion goes back to prehistory and even crosses over into parascience; scientist from all corners of the globe attend he project, and so forth.

Understanding the world then means opening channels for manipulation and exploitation, as the novel points out by constructing an elaborate conspiratorial subtext. A Honduran cartel, headed by the elusive Elux Troxl, is secretly trying to buy out the entire scientific mission.[26] Unlike the conspiracies, the scientific discourse is intelligible and clearly ordered. Recapitulating the genealogy of scientific knowledge and its culmination in the current state of affairs, *Ratner's Star* sets up rigid historical and typological systems of classification.[27] Again, DeLillo undercuts the integrity of the twofold scientific project, this time by revealing that the mysterious signals do not originate in outer space and that Logicon must necessarily fail. Yet the novel's essential purpose is still to unfold abstract scientific history as a metaphor for the concrete yet unrepresentable multiplicity of data comprised in the totalizing vision of encyclopedism. Only that, given its demonstrable failure on both counts, the significance of these data is shifted from mimesis to allegoresis: what does the urge to understand mean? Why believe in results that are obviously flawed or pragmatically useless?

The metaphoric center and structural integrity of *Ratner's Star* also manifests itself in the novels' settings and their spatial arrangement.

Abstracted from natural space in the huge, labyrinthine, and sealed institute, a city of information owned by a multinational and global cartel that uses advanced science to manipulate financial markets. . . [28]

DeLillo's characters inhabit a small-scale version of the postmodern world; the kind of synecdoche which, in this form, would be almost impossible to find in *Women and Men*. The physical structure of the Project has all the features of the global totality the novel attempts to represent. It is the proverbial Ship of Fools, or the room full of suspects in detective fiction. In this symbolic landscape, however, vast economic markets, which are dependent on technology as a means of production and distribution, peddle that same technology as a commodity. Human nature is not at stake here. Knowledge and power come together in the microcosm of the Project itself. Following the nature of abstraction, the Project--both as a physical structure and as the discourses it contains--functions as the central metonymy that the novel unfolds through a bewildering multitude of individual characters, scientific theories, historical references, and so on.

Just as the spatial abstraction allows DeLillo to launch his investigation into "planetary consciousness"[29] from a small space within which all structure is reduced to an intelligible scale and complexity, the discourse on mathematics allows him to address the collective project of human (scientific) knowledge through a similar synecdochal reduction. According to its more optimistic theoreticians in the novel, mathematics is abstract enough to accommodate for all kinds of informational systems. Mathematics can give voice to the fearful and intimidating childhood experiences of the protagonist, just as it can describe the mystic experiences of Australian Aborigines. Mathematics is a language without a concrete signified. In this sense, the novel attempts to elevate mathematics to a kind of universal meta-discourse, which would then, of course, also include *Ratner's Star* itself. By projecting mathematics onto the encyclopedic novel, one abstract and supposedly universal informational system is grafted upon another.

However, it is this theme itself--the universality of abstraction and its relation to literary encyclopedism--that sets *Ratner's Star* apart from other, more conventional encyclopedic novels. As DeLillo addresses problems of encoding and deciphering, abstract representation, and the desire to construct a system of thought that explains the world in its totality, the book's own metafictional impulse is turned inward. Any novel that wants to be simultaneously "an experimental novel, an allegory, a lunar geography, an artful autobiography, a cryptic scientific tract, a work of science fiction"[30] must somehow account for its own ambitions to cover all of these areas. What degree of abstraction is necessary in order to maximize the inclusiveness of a statement; no matter if it is a scientific axiom, a logical hypothesis, or an artistic statement made within a piece of fiction? At what point does abstraction become redundant, spreading itself so thin that its conceptual categories become virtually meaningless? At what point does it become counterproductive, generating a genuine metaphysics or sense of the sublime, while it consciously attempts to erase all forms of mysticism by making the world transparent for the enlightened, rational mind?

Significantly enough, DeLillo addresses most of these questions in a passage that discusses the difficulty and transparency of abstract representational systems.

> There's a whole class of writers who don't want their books to be read. This to some extent explains their crazed prose. To express what is expressible isn't why you write if you're in this class of writers. To be understood is faintly embarrassing. . . .. The friction of an audience is what drives writers crazy. . . .. The more they understand the crazier you get.[31]

Judging from LeClair's and Karl's description of postmodern encyclopedic novels, encyclopedism is one possible means to insure the incomprehensibility of the writing; regardless of whether it is accomplished by overextending the level of abstraction like DeLillo or delimiting the epistemological categories like McElroy. To write "in a style best characterized as undiscourageably diffuse"[32] can be a method of undercutting the positivistic and imperialist agenda of conventional encyclopedic fiction and displacing its agents.

Obviously, mystifying the reader carries positive connotations for DeLillo. Thus he allows Jean Venable, in one of the frequent allusions to Lewis Carroll, to state categorically, "I'm free to make whatever rules I want as long as there's an inner firmness and cohesion."[33] Like Humpty Dumpty, Jean's insistence on self-determination jeopardizes the communicative function of language for the sake of a more aesthetic and less pragmatic agenda; to make a rule that is only private property--no matter if it is coherent with other rules in the same private system or not--allows for the creation of a meaningful, yet potentially mystifying utterance. Unlike the path to heightened complexity and extended range, the path inward, into privacy and the self, leads to a state of catatonic paralysis that so many of DeLillo's characters experience at some point in their development. Billy's mentor, Henrik Endor, whose name signifies the uncomfortable ambiguity between mutually exclusive choices (and/or), is a representative of the decision in favor of privacy. Living in a hole in the ground, either because he did find the solution to the alien messages, or because he went crazy over not finding it, Endor withdraws from the complexity of the systems and communities that used to surround him, only to be persuaded by Billy to re-enter the world later on. Since he refuses to explain both the experience that made him decide to abandon all communication and the subsequent change of heart, his primitive, atavistic lifestyle has dramatic, maybe even melodramatic weight. Yet it remains vague and ultimately meaningless for anybody but himself. Consequently, his final decision to leave the hole has very little impact on the events to follow. In the closing scenes of both *Ratner's*

Star and *Women and Men* the way in and the way out culminate in a grave scenario each: either readers are lead down the rabbit hole toward regression, catatonics, and isolation, or they are left staring toward the far horizon, in awe of a mystifying yet potentially explicable mirage.

In realizing that both novels try to undercut certain key-objectives of conventional encyclopedic fiction, readers are led to consider the novel as a self-conscious artistic equivalent of scientific inquiry itself. The most prominent goal for both art and science, from this perspective, is to acknowledge their respective lack of autonomy by discussing their relation to problems of economic exploitation. For McElroy, this goal can be accomplished by first abolishing the constitutive categories by which scientific thinking defines its object and then encouraging and accelerating the exchange of information and data across these now permeable borderlines. For DeLillo, there are three viable strategies to that same effect. First, *Ratner's Star* extends the abstract language that allows for the encyclopedic range of the novel to a point where it becomes so general that its statements are virtually meaningless. Second, it increases the complexity of the information handled to a degree that renders the text equally unintelligible. And third, it proposes a private alternative to these two communicative options, which ultimately collapses the novel as a communicative act between text and reader by drawing it into the hermetic, solipsistic interiority of a secret code.

While DeLillo's tone is unmistakably ironic and satiric of scientific thought in general and the economics of science in particular, McElroy seems to be the one who is still willing to work within the scientific traditions for a reformulation of their more confining and outdated conventions.[34] Satire may very well be the generic convention that links *Ratner's Star* more strongly to other encyclopedic fictions that are unlike *Women and Men*. William Gaddis' *JR*, Pynchon's *Gravity's Rainbow*, or Coover's *The Public Burning* are all applying a "hyperbolic metonymizing of reality"--Patrick O'Donnell's term for the effects of conspiracy--to distort through exaggeration, in other words, to satirize. While the element of hyperbole connects satire and conspiracy in this class of novels, McElroy's approach characterizes him as less of a satirist and more of a reformer. For both writers, however, encyclopedism has ceased to be what Leo Bersani claims it once was. Instead of being "literature's defense against its exclusion from (or its marginal place in) the information systems; the political, economic, and scientific networks of power; and even the symbolic orders by which a society defines itself,"[35] encyclopedism has self-consciously transformed itself into a way of codifying knowledge which defies the existence of all barriers between the categories Bersani lists. Whether satiric or revisionist, encyclopedism can now be deconstructed with the same rigorous scrutiny as science, politics, and economics.

At this point in its generic history, it must seem as if the encyclopedic novel has become a difficult, even impossible model for writers like DeLillo or McElroy to emulate. On the one hand, encyclopedism has rid itself of the purpose of stabilizing the ceaseless and vaguely threatening flow of information that constitutes reality for the bourgeois observer. It has ceased to legitimize his stand-in's central position in this world (from Conan's Doyle's gentleman detective to Robert Heinlein's universally gifted amateur scientists, all of them invariably white Western males), and does not subjugate the world to his political and economic intentions any longer. This socially and ideologically pragmatic side of encyclopedism has been made impossible in novels like *Women and Men*. On the other hand, however, a novel like *Ratner's Star* makes a convincing case that it has become equally impossible for encyclopedic fiction to stand aside from, to quote Leo Bersani again, "the political, economic, and scientific networks of power." Neither McElroy nor DeLillo want their novels to stand aside from "the symbolic orders by which a society defines itself" and to remain confined to an elevated, yet ineffective and ultimately irrelevant realm of art which keeps it separate and safe from the mechanisms of power, and vice versa. It becomes difficult to imagine how novelists would chart a course that will take them past the implications of both extremes, yet still work within the conventions of encyclopedism at all. How is one to continue writing encyclopedic fiction that is neither elitist and solipsistic, nor contaminated by a questionable pragmatics of power?

Knowledge and power mark the point where the theme of conspiracy and paranoia comes up again; a theme that all encyclopedic novels mentioned here share and work through with some intensity. Once the question of literature's exceptional status and the corresponding question of its co-optation are struck from the agenda, it becomes possible to have a fresh look at conspiracy as a means of introducing hyperbole into encyclopedic fiction and of conflating theme and structure in novelistic discourse. A newly defined form of aesthetic organicism might emerge from this process. So far, it has become obvious that the conspiracy theme introduces or supports the element of hyperbole, which is structurally essential to all encyclopedic and thematically essential to most postmodernist fiction. Just as any postmodern conspiracy carries the implication that its reach is potentially unlimited, all encyclopedic fiction considers itself necessarily incomplete; despite their complexity, novels like *Tristram Shandy* or *Flegeljahre* remain fragmentary, while *Women and Men* or *Gravity's Rainbow* communicate a sense of incompleteness. This sense of having "magnitude rather than final shape" or of being "all middles or extensions"[36] corresponds to the paranoid suspicion, structurally inherent in the conspiracy theme, that conspiracies are fundamentally mysterious and residually unknowable so that the process of their detection is potentially infinite. The full extent of any conspiracy can never be established beyond the shadow of a doubt, just as the totality of the world can never be fully represented, even in the most ambitious of all encyclopedic novels.

Despite the superficial congeniality between the conspiracy theme and the encyclopedic vision, however, the two novels discussed here tend to emphasize all those specific qualities of conspiracy that stand in graphic contrast to the original intentions of encyclopedic fiction. Conspiracy fiction may be concerned with finding the truth, but in *Women and Men* it is a truth that is of little pragmatic value. Conspiracy fiction may be concerned with explaining potentially unlimited systems, but in *Ratner's Star* it is the failure to accomplish this task that is more significant than its original agenda. Conspiracy fiction may be concerned with placing a supreme consciousness at the center of the universe, but in *Women and Men* the centers are either multiple, instable, or incomplete (James Mayn/Grace Kimball, the two colonists merged into one, Larry giving himself to Amy in the act of establishing individuality, etc.). Conspiracy fiction may be concerned with superimposing order upon the chaotic randomness of the world, but in *Ratner's Star* this superimposition is driven to an extreme, leading to solipsism and the collapse of communication. Conspiracy fiction may be concerned with metonymy (the market as conspiracy, global communication networks as conspiracy, cyberspace as conspiracy, etc.), but in *Women and Men* the oscillation between opposites (large/small, public/private, myth/history, sign/referent, etc.) undercuts the basis for metonymy.[37]

The list could be conveniently extended, but it becomes obvious that encyclopedism is not being merely supplemented or reinforced by the conspiracy theme. It is being radically redefined. Both McElroy and DeLillo make use of the structural congeniality between the two aspects, inconspicuously inserting one into the other and then working out the consequences of this recombination. The results are reminiscent of the conclusions regarding the use of hyperbole and its decline as a significant feature of the new conspiracy fiction presented in the preceding chapter. If "on first acquaintance, some readers react with daunted impatience to the proliferating variation or to the plenum of incident and unanticipated detail"[38] in these encyclopedic fictions, then their response has been anticipated by an author, who wants the reader to experience hyperbole as an expression of the world's vastness and not as an expression of the reader's power to subjugate this vast terrain. Emphasis is shifted from paranoia as a device to induce order to its potential as a means to induce ambiguity, creating unexpected correspondences to more minimalist fiction like *Plus*. The issue of empowerment, which was crucial, though only through its radical negation, even for the first postmodern incarnations of the encyclopedic novel like *Gravity's Rainbow* or *JR*, has been dropped in the old sense in order to redefine a new state of "being in the world." For that reason alone, the encyclopedic novel has definitely ceased to function as a bourgeois power-fantasy.

Notes

[1] Joseph McElroy, *Women and Men: A Novel* (New York: Alfred A. Knopf, 1987).

[2] Robert Walsh, "A Wind Rose: Joseph McElroy's *Women and Men*," *Facing Texts: Encounters Between Contemporary Writers and Critics*, ed. Heide Ziegler (Durham: Duke UP, 1988) 263.

[3] *Women and Men* 301.

[4] *Women and Men* 297.

[5] *Women and Men* 287.

[6] *Women and Men* 295.

[7] *Women and Men* 699.

[8] Frederick Karl, "*Women and Men*: More than a Novel," *The Review of Contemporary Fiction* 10.1 (Spring 1990) 183.

[9] In a later chapter that will deal primarily with *Hind's Kidnap*, written in 1969, it will become clear that McElroy's work as a whole is striving toward an increasing permeability of these conceptual categories. As much as the earlier novel already incorporates elements that *Women and Men* will come to refine, it is still based on a more conventional epistemological model, which generates conspiracy and paranoia from within a different, less holistic epistemological mechanism.

[10] *Women and Men* 586.

[11] see Jean-Francois Lyotard, *The Postmodern Condition: A Report on Knowledge* (Minneapolis: University of Minnesota Press, 1984). Though Lyotard is not so much concerned with ideological fictions outside of the production of (scientific) knowledge, his notion of postmodernism as a period characterized by the collapse of great unifying theories applies very well in this context. See also Fredric Jameson, *The Political Unconscious: Narrative as a Socially Symbolic Act* (Ithaca: Cornell UP, 1981).

[12] Harry Mathews, "We for One: An Introduction to Joseph McElroy's *Women and Men*," *The Review of Contemporary Fiction* 10.1 (Spring 1990) 221.

[13] Antonio Marquez, "Everything is Connected: Paranoia in *Gravity's Rainbow*," *Perspectives on Contemporary Literature* 9 (1983) 94.

[14] Patrick O'Donnell, "Engendering Paranoia in Contemporary Literature," *boundary 2: An International Journal Of Literature and Culture* 19.1 (Spring 1992) 182.

[15] Frederick Karl, "*Women and Men*: More than a Novel," *The Review of Contemporary Fiction* 10.1 (Spring 1990), and Tom LeClair, *The Art of Excess: Mastery in Contemporary American Fiction* (Urbana: University of Illinois Press, 1989).

[16] These idiosyncrasies indicate that Tony Tanner's insights in *City of Words* about the American writer's rejection of community standards is exactly to the point. They also attest to the continuing traditions of a Romantic poetics, in which, historically speaking, conspiracy fiction has always been anchoring its rhetorics and ideological positions.

[17] Karl 183.

[18] LeClair 2.

[19] Tom LeClair, "A New Map of the World: *Ratner's Star*," *In the Loop: Don DeLillo and the Systems Novel* (Urbana: University of Illinois Press, 1978) 113.

[20] Joseph McElroy, *Plus* (New York: Alfred A. Knopf, 1977).

[21] Don DeLillo, "Human Moments in World War III," *Esquire* (July 1983) 118-26. The reference to Baudelaire is, of course, mediated through Walter Benjamin's description of the *flaneur* as a specific social and historical type in his own work.

[22] Karl 184.

[23] for further development of these concepts and corroboration of the ideas presented here, see Christine Brooke-Rose, "The New Science Fiction--Joseph Mc Elroy: *Plus*," *A Rhetoric of the Unreal: Studies in narrative and structure, especially of the fantastic* (Cambridge/New York: Cambridge UP, 1981) 268-88; Alicia Miller, "Power and Perception in *Plus*," *Review of Contemporary Fiction* 10.1 (Spring 1990) 173-180; and Pamela White Hadas, "Green Thoughts on Being in Charge: Discovering Joseph Mc Elroy's *Plus*," *Review of Contemporary Fiction* 10.1 (Spring 1990) 140-155.

[24] Leo Bersani, "Pynchon, Paranoia, and Literature," *Representations* 25 (Winter 1989) 117.

[25] Don DeLillo, *Ratner's Star* (New York: Alfred A. Knopf, 1976).

[26] The theme of economic exploitation and infiltration is also repeated in a significant number of proper names, which DeLillo borrows from business or individual products: Mainwaring or Braun are named after companies manufacturing kitchen and household appliances; Evinrude after a company manufacturing outboarders; F.A.O. Schwartz after a toy store on 5th Avenue. Ratner himself, the fictive scientist giving the novel its title, is named after a famous kosher deli on the Lower East Side.

[27] see LeClair's listing of mathematical theories as a structuring device for the chapter in "A New Map of the World," 125.

[28] LeClair, "A New Map of the World," 135.

[29] *Ratner's Star* 21.

[30] *Ratner's Star* 57.

[31] *Ratner's Star* 411.

[32] *Ratner's Star* 306.

[33] *Ratner's Star* 352.

34 In two articles, one of them quite recent, McElroy has explained in some detail his attitude toward science and scientific thought; see "Neural Neighborhoods and Other Concrete Abstracts," *TriQuarterly* 34 (Fall 1975) 201-17; and "Fiction as a Field of Growth: Science at Heart, Action at a Distance," *American Book Review* 14.1 (April/May 1992) 1/30-31.

35 Bersani, "Pynchon, Paranoia, and Preterition," 117.

36 Karl 183.

37 In conversation, McElroy has suggested to me that, in the relation between the "Breathers" and the small interpolated chapters in *Women and Men*, his goal was to undercut the distinction between small and large altogether; a goal that, in my opinion, he has achieved to the extent that the confines of language itself permit. Since the small chapters are not supposed to be miniatures of the expansive "Breathers," the novel is impossible to summarize properly (as I myself have done by singling out Larry and his story--an effort that has remained as incomplete and perfunctory as McElroy would have suggested). The problematic status of metonymy for the significance of the novel seems to me an adequate reflection of McElroy's intentions as to its inner organization.

38 Robert Walsh, ""A Wind Rose,"" 266-67.

3. Running Dog *and* Hind's Kidnap*: The Dissociation of Conspiracy and Paranoia*

In a brilliantly poignant discussion of intertextuality in Don DeLillo's *Running Dog*, critic John Frow arrives at the following conclusion about the novel's preoccupation with the politics of representation.

> One of the advantages offered by the popular thriller is a workable *formal* solution to the question of how to write a novel: it delivers certain resources of story and plot construction, a repertoire of *topoi*, a ready-made thematics of conspiracy and paranoia, and so on. [Postmodernism uses it] as a machine for generating words and representations, but it then reworks the genre in such a way as to refuse and expose its ideological implications. In the place of Ludlum's "good" plotting we are given a "bad" plot . . . What is performed is not an ideologically "correct" contestation of the certainties of the Ludlum novels . . .[1]

Consistent, however, with his assumption that it is the conventional thriller alone that *Running Dog* harks back to, Frow concludes that DeLillo's achievement consists of what he calls an "inventive negativity." Frow is not entirely sure whether the inversion of certain aesthetic standards is a praiseworthy enterprise in itself. Other critics share this sense of unease. John Kucich, for example, notices that the act of ideological subversion, which DeLillo knows to performs with a great deal of creativity and panache, leaves a kind of uncomfortable vacuum, which DeLillo appears hesitant or unable to fill.[2] Unlike Robert Ludlum's novels, in which "the ideological burden is carried most forcefully at this level of formal structure than at the level of an overtly thematized political ideology . . . or the level of a cliché-ridden verbal texture,"[3] DeLillo's ideological deconstruction is viewed as a gesture of inversion or negation that is aesthetically successful yet politically lacking in substance and involvement. It is not enough to undermine one ideology, so Kucich, without supplying another, perhaps more humane and constructive one to take its place.

As the passage quoted above demonstrates, this attack on novels like DeLillo's own *Running Dog* requires some sort of ideological scaffolding to place the text in its supposedly "proper" environment. The mechanism used for that purpose must fulfill two requirements. First, it must establish links and analogies in order to place the text in a historical setting; second, it must employ hierarchical distinctions to signal to the reader what genre the text belongs to. Not only does *Running Dog* therefore figure as "a kind of palimpsestic commentary on the genre it mimes, the "thriller,""[4] but it also responds to and comments on one characteristic feature of the genres it is associated with. Common to those genres is a close association between paranoia as an individual feature, and conspiracy as a political and social reality.

Following Frow's argument, any reader might come to the conclusion that, given its "ready-made thematics," *Running Dog* does little else besides elaborate upon strategies of negation or subversion. The question that Frow's reading suggests but never addresses is, of course, what exactly is being subverted with regard to conspiracy and paranoia. What is the essential ideological statement around which all thrillers, give and take some individual variations, revolve? Also, if a novel like *Running Dog* does, in fact, thematize its own genealogy, how does it then construe its own synchronic and diachronic context? How does it signal to the reader in which context it wants to be perceived and which part of all possible traditions it wants to be considered of?

The case which *Running Dog* seems to make most urgently is the one for the dissociation of conspiracy from paranoia; a gesture of conceptual separation which is muted in Frow's account of historical sequence but resurfaces in his description of the transformations that the new form performs upon its generic antecedents. Refusing and exposing the thriller's ideological implications cannot leave untouched what Frow still conveniently lists as one, and only one "thematics." Conspiracy and paranoia are two sides of the same coin, as far as the writing and reading of fiction is concerned.

Obviously, both terms derive from different, if not incompatible disciplines and their respective vocabularies; one from psychology, the other from sociology or historiography. They are linked by a rhetorical gesture which is more metonymic than merely analogic in nature. Usually, one term can be resolved through the other. On the one hand, the thriller tells stories about conspiracies that eventually turn out to be purely imaginary. The anticlimactic revelation that the reader has been tantalized by a promise that the text will not keep is reserved for novels outside of popular fiction, such as Stanley Elkin's *The MacGuffin*.[5] On the other hand, the protagonist's alleged paranoid state of mind can be validated as the belated or ignored recognition of the existence of a real conspiracy. In this latter case, what appeared like a delusion turns out to be a narratively latent conspiracy, so to speak. Both terms, however, are either mutually inclusive, or can be subsumed under a third, mostly silent category, depending on the reading the individual text decides on.

To discuss the conceptual dissociation of paranoia from conspiracy, the mysterious film, around which all activities in DeLillo's *Running Dog* revolve, provides a perfect test case.[6] Film and representational politics are two of the more prominent subjects of formal subversion that the novel is targeting. For the contemporary American reader, the events in the *Führerbunker* in the last days of WW II are historically and geographically so far removed from ordinary experience that none of the conspiratorial activities has any immediate bearings on the present. Whatever the object of contention is, history is hardly at stake here. The novel opens with a scene in which Ludecke is killed. He is the only character whose biography touches personally on the period in which the film originates. With this link between past and present severed in the opening scene, the film assumes the status of a commodity. Its value is determined by extrinsic forces, such as the market, demand, sexual desire, political ambition, and so on. Its inalienable intrinsic features, such as, for instance, its value as a historical document or its integrity as a work of art cease to count for the purpose of the novel. In this sense, it lacks individuality, even though there is no other one like it. None of the characters, as urgently as their pursuit of the film may be, is capable of overcoming this epistemological ambiguity that DeLillo has placed on the McGuffin of his story. Characters like Lightborne cannot chose to look beyond the film's status as commodity. Accordingly, nobody can regard the film with an interest justified by personal relevance. And since the film as a text is randomized so radically that not even an imaginary bond can be forged between an individual and the object, the necessary prerequisite for paranoia is lacking altogether.[7]

The second indication that paranoia is not what is at stake in *Running Dog* is the deliberate marginality of figures that function as iconic representations of paranoia. Unlike, for example, the work of Thomas Pynchon, DeLillo's novel does not assimilate the paranoiac's particular set of epistemological and conceptual problems and their possible solutions in order to transform them into central concerns for the formulation of its own narrative premises. Apart from Senator Percival's wife, who "curls up with the Warren Report"[8] and an unnamed customer at Frankie's Tropical Bar, who delivers a long monologue revolving around his fears that he has become the target of a highly sophisticated and technologically advanced system of surveillance by the FBI, none of the other major characters is subject to a noticeable state of paranoia.[9]

Some critics have already remarked on "DeLillo's capacity to render character as a function of a certain speech pattern,"[10] his preference for creating a "novel of language" in the Bakhtinian sense rather than a realist, mimetic fiction that critics like Gerald Graff would like to see more often in contemporary American fiction. Therefore, no reader would recognize figures like the nameless man in the bar as "characters" in the strictest sense of the word, as John Frow does when he refers to characters in Robert Ludlum's thrillers. The degree of abstraction and lack of individuality that applies to these marginal paranoiacs in *Running Dog* affects not only their essence but also how they function in the text. Devoid of depth, they hardly contribute to the advancement of the narrative. Their presence, at best, endows the narrative with a mood, a sense of space or depth, but hardly ever exceeds these more decorative functions.

Obviously, these figures are significant because they self-consciously represent paranoia, both as a phenomenon associated with characters that are not at the center of the mystery, and as a signal toward one of the genre's most highly visible conventions. Although they point back to the thriller, their deliberate functional marginality brings the redefined relationship between conspiracy and paranoia to the reader's attention. They attempt to expose the convention that only central, individualized characters can represent a state of mind encompassing the entire narrative microcosm. In this double function, the icon comments simultaneously on the novel's syntagmatic position in the genre history and on its paradigmatic position in relation to adjacent genres. While Frow is focusing on the deconstruction of thriller conventions, DeLillo steers toward an idiosyncratic genre of his own; a thriller that is not based on the ambiguity between two categories of experience but on the capacity to include this ambiguity as an intrinsically coherent phenomenon in the text.

To explore the content of this icon beyond its superficial operational value--that it, to describe the exact nature of the conceptual relationship between conspiracy and paranoia as it is redefined by *Running Dog*--the reader must turn to the narrative processes into which these iconic figures are being inserted. If paranoia has indeed ceased to be a central concern of the narrative, or if it is at least thematically and functionally distinguished from conspiracy, then the driving force behind the narrative is not likely to be the one operating in texts that are powered by the metonymic operations of mutual inclusion or subsumation. What can a conspiracy novel be about if not the disambiguation of paranoid suspicions, or the careful description of a deranged state of mind? What can be the goal of such a narrative, its *telos*?

The plot of *Running Dog* is a movement toward the solidification or concretization of rumor. Rumor itself is intimately associated with myth and therefore functions as an opposing force to history. While an increasing number of fiercely competing and shifting alliances struggle for access to the film and control over it, rumors abound as to the source of the footage, its subject matter, and the history of its being passed around. Handed down from the source, it has circulated among a number of dealers and intermediaries, who are increasingly ignorant of the nature of their commodity, if they are not downright indifferent instead. One character notices that events seem to happen "as in a fairy tale;"[11] a remark that accurately describes the novel's prevailing narrative logic. The historical distance, which readers are made to experience through an increasing lack of information about the film's owners the further they are removed from them, contributes to the mythical nature of the narratives it generates. As expected, rumor as a form of semi-public collective discourse becomes the locus of conspiracy.

This mythic "history" of the film--one is almost tempted to call it the film's biography--is coupled with a myth of origin in which the last days of the Third Reich are dramatically recast as The Last Days; an apocalyptic, carnevalesque moment in which "myths, dreams, memory. . . . The violence, the rituals, the leather, the jackboots"[12] converge in a picture that has little to do with historical accuracy or the disinterested pursuit of knowledge. During this preliminary absence of a properly historical perspective on the film, the narrative nevertheless proceeds to demystify the object of contention. At the moment of the long-awaited screening toward the end of the novel, the film's proper historical categories have been restored. Long before this ambiguously climactic moment, however, all ambiguities about the nature of the different interlocking conspiracies have been resolved. The screening itself only confirms what any reader familiar with postmodern conspiracy fiction suspected all along. The content of the film is not really of any concern for the resolution of the plot. Instead, the anticlimactic denouement retrospectively sheds light on the driving force of the narrative, which itself has not been any less suspenseful for that matter.

While paranoia has been assigned a secondary function in *Running Dog*, the narrative concentrates on gradually disambiguating the rumors that its own sense of suspense is based upon. Whereas it categorically resists returning to a purely psychological frame of reference, the narrative instead goes back to history as a form of validation. There is never any question if the footage of Hitler imitating Chaplin is genuine; what counts is that its content disqualifies it from becoming a marketable commodity. Once the prevailing notion of history has been exposed as a myth, the narrative rests comfortably with the insight that myth and history have never been mutually exclusive categories.

Unlike the conventional thriller, which John Frow had identified as the target for DeLillo's deconstructive criticism, *Running Dog* does not attempt to rewrite history as myth or vice versa. Despite their epistemological differences, both representational forms are only separate in theory. According to DeLillo, conspiracy as an American phenomenon has always been accepting of the fact that the distinction between history and myth is provisional at best. Like rumor, they are public displays of ideological self-definition, and like commodities in an open market, their value is determined by extrinsic forces. In an arena marked by exclusively collective forces (rumor, history, myth), the distinction between conspiracy and paranoia, between the psychological and the political, or individual and collective loses most of its significance. The sphere of privacy has been overwhelmed and consumed by the public sphere.

In order to complement the interpretation of *Running Dog*, the reading of a second novel could possibly reveal the other side of this dichotomy. What would a text look like in which conspiracy and paranoia are dissociated from each other, but now the emphasis is shifted toward the aspect of paranoia? Would this mean that the novel must select a genre that is more personal and private, perhaps even biographical or confessional? Unlike *Running Dog* with its interlocking spheres of public discourse, Joseph McElroy's novel *Hind's Kidnap*[13] focuses intensely on only one protagonist, Jack Hind. As the privileged position in the narrative network, Hind's consciousness establishes the parameters in which the narrative twists and turns while it moves toward the solution of a kidnap case which Hind has taken upon himself to solve. As in so many other of McElroy's novels, most notably among them *Plus*, the story is being told by a third-person omniscient narrator. But the attention to just this one person is so intense that there is hardly an room for dissenting viewpoints. It is by virtue of this centrality alone that a sense of paranoia begins to invade the narrative.[14]

Not unlike the narrative mechanism in *Running Dog*, however, McElroy's text presents an ideological construct in the making. Whereas DeLillo's critique was directed at myth as functional equivalent of history and the processes necessary to undercut this relation in order to superimpose one upon the other, *Hind's Kidnap* revolves predominantly around paranoia. To question paranoia as to its epistemological limits does not in itself undercut the conventions of conspiracy fiction; novels by Pynchon, Coover, or Gaddis have been doing this all along. Eschewing the conventions of the psychological profile or biography, McElroy starts with the assumption that paranoia must be reaffirmed first and can then be examined from the outside as a working, pragmatic philosophy. At some point in the novel, Jack Hind makes the decision to "de-kidnap" not only all human beings whom his pursuit has implicated into the abduction of Hershey Laurel, but also all places, objects, and even abstract concepts. Thus McElroy reverses the driving-force behind paranoid fiction as if it were, literally, an expression of "the Cartesian project of acquiring empiricist knowledge."[15] What can be learned, can be unlearned or forgotten. The damage that one has done can be repaired.

Apart from the fact that Hind's conscious decision to "quit" paranoia completely breaks with any concept of psychopathological verisimilitude, the disambiguation announced and seemingly initiated is one from which paranoia and conspiracy are conspicuously absent. The novel strictly refuses to provide a clear-cut resolution or explanatory recapitulation which would provide the reader with a sense of closure by sorting out what is real from what was merely imagined. Instead, it announces that, in a way, the narrative will now go backwards, regress through the dichotomies of connecting and isolating, linking and severing, emplotting and disentangling, encoding and decoding.

Despite Hind's best intentions, however, his efforts fail to produce the results he hopes for; at least, this is what he himself believes. The reader of the novel, however, must recognize that, in a way, he accomplishes to create something that is still diametrically opposed to paranoia. It just so happens that the double negation of clarity, in this case, does not allow him to backtrack toward the point where all confusion started. Successful or not, Hind's efforts foreground the paranoid view as an epistemological framework that generates categories for the conceptualization of observations and experiences on the one hand, and the establishment of a libidinal economy on the other. It enables Hind to make sense of "the wilderness of phenomena"[16] by which he finds himself surrounded. He is empowered to make decisions in a field of "multiple choices"[17] and position himself in the center of a "concentric vegetational growth,"[18] which the novel readily identifies as "narrative vegetation."[19]

McElroy's achievement consists of the novel's insistent refusal to reinstate conspiracy whenever the paranoid point of view is relativized or weakened. One could easily imagine instances in which the relevance of a paranoid perspective is, at least measured against, if not grounded in, the validity of its constructs alongside reality. So the question remains unanswered, for example, to what degree the omnipresent Santos-Dumont company, together with her affiliated "Center for Total Research,"[20] are involved in the events; or what significance Dewey Wood's insurance company, which is ominously called "The Group," has in the overall scheme of things. Their functional irrelevance, or at least marginality, suggests that these details have the same iconic status as similar elements in *Running Dog*. They testify to the presence of conspiracy, but do not establish grounds for a conceptual link between both terms.

Similarly, Hind's apparent ability to switch his paranoia on and off at will deflects the narrative's attention from the search for an ontological ground level. Instead, it directs the narrative toward the function that the presence or absence of paranoia may assume in order to determine the conceptual categories that the narrative will then rest on. The "complicated circuit" that loops back into "the heart of the revived kidnap"[21] is a trope that clearly addresses matters of narrative *gestalt* instead of offering a plausible motivation for the character's crucial decision to subject the reader to "a series of unmanageable distortions."[22] That paranoia is dissociated from conspiracy, not unlike the basic paradigm that DeLillo's *Running Dog* is constructed on, remains a given from the outset. As far as the functional value of these conceptual and organizational categories is concerned, they can best be described by what Roland Barthes in *S/Z* refers to as "codes," a number of distinct patterns that operate alongside each other in any given text and organize the flow or play of information.[23]

Being built out of an accumulation of "clumps of data,"[24] the novel organizes its diverse pieces of information primarily around rhetorical concepts. True to the slogan "Get your roots right and rich vocabularies will open to you,"[25] discursive codes are not only derived from but also linked by metaphor, metonymy, and so on. This process leads to the spreading of what critic Brian Mc Hale calls "metonymic chains" throughout the narrative. It is a metaphor that links, for example, memory with the kidnap when Hind thinks of memory in terms of "abductions of past into present."[26] This image creates a linear connection that will, in fact, lead Hind to an exploration of the bearing that the past has on the present. This particular branch of his investigation will be equally concerned with Hind's own troubled family history, past and present, as it will try to clarify what happened to the other lost child, Hershey Laurel. Hind's own and somewhat pathetic identification with the lost child becomes more convincing when the reader is allowed to glimpse the argumentative pathways that lead Hind toward responsibility and maturity.

Another type of metaphoric association branches off in more than two directions at the same time. Hind's physical height is, for example, associated with him being a "city shepard,"[27] as well as the "magic narrative communications"[28] of fairy-tales. Particularly the story about Jack and the Beanstalk, with its protagonist being led on by curiosity, keeps coming up as Hind's height and superior field of vision are being described. The narrative then goes on to pursue all of these concepts in detail so that each eventually turns into "a subcounterplot thriving in a style its very own."[29] The shepard motif is being contextualized by a whole series of pastoral tropes, as the random quotes used above and the novel's subtitle "A Pastoral on Familiar Airs" already indicate. Fairy-tales and the historically outdated pastoral are linked up with contemplations on childhood. The notion of vision is being channeled into extensive discussions about perspective and its significance in art, which, not surprisingly, turns out to be painting devoting itself primarily to pastoral motifs.[30] The list can be extended into infinity since all stories eventually come full circle, link up, and continue.

With just this brief sketch of the novel's narrative texture, it should become clear that the material of every single code (which for the purpose of clearer presentation I have somewhat artificially disentangled and set apart here) could equally be recast in terms of any of the other codes.[31] Space, for example, is a narrative function of time. Memory recreates past events in the landscapes that were the necessary precondition of the possibility of their occurrence. This way, elements of one code can meaningfully be integrated into another, creating chains of meaning that eventually loop back onto themselves.

The plot of the novel itself, which does not move toward gestures of closure or resolution, is therefore not concerned with narrative as an account of things as they happen but with what Hayden White has called "transcodation,"[32] or with what Roland Barthes describes thus:

> To read is to find meanings, and to find meanings is to name them; but then named meanings
> are swept toward other names; names call to each other, reassemble, and their grouping calls
> for further naming: I name, I unname, I rename: so the text passes: it is a nomination in the
> course of becoming, a tireless approximation, a metonymic labor.[33]

Since a "narrative account is always a figurative account, an allegory,"[34] *Hind's Kidnap* turns its own mechanism for textual production into the object of *allegoresis*. Sharing the circulatory capacity for the exchange of metaphoric properties and participating freely in the novel's ongoing process of transcodation, conspiracy and paranoia constitute elements--or possibly one single distinct entity--in this system of interlocking codes. In regard to their functional value, they appear to constitute what Barthes calls the hermeneutic code, consisting of "the various (formal) terms by which an enigma can be distinguished, suggested, formulated, held in suspense, and finally disclosed."[35]

However, Barthes' definition derives from the context of a more conventional narrative situation and is therefore likely to fall short of any text that foregrounds a different object of *allegoresis* than the one of conventional literary realism (Barthes' point of reference is, after all, a text by Balzac and not, say, by William Gaddis). It becomes obvious that any effort to reinstall paranoia as a kind of ontological ground level for the rest of the narrative must necessarily fail because transcodation in itself describes a process of syntagmatic organization. Its elements are not questioned for their origin, and thereby their relative proximity to what is real or authentic or epistemologically trustworthy, but only for their relative position toward each other.

What paranoia does accomplish, however, is to pose a challenge to this predominance of the syntagmatic. Its mere presence as one of the novel's numerous codes and its association with latent meaning or depth constitutes a gesture of temptation or seduction toward the reader. Paranoia insinuates that it could be the one code that contains the key to crack all other codes. It distracts the reader from the fact that what is encoded does not reside in the concealed "true" arrangement of codes but in the process of transcodation itself. The insertion of paranoia suggests that traces of a different, more conventional kind of *allegoresis* are present in the text and threaten to disrupt the animated suspension McElroy has so carefully established.[36]

To embrace this temptation and follow the disruptive, residual presence of paranoia to its logical extension would mean to arrive at the *aporia* that the novel, as a sound piece of postmodernist fiction, is based on. If paranoia could, indeed, be established as the secret master-narrative, which the author has cunningly hidden in the midst of irrelevant or inessential information, then all other codes become its secondary manifestations. Everything else would turn into a lesser paradigmatic substitution of the master-code. The question of genre is thereby conveniently resolved. The novel's decision to prioritize paranoia now suppresses all other codes that have claims of equal validity, which means that paranoia would have asserted not only its functional, but also its essential dominance over the entire text. Things fall into place and the novel turns, before its readers' very eyes, into a perfect specimen of the conspiracy novel as they know it.

Unfortunately, the decision to prioritize paranoia is arbitrary, considering that the novel does not support this choice even though it self-consciously baits its reader with it. *Hind's Kidnap* may either be all surface, in which case it incorporates a multitude of syntagmatically arranged genres, or it is all depth, in which case all codes dissolve into a series of paradigmatic substitutions of one genre, probably that of the conspiracy novel. Unlike other conspiracy novels, such as John Crowley's beautifully nostalgic *Aegypt* or *Little Big*, in which the moment of historical change is always irretrievably past, *Hind's Kidnap* construes this situation as always about to happen. It presents itself as permanently on the verge of falling from one mode into the other, as occupying exactly this precarious, infinitesimally short moment of change.

Reminiscent of DeLillo's preoccupation with the function of myth within history, McElroy is concerned with transforming Patrick O'Donnell's dictum of paranoia as "a mode of *perception* that notes the connectedness between things in a hyperbolic metonymizing of reality" [my emphasis] into one code of *expression* among others, derived from perception by a set of complex procedures. Whereas DeLillo explodes the duality which O'Donnell's definition is based on from the outside, McElroy dissolves it from within by putting it into an "impossible" situation; a postmodernist *mise en abyme*, which, once its untenable premises are revealed, defies the reader's efforts to stabilize its meaning within a cohesive, all-encompassing interpretation.

Both novels can therefore hardly be read as conspiracy novels any more. Rather, they are novels that deal with the consequences of the paradigm shift from a mode of perception to a mode of expression, which is simultaneously a historical and a generic transformation. Since the dissociation of conspiracy and paranoia has opened a space that can now be reinscribed according to a new ideological agenda, it seems reasonable, in following up on these two aspects of the paradigm shift, to try to determine what is being substituted to fill this empty space. Here, the novels themselves suggest the further course of analysis. Subtitled "A Pastoral on Familiar Airs", *Hind's Kidnap* is obviously concerned with issues of genre, that is with the synchronic position that the new conspiracy novel ascribes to itself, while *Running Dog* obviously takes sides with the diachronic aspect of its own position.

Given John Frow's observation that DeLillo's novels function primarily on a principle of "inventive negativity," *Running Dog* seems to suggest to some readers that, in fact, nothing is being substituted for what has been erased. Since Frow's argument appears more sound from the perspective of a synchronic reading, however, a more historizing approach may turn up what Frow must necessarily overlook. The novel itself supplies the first clues when, in conversation with Moll, Grace Delaney admits that she misses conspiracies. Without a "sense of evil design,"[37] she admits, something essential is lacking from her life. Despite the obvious irony of the statement--a conspiratorial scheme is, after all, being installed against her as she speaks--the remark represents a consistent mood of nostalgia for a time when things were different. Again, ironically this yearning for a prelapsarian moment of almost mythical dimension is focused on the possibility of conspiracy, i.e. on fear, ambiguity, manipulation, and so on. But the complaint that intrigues are not what they used to be is pervasive; she is not the only character who feels this way.

Moll Robbins herself is defined by a brief involvement with radical politics in the 60s, just as the magazine she works for, a thinly disguised version of *Rolling Stone* called *Running Dog*, has acquired its current status by virtue of its accomplishments in the past. Pandering to its readers' hunger for "Worldwide conspiracies. Fantastic assassination schemes,"[38] the magazine's standards appear thoroughly co-opted, closer to those of a tabloid than those of an underground publication. Similarly, ex-agent Earl Mudger's nostalgia is geared toward the Vietnam War, which his memories have transformed into an opportunity for active involvement, perceptual clarity, transcendental commitment, or some other form of authenticity.

Only characters like Senator Percival appear immune to this pervasive mood of nostalgia. As a man with a strong sense for *Realpolitik*, Percival tries to distract his wife from her justified suspicions that he might be with another woman by defending the lone-gunman theory in the context of the Kennedy assassination in a phone conversation. Although the topic of the conversation has little relevance for the plot, it is another reminder of conspiracy schemes so grand that they enter the collective cultural memory. Paradoxically, his attempt at distraction only returns the conversation, which threatens to drift into paranoia of a personal nature, back to the realm of general conspiracy.

But no matter if characters like Moll and Grace are positively associated with the nostalgia for paranoia and conspiracy, or characters like Lloyd Percival negatively, the novel insistently points to "the Sixties" as a point of reference. It is tempting to take the specific form of nostalgia displayed by characters in the course of the narrative at face value and read *Running Dog* as a step away from one narrative paradigm toward another with a guilty conscience and in bad faith, so to speak. The remnants of the Sixties appear in this context as reminders of a time when a genre like conspiracy fiction was still intact. One must, however, give DeLillo credit for not confusing the map with the territory. The way in which "The Sixties" are evoked in *Running Dog* leaves little doubt that the narrative does not try to recreate a true sense of the decade itself. As a screen against which the present moment can project its wishes, fears, and desires, the Sixties function as a commodity that allows the gratuitous and ahistorical reliving of a mythical moment.

The myth that "The Sixties" have come to represent is therefore not unlike the one concerning the origin and history of the supposedly pornographic film involving leaders of Nazi Germany. It is a myth about authenticity and about the possibility of not being caught within prison-houses of language, simulacra, and chains of signifiers liberated from their signifieds--at least according to a kind of critical consensus that must necessarily assume that DeLillo's achievement is restricted to "inventive negativity." However, the possibility of the mutual legitimization of conspiracy and paranoia appears in this context as an indication of this kind of authenticity. The duality Pynchon could still indulge in *The Crying of Lot 49* with a character like Oedipa Maas and a conspiracy like the Tristero, has been dismantled. It has to make room for each one of its components to exist in its own right. DeLillo's ironic twist on this development is the fact that neither the individual's psychopathological condition nor the collective political fact are particularly desirable in themselves. If one can only construe paranoia as an impossible, hopelessly past condition, then the only remaining option is to focus on conspiracy instead and shift one's ideological concerns to this new, largely unexplored territory; a territory that has been staked out by an act of definition through elimination or exclusion. In a way, this shift constitutes a rescue of one phenomenon from the categories in which it does not properly belong.

McElroy's synchronic twist on this theme is less concerned with the critique of a mythological reinscription of history. Instead, it focuses on the possibility to play out the dissociation of conspiracy and paranoia between narrative codes and their associated historically determined genres. The recurring image of the "painfully slow map"[39] of the New York City subway system on a pier along the river will remind the reader of *Hind's Kidnap* of the perceptual and conceptual challenges posed by the novel and the striking resemblance they bear to the experience of the postmodern city. On the postmodern experience of urban space, Fredric Jameson comments that

> the alienated city is above all a space in which people are unable to map (in their minds) either their own positions or the urban totality in which they find themselves.[40]

This description not only fits the novel insofar that it translates sequentiality into a spatial trope, but also that it formulates the overall spatial grid as resistant to any effort to be grasped from the inside or the outside. Any single definable feature within this artefact, be it a city block on the urban map or a narrative code in the novel's grid, can therefore be maintained unchanged and intact, while the arrangement of all features taken together defies synthesis. In accord with the predominantly spatial tropology in *Hind's Kidnap*, one character in the novel tells the other in a discussion on architecture that "America is open-ended. . .. You build the American house unfinished."[41]

This undecidability, which stands in sharp contrast to notions like Santos-Dumont's "Total Research," seems to insist by implication on the basic sameness of all the narrative codes employed in *Hind's Kidnap*; a notion that is certainly true to the extent that no single code can legitimately claim precedence or superiority over the others.[42] Hind's decision to de-kidnap elements of his paranoid plot and its partial failure indicates that McElroy believes that conceptual categories can be manipulated but never erased completely. The inadequacy of the culture's means of expression in relation to the richness of its perception cannot be remedied by establishing a master-code according to which all categorized knowledge can be arranged in a meaningful way. No single gesture can put an end to the potentially unlimited syntagmatic accumulation of knowledge or experience. This does not mean that the individual's experience of depth, which, not incidentally, corresponds to what appears as "authenticity" in DeLillo's approach to the same problem, constitutes a state of deliberate mystification in American postmodern fiction. Neither one author believes that postmodern narrative is merely based on a logocentric ruse that needs to be exposed for what it really is. The later novel, *Women and Men*, demonstrates more poignantly that power flows among multiple centers. A novel like *Hind's Kidnap* suggests that the only way to contextualize the categories of perception and codes of expression without privileging any single one of them is to construct a "para-story,"[43] which hits the mark exactly by being "beside the point;"[44] by having "foreground and background like interpenetrating sieves;"[45] by building "the American house unfinished". A "painfully slow map" is, after all, not unreadable, but simply resisting superficial perusal.

In order to summarize both novels' efforts to position themselves historically and generically on the map of American postmodernist fiction, DeLillo's image of the "Radial Matrix" comes to mind. Originally the name of a clandestine unit embedded in the rich strata of American secret services and doomed to failure at the moment it attempts to diversify its operations, Radial Matrix can be read as a trope that reconciles old and new perspectives on the conspiracy novel at a crucial juncture of its development. On the one hand, the interpretation of this image rests on the colloquial, familiar, well established use of both terms. In this context it comes to represent the surface structure of conventional narratives in which clearly discernible centers, origins, beginnings, and endings govern the textual play. It promises the reader the ability to presuppose, occasionally even to penetrate "the heart of the revived kidnap" in *Hind's Kidnap*, or to get to the truth behind the rumors, the history behind the myth in *Running Dog*. It refers to Jack Hind's consciousness as the necessary instance in which paranoia is anchored and from which it permeates the entire narrative; or to an ever more complicated web of government agencies whose true nature only manifests itself in its smallest possible unit of organization.

On the other hand, "Radial Matrix" attempts an oxymoronic combination in which one term is defined by what is lacking from the other. Just as a matrix, in the mathematical sense of the word, is not centered, any definition of what "radial" means is always going to include the notion of centeredness. A reconciliation of both terms within this oxymoron is only possible on the level of their rhetorical and not their referential properties. With both meanings existing simultaneously, Radial Matrix represents an intermediate position between two stages of which each one will contain traces of the other. Only in a mood of profound nostalgia can one conceptualize its diachronic position in regard to the other; its synchronic position only in refusal to privilege either one of its conflicting aspects. The shift or change implicit in this model is one from an intrinsically cohesive, well solidified mode to one that is just barely emerging and consolidating itself.

Notes

[1] John Frow, *Marxism and Literary History* (Cambridge: Harvard UP, 1986) 146.

[2] In "Postmodern Politics: Don DeLillo and the Plight of the White Male Writer," *Michigan Quarterly Review* 27 (Spring 1988), John Kucich argues that DeLillo's political position is determined by a feeling of helplessness in the face of an overwhelming ideological opponent. This entrapment translates for Kucich into the impotence of DeLillo's characters, whose "attempts to oppose the power of mainstream American culture always involves the appropriation of gestures and poses that they cannot legitimately claim as their own . . . And in this agony of social distance lies their impotence." (337) What Kucich calls the "social distance" of DeLillo's characters is a result of, in John Frow's words, his "inventive negativity".

[3] Frow 141.

[4] Patrick O'Donnell, "Obvious Paranoia: The Politics of Don DeLillo's *Running Dog*," *The Centennial Review* 34.1 (Winter 1990) 63. For further reading into the nature of the thriller as a popular form, see John Cawelti, *Adventure, Mystery, and Romance: Formula Stories as Art and Popular Culture.* (Chicago: Chicago UP, 1976), as well as James Fulcher, "American Conspiracy: Formula in Popular Fiction," *Midwest Quarterly: A Journal of Contemporary Thought* 24.2 (Winter 1983) 152-164.

[5] Stanley Elkin, *The MacGuffin* (New York: Viking, 1991). Elkin's novel deliberately steps outside the genre conventions as well when it foregrounds the purely psychological instead of following through with narrative sequence and suspense.

[6] Don DeLillo, *Running Dog* (New York: Alfred A. Knopf, 1978).

[7] Curiously enough, the film construes only one ideal reader who would perceive it as an item of genuine authenticity--the consumer of pornography. This consumer would accomplish such a degree of suspended disbelief that, for a moment, the ambivalence between uniqueness and mass-produced commodity is being resolved. An authentic projection of libidinal power would allow for a fetishization which could erase these ambiguities. However, all characters in the novel reorganize this potentially authentic projection according to some secondary principle; sexuality is directed first toward economic, informational, or political power and only secondarily toward the sexual.

[8] *Running Dog* 71.

[9] Richi Armbrister seems to be the only exception, but his case may be considered a remnant of the preceding model that DeLillo is elaborating on (I will elaborate at a later point on the notion of the historic trace that is embedded in a text, which has progressed beyond its own stage of development). My own reading of the text is indebted to the Russian Formalist idea of the historical dominant. In this case, the dominant may also be a generic one, considering that the analysis attempts to focus equally on synchronic and diachronic aspects of this paradigm shift.

[10] John Johnston, "Generic Difficulties in the Novels of Don DeLillo", *Critique* 30 (Summer 1989) 263.

[11] *Running Dog* 100.

[12] *Running Dog* 52.

[13] Joseph Mc Elroy, *Hind's Kidnap: A Pastoral on Familiar Airs* (New York: Alfred A. Knopf, 1974).

[14] *Hind's Kidnap* includes a long passage, reminiscent of an interior monologue, by Jack Hind's wife. This passage constitutes the only exception to the seamless personalized surfaces of McElroy's novels.

[15] Carl Freedman, "Towards a Theory of Paranoia: The SF of Philip K. Dick." *Science Fiction Studies* 11 (1984) 17.

[16] *Hind's Kidnap* 471.

[17] *Hind's Kidnap* 169.

[18] *Hind's Kidnap* 410.

[19] *Hind's Kidnap* 272.

[20] The idea that any kind of research could, in fact, be "total" suggests the rhetoric of hyperbole, of potential unlimitedness, which I have already discussed as a feature of the demoted paradigm in the preceding two chapters. Consequently, the marginal or mostly unexplored significance that this institution has for the course of the narrative conforms to the assumption that *Hind's Kidnap* has already shifted its focus of attention so that elements like these remain as atrophied remnants of the old paradigm.

[21] *Hind's Kidnap* 198.

[22] *Hind's Kidnap* 33.

[23] Roland Barthes, *S/Z* (New York: Hill and Wang, 1974)

[24] *Hind's Kidnap* 29.

[25] *Hind's Kidnap* 158.

[26] *Hind's Kidnap* 102.

[27] *Hind's Kidnap* 10.

[28] *Hind's Kidnap* 489.

[29] *Hind's Kidnap* 147.

[30] For a more in-depth discussion of the organizational patterns in McElroy's work, specifically in reference to *Women and Men*, see Brian McHale's insightful article "Women and Men and Angels: On Joseph Mc Elroy's Fiction." *The Review of Contemporary Fiction* 10.1 (Spring 1990) 227-47.

[31] In references to Barthes' *S/Z*, I have tentatively identified and named these codes as the pastoral, the mnemonic, the technological, the geographic or, more narrowly, the topographic, the architectural, the familial, and so on. However, since this interpretation is more concerned with establishing the text's general

organizational principles, an exhaustive listing and analysis of all the codes present must remain as a task for another critical reader.

[32] Hayden White, "The Question of Narrative in Contemporary Historical Theory," *The Content of the Form: Narrative Discourse and Historical Representation* (Baltimore: Johns Hopkins UP, 1987) 47.

[33] Barthes 11.

[34] White 48.

[35] Barthes 19.

[36] The strategy is highly reminiscent of the process by which *Running Dog* arrives at the creation of icons. The redoubled step from from the topos that serves as a historically or generically marked signifier to the topos that also encompasses its own position toward its historical or generic antecedent may well constitute the step from modernism to postmodernism.

[37] *Running Dog* 57.

[38] *Running Dog* 111.

[39] *Hind's Kidnap* 45.

[40] Fredric Jameson, *Postmodernism or The Cultural Logic of Late Capitalism* (Durham: Duke UP, 1991) 51. Jameson's account is indebted to Kevin Lynch's *The Image of the City* but already transforms Lynch's literal description of urban *gestalt* and the perceptual problems it poses into a trope for what Jameson himself calls "cognitive mapping," i.e. a trope of expression rather than cognition.

[41] *Hind's Kidnap* 59.

[42] All in all, this description of the novel is more reminiscent of certain canonical texts of modernism than postmodernism. The discussion where McElroy's work rightfully belongs in terms of its historical significance must be postponed, however, to a later point of this argument.

[43] *Hind's Kidnap* 272.

[44] *Hind's Kidnap* 300.

[45] *Hind's Kidnap* 500.

4. Great Jones Street *and* Ancient History: *The Construction of Genre*

In the previous chapter I have tried to demonstrate, with the example of DeLillo's *Running Dog* and McElroy's *Hind's Kidnap,* how texts operating within the new paradigm of conspiracy literature construct either their predecessors or their generic equivalents in order to situate themselves in relation to these constructs. This act of situating or positioning is performed indirectly by constructing "the Other," i.e. the outdated form and the marginalized genre, within the limitations of the texts themselves. In this context, the thriller appears as an adjacent genre, displaced along lines of readership, complexity, conventionality, and ideology. Constructed as historically preceding, the reader is confronted with a different kind of postmodern narrative, associated with the 1960s and the nostalgia for a culturally more pervasive sense of paranoia. These disruptive elements--either seen as remnant or latent possibility--must then be controlled or managed and a whole textual machinery is installed for that purpose. The most notable element in this machinery is the dissociation of paranoia and conspiracy.

The preceding reading of *Running Dog*, however, may have invoked a new conspiracy literature in which the management of the repressed is almost exclusively an act of erasure or elimination. It may even suggest that some kind of radical break has taken place from which it is impossible to go back and retrieve what apparently has been lost; the kind of "radical disruption" that Jerome Klinkowitz is so taken with, as mentioned before. This is further supported by the distinctly disruptive effect that the repressed is allowed to develop within the given text; one may only need to mention the presence of the genre of conspiracy literature in *Hind's Kidnap* and the implicit challenge it poses to the order of the narrative.

In discussing two novels by the same authors, DeLillo's *Great Jones Street* and McElroy's *Ancient History: A Paraphase,*[1] whose most conspicuous characteristic it is that they do *not* attempt to erase the traces of the discarded paradigm--whatever their strategies of containment may actually be--I would like to present a more balanced view of what the paradigm shift within contemporary American conspiracy fiction means and how it manifests itself.

The presence of textual elements, which are construed as historically or generically exclusive, does not in itself create the disruption or scandal that needs to be contained and controlled. Any less sophisticated model of change in the history of ideas does, after all, account for works that mark a period of transition. Ford Madox Ford's *The Good Soldier*, for example has elements of both realism and modernism; Robbe-Grillet's *The Erasers* is a generic hybrid in which the *noveau roman* and the classic detective novel intersect. It is the meticulous concern that texts which can be arranged around this paradigm shift display--the elaborate "strategies of containment," to use Fredric Jameson's term--for sustaining control over these disparate elements that indicates that it is no shift toward something known and well-defined that is taking place. Instead, novels like *Great Jones Street* or *Ancient History* betray a revealing insecurity and tentativeness in the face of change. Perhaps as works of an intermediary phase, they operate within a territory that has not been fully staked out yet.

Unlike *Running Dog*, written in 1978, which is already much more accomplished in the suppression or marginalization of these historical traces, an earlier novel by DeLillo, *Great Jones Street*, which was written in 1973, still presents what is to be repressed later on as a historical presence; as a valid option that the present has to be measured against. Consistent with the prevailing attitude in the novel DeLillo is to write five years later, the world of *Great Jones Street* is primarily defined by a pervasive commercialization, a world of wheeling and dealing, buying and selling. Its machinations are merciless in their total sweep of every aspect of human existence within society. In this coherent market land-scape, Globke's company "Transparanoia," aptly named by the novel's protagonist himself, musician Bucky Wunderlick, after experiencing hashish as "a puppet drug of technology, made and marketed under government supervision,"[2] represents an economic runaway system, defined by "diversification, expansion, maximizing the growth potential,"[3] synonymous with the market itself. As this system is striving toward ever-increasing and potentially unlimited growth, Bucky himself has obviously lost control over Transparanoia's transactions. The company's accumulation of property, unbeknownst to Bucky himself on whose creative output and financial resources it was originally based, includes his girlfriend Opel's apartment, which ironically Bucky chooses as a safe haven to withdraw from the world. Transparanoia's activities and structure, "with subsidiaries and affiliates all over the place,"[4] are highly reminiscent of William Gaddis' business conglom-erates in *JR* and *Carpenter's Gothic*, William Gibson's ideas of "cyberspace" as a form of consensual hallucination, or Milo Minderbinder's bizarre war-profiteering enterprise in Joseph Heller's *Catch 22*. Given the ubiquity of such images of total economic power in postmodern American fiction, DeLillo is tapping into a paranoid theme that takes him right into the mainstream of American culture and politics.

Unlike these potentially totalized systems, however, which belong to the outmoded paradigm of conspiracy literature, *Great Jones Street* pays considerable attention to the marginal or microscopic sites of the market. Like Pynchon in his latest novel *Vineland*, DeLillo focuses specifically on what he refers to as "the underground," a term that under-goes significant semantic transformations in the course of the novel. A typical example of such a marginal site in a free market economy is the nameless apple salesman, which appears as an element within the city landscape in the closing section of the novel. Insistently yelling "YOU'RE BUYING, I'M SELLING,"[5] he represents the limited, socially marginal presence, which, unlike the "Preterites" that populate *Gravity's Rainbow*, is still given a place in the overall system of power which validates this presence. This single element, even though it is defined by its qualitative insignificance in the grand scheme of things, functions according to the same principles and ideologies as the system that surrounds it. The possible significance of these small entrepreneurs is differentiated further by the figures of Hanes and Skippy, who both, with different degrees of success, break away from their rivalling economic base structures (Transparanoia and the Happy Valley Farm Commune) in order to become independent agents. With Hanes as the renegade whose acts endanger the power structures themselves, and Skippy as the dealer who is branching off into a mere sideline of profit and independence, DeLillo clearly defines the role that these alternatives to the runaway conglomerates can play and the niches they have carved for themselves.

Such small, independent entrepreneurial efforts are also translated into other aspects of the characters' lives. With Opel Hansom's involvement in the novel's central drug deal, the economic motive invades personal relationships. With Ed Fenig's incessant attempts to court success as a writer, the novel presents an example of obsession with "the market" that reaches a degree of absolute orientation toward economic success as the one goal that defies paradox and personal identity. On an even deeper level of the text and as a kind of foreshadowing of *Ratner's Star*, characters' names are clearly identifiable as commodities. Thus, one figure is named after a brand of peanut butter (Skippy), another after a registered trademark of artificial fibers (Lycra Spandex), yet another after a soft drink (Dr. Pepper).

In what appears to be a sharp contrast to these institutionalized or culturally legitimized representations of "the market," the novel introduces the Happy Valley Farm Commune as an example of "the underground"; a countercultural manifestation of resistance to "the establishment." Critic Anthony DeCurtis calls the Commune "the book's major image of counterculture's idealism gone berserk" and adds that the gap between underground and mainstream seems to close as "undergrounds . . . begin more and more to resemble flaky, sinister spin-offs of the dominant culture, rather than rebellious or subversive alternatives to it."[6]

Even though explicit references to the group's genesis and genealogy are made in a more mythical than truly historical rhetoric, the connotations of the descriptions and self-stylizations are unmistakably geared toward the Sixties yet again.[7] Defining itself as an "earth family" that does not appear "too well organized"[8] to the outside observer, Happy Valley eventually reveals itself as yet another aggressive business enterprise which competes in the appropriation, distribution, and marketing of "the ultimate drug."[9] However, Happy Valley does not produce anything, but then neither does Transparanoia. The drug has been developed by "US Guv" and has been merely stolen from one of its research facilities. Similarly, Transparanoia is basically a bureaucratic apparatus to manage and distribute Bucky's and other artists' creative efforts. Happy Valley is willing to overstep legal boundaries, but so is Globke: violence, deception, or fraud appear as a continuation of business with other means for both the mainstream businessman and the counterculture operation. And both official and unofficial enterprises are concerned with secrecy, reflected in their use of emissaries, intermediaries, front men, and negotiators.

Yet, the connotations clearly point to a difference in ideology. Within this landscape of the market, in which every microscopic site of potential resistance has been colonized either by the one system, which strives for total appropriation, or by a multitude of small commercial efforts, which are allowed to exist in its folds and margins without excessive harassment, the Happy Valley Farm Commune appears as a remnant of counterculture and thus as a memory or trace of resistance. Strangely enough, however, the sense of nostalgia for the moment of prelapsarian innocence, generally associated with "the Sixties," that was such an integral component in *Running Dog*, is completely missing from *Great Jones Street*. Talking about the presence of the Commune as a historical remnant is misleading in itself, given that only a historical perspective that is much further removed can, in fact, read the Commune as a "hardening" of historically determined forms.[10] In contrast to DeCurtis' observations, the novel does not concern itself with the Commune's transition from underground to mainstream, its fall from grace or loss of innocence. It presents the commune's organization and objectives as an accomplished fact, even as the result of design and manipulation right from the very start. This degree of co-optation poses the question if the belief in such historical narratives of rise and decline is not an ideological fiction that is most dangerous for its lack of content. As Happy Valley demonstrates, legends of the fall are self-legitimizing arguments that are readily available even to those who have never experienced prelapsarian innocence.

The reader's first impression may be that DeLillo has merely failed to endow the Commune with an appropriate history; the author is, after all, conspicuously silent on this issue. What was it like, what were the commune's goals before leaders like Chess or Bohack took over, or before it made the move from the country to the city? The only genuine development that the reader is allowed to witness is the split of the violent faction from the group's mainstream, which eventually turns out to be, first, a fabricated story in order to maintain a firm hold on the leadership's power over the commune's members, and, second, merely a pattern of power distribution that had been an integral part of the group's dynamics all along.[11] Whatever else is known about the group's history sounds like well-rehearsed, prefabricated pieces of mythology which are uttered over and over again by different characters. Members repeatedly and somewhat mechanically mention that they "believe in the idea of returning the idea of privacy to the idea of American life,"[12] that they are "a rural group that came to the city to find peace and contentment,"[13] and that they own "the whole top floor of one tenement."[14] All of these characteristics are superficial reflections of issues deeply embedded in the culture, such as questions of property rights, the contrast between city and country, or the intrusion of public into private life. Yet none of these distinguishing marks seems to contribute a truly unique or authentic feature to the group's outward appearance. Their alleged characteristics remain semantic variations on the rhetoric of certain political themes rather than intellectual variations on these themes themselves.

With the conspicuous absence of a truly historical perspective held either by the narrator or by institutions like the Commune or Transparanoia, even an attitude like nostalgia, which was such a pervasive presence in the later novel *Running Dog*, becomes impossible to sustain.[15] What is one to yearn for, after all, if one holds a belief that the past is merely a backwards extension of the present? As much as nostalgia creates its object, which it then removes to a save distance in order to project the subject's desires onto, one must not forget, however, that exactly this sense of nostalgia was presented as a viable political option in *Running Dog*. DeLillo had taken great care to demonstrate how it was part of a historical and cultural mystique; an ideology that, once integrated into mainstream culture, functioned as a means of mystification, replacing history with myth and legitimizing and finalizing the historical transition, which it pretended merely to reflect.

Since *Great Jones Street* is so adamant in its totalization of market forces, any reader coming from *Running Dog* will wonder if DeLillo himself has made a transition from complete disillusionment in the earlier to a sense of nostalgia in the later novel. But is the world of *Great Jones Street* really so seamless? Or is there an "Other" in the novel that motivates such strict control and total ideological closure? One could suspect that, if there was nothing to suppress, then no such textual machinery would be necessary in the first place. This somewhat paranoid conclusion also suggests that what masquerades as totality is, in fact, the means by which the text controls all disruptive or dissenting interpretive options. This line of approach seems more productive and certainly more relevant if one considers Fredric Jameson's definition of the factors that constitute what he has called a "strategy of containment." Instead of seeking

> a system of allegorical interpretation in which the data of one narrative line are radically
> impoverished by their rewriting according to the paradigm of another narrative, which is

taken as the former's master code or Ur-narrative and proposed as the ultimate hidden or
unconscious *meaning* of the first one,[16]
the critic must assess the "particular interpretive master code," which constitutes the necessary precondition for both contradictory lines of narrative to coexists. Further, Jameson
calls for a critical evaluation of the narrative's capacity to suppress any other interpretive
options to a degree that these otherwise legitimate alternatives disappear from the viewer's
perspective and only itself remains as the "natural," "logical," or virtually inevitable choice.
In its paraphrasing and reworking of Northrop Frye's cyclic mythical patterns of literary
history in the *Anatomy of Criticism*, Jameson's account is primarily focused on narratives
that are deeply embedded in traditional Western thought. The postlapsarian nostalgia for a
lost moment of authenticity and metaphysical presence, which was such a characteristic
feature of *Running Dog* and which is so conspicuously absent from *Great Jones Street*, is
closely associated with those narratives, harking back to the biblical account of the Garden
of Eden and persisting in Western culture in such canonical texts as Milton's *Paradise Lost*.

If one talks about the absence of nostalgia as an indication of the paradigm shift that
is reflected by novels like *Great Jones Street*, one must concede that other texts which are
roughly contemporary to DeLillo's novel do not necessarily share this quality. Joseph
McElroy's *Ancient History: A Paraphase* is, by virtue of its form alone, concerned with the
mourning of what has passed. Formulated along the generic conventions of the confession
or, to a lesser degree, the autobiography, the novel consists of an extended monologue,
written by a man who is hiding inside his neighbor's apartment after its proper occupant
has committed suicide. The narrator's paranoid, obsessive, and intensely private concerns
and conspiratorial schemes are addressed to the dead man, whose own life as a celebrity
represents quite the opposite to that of the narrator: open to public scrutiny, obsessively
self-conscious, and deliberately defined as a succession of meaningful acts and gestures.
Most of these qualities are transferred, in some form or another, to the narrator himself, as
he discovers the abstract patterns in his own life through the act of writing and speaking.

McElroy himself, often one of his own shrewdest readers, describes the novel as a
book "about disintegration and reintegration", a "psycho-philosophical mystery about the
self putting itself back together again."[17] In this process, the narrator is initially concerned
with discovering doubles and hidden correspondences: his wife's former husband's suicide
and Dom's suicide; himself as Dom's replacement, and so forth. Even the two elevators on
opposite corners of the building are a constant reminder that all things come in pairs. Once
he discovers, however, that he suffers from a kind of conceptual disease that "shrinks Field
to Dichotomy,"[18] he redirects his efforts to account for the full complexity of the events

"out there"--spatially as well as temporally. His hero's apartment becomes a "para-site," the time it takes to complete "this long memorial arc" of memory and monologue becomes a "para-phase,"[19] since only from a point "outside" or "alongside" reality can he do justice to a world for which he is the "Unknown Survivor."

As its title already indicates, the novel is very much concerned with the issues of history and the possibilities of recovering what is irredeemably past. Its agenda is never far from nostalgia as an appropriate response to the feeling of loss. The narrator, Cy (short for Cyrus) wishes to have Dom, the addressee of his monologue, back in person now that he has committed suicide. Explaining the distance between the dead man and himself, Cy is reminded of other relationships based on separation. Trying to recover a sense of order between himself and two of his friends, whom he has deliberately kept apart all of his life, it dawns on him that not all is past and that amends can still be made. This realization also leads him to the decision that will eventually take him out of the stranger's apartment.[20] But just as his friends Al and Bob have finally met during the course of the narrative, and have thus brought about the failure of the narrator's tireless efforts since their common childhood, Dom's suicide cannot be reversed and constitutes in its finality an abrupt break in the narrator's conception of time. Events now fall into the mutually exclusive categories of before/after, and even the moment of transition, or, as the narrator himself would have it, "welcome interruption," cannot be recuperated by experience but only by memory.

The narrative itself revolves around this break, returning almost obsessively to the questions of why Dom killed himself and what follows from Al's and Bob's meeting. To the same degree that these two events, which are mysteriously linked in the narrator's mind, upset the order of his world, they also threaten his sense of self, of personal identity. His efforts to establish the narrative in all its complexity as either a barrier between himself and this threat, or as a mechanism, which produces new meanings, generates links where the old ones have been dissolved, and superimposes an, at times, more than desperately random order, suggest to the reader the same familiar "strategies of containment" that already governed textual play in *Hind's Kidnap*. Only in this particular case, the same strategies seem to have been raised to a more conscious, explicit level, closer to the surface of the text.

What is it then that is being managed and/or repressed by this elaborate textual machinery? The first response, in accordance with the preceding argument, would be to link the time before the change to the same mythic image of prelapsarian innocence that was such a determining presence in *Running Dog*; to an image of "The Sixties" as a cultural-political entity, or to an image of the demoted paradigm of postmodernist fiction as a literary entity. With Dom's suicide and his resurrection in the narrator's monologue, a figure is removed and reinstalled that has many characteristics of figures representative of that decade. The note on Dom's icebox, for example, which says "EARTH=SPACECRAFT" points to Buckminster Fuller; another reference links him to Norman Mailer,[21] both public figures that embody a curious mixture of political activism and public self-display, iconoclasm, and a dash of charlatanries. As divided as one may feel about cultural phenomena of this order, the narrator, addressing Dom as his "ideal audience," still laments the passing of his "American greatness," and endows his activities and ideas with a sense of nostalgic glorification.

Comparing *Ancient History* to *Great Jones Street*, it seems as if a certain period of coming to terms with the Sixties was necessary for both DeLillo and McElroy in order to get to a point where the decade could be interpreted in terms of genre rather than history. The complexity of the texts themselves suggests that the model used so far does not quite accommodate the variety of characteristics of the new conspiracy fiction. The crossover of synchronic and diachronic readings with the generic dichotomy of "equilibrium" and "nostalgia" (*Hind's Kidnap/Running Dog*, and supposedly *Great Jones Street/ Ancient History*) does not do justice to the unique qualities of every individual novel. In order to pursue the "strategies of containment" any further, it seems likely that Jameson's notion of "containment" needs to be augmented with a principle that does not silence but incite discourse; a kind of positive restriction that generates the kind of rhetoric it wants to see as dominant. A glimpse of this affirmative containment can be witnessed at the grand party scene in *Running Dog*. An unnamed character, who remains largely out of the reader's sight but will later reveal himself as the underground's narcotics expert and man of many disguises, Dr. Pepper, describes himself as the "Morehouse Professor of Latent History at the Osmond Institute." He goes on to explain that his profession

> deals with events that almost took place, events that definitely took place but remained unseen and unremarked on . . . and events that probably took place but were definitely not chronicled.[22]

Apart from the fact that this account takes the reader back immediately into the slightly slanted realities of the paranoid view, the question remains what purpose this kind of historical record could possibly serve. According to the speaker "latent history never tells us where we stand in the sweep of events but rather how we can get out of the way."[23] This, of course, means that history is not only implicitly conceived as hostile--a natural assumption since the text does, after all belong to the genre of conspiracy fiction--but also that there is a realm parallel to the one appropriated by discourse which has remained free from its trappings. Characterized by the mutually reinforcing degree of insecurity for both the event itself and its account, latent history becomes a stage for pure possibility, a realm outside of, but not completely severed from, official history and its records.

This same idea is taken up by a character named Chess, who, after setting aside his front man and revealing himself as the Commune's real leader, tries to tempt Bucky with "the paranoid man's ultimate fear."

> Everything that takes place is taking place solely to mislead you. Your reality is managed by others. Logic is inside out. Events are delusions.[24]

Chess goes on to summarize and rephrase the whole of the preceding narrative in terms of a conspiracy fiction: what if he were Dr. Pepper? What if every suspicion were true? What if we couldn't trust our senses? Events suddenly acquire double meanings, ambiguity is retroactively installed in the text as the dominant theme, and for the reader a second, momentarily valid reading is opened up alongside the straightforward and coherent one that the text has been encouraging all along. As unsettling as this moment may be, Chess himself quickly settles matters by reassuring Bucky that he is not Dr. Pepper; a promise that is made on the shaky ground of non-matching physical height--Pepper is after all an expert of disguise--yet is left unquestioned by the rest of the narrative. Seemingly, the scene remains a brief and isolated exercise in paranoia.[25]

Connected by Dr. Pepper, who appears in both of them as an allegorical figure of deceit and indeterminate identity, the two scenes provide two aspects of a vision of a narrative alongside the official narrative which seems to fill the conceptual gap that the absence of a non-repressive strategy of containment had opened up in the novel. If "the Other" cannot be projected within the text as a presence that needs to be repressed and managed, distanced and desired through nostalgia, then it can perhaps be construed as an absence that can only be detected from a perspective of latency or possibility. Thus, repression is transferred into "latent history" as one of its potential subjects (what was not reported? what did almost happen?). The whole of "latent history" itself appears now as a kind of Utopian vision or impulse, asserting the legitimacy of what could have happened. For *Great Jones Street* as a piece of fiction self-conscious about its own historical status, this means that, all of a sudden, in the midst of a conspiracy novel, a space opens up in which a traditional narrative of conspiracy and paranoia is unfolded as something other than the novel itself. The result is perplexing: what else is the novel supposed to be when that which it so insistently claims to be appears only as an unrealized alternative to itself?

Significantly enough, a similar concept appears in McElroy's work. The full title of the novel is, after all, *Ancient History: Paraphase*. The novel's narrator extends the meaning of the term further and further until it includes every concept--spatial, temporal, and abstract-- which can be seen as being located "alongside" the authoritative version of any narrative "site": Dom's apartment as a "para-site" to the public space in which its owner used to be such a skillful manipulator; time spent in the apartment as a "collapse into paraphase"[26] without knowledge of clock-time or duration; and finally the narrative itself, more in the sense of *discours* than *recit*, which positions itself alongside the events it conjures up.

Joseph Tabbi, one of McElroy's insightful commentators, reads this insistence on "putting oneself outside" in McElroy's fiction as an expression of what he calls "*literary* paranoia".

> For McElroy, correspondences, analogies, and significant junctions make up the central substance of what he called in the LeClair interview a "collaborative network," and the paranoid's salvation, a condition to be realized within the design of the fiction, begins for him not in any withdrawal or attempted escape from structure, but in the confirming "fear that I might be outside the network--therefore it exists."[27]

Despite Tabbi's differing interpretive interest, his account of McElroy's attitude toward the trappings of structure confirms the existence of a Utopian mechanism ("the paranoid's salvation") that regulates the inside/outside metaphor within a perspective that conceives of "structure" as always already fully realized and potentially totalized. Not unlike DeLillo's notion of "the market" in *Great Jones Street*, McElroy's "collaborative network" has invaded and colonized all microscopic sites of resistance so that only a "paraphase," which is simultaneously removed from and tied to the reality it describes, can give the necessary leverage to affect change or provide the liberty to speak truthfully and unencumbered by paranoia..

Granted that McElroy's notion of structure seems to lack the concrete political and historical content which DeLillo has already invested in his text by filling in the concept of a free market economy. But even though McElroy still speaks in the abstract about such a space, both novels share a Utopian impulse which brings the argument back to Jameson's "strategies of containment." In the conclusion to *The Political Unconscious*, Jameson argues that, very likely, the mechanism of such strategy can be divided into two distinct modes of persuasion, one based on repression, the other on a principle of hope, fulfillment, and reward.[28] The notions of "paraphase" and "latent history" clearly fall in the latter category. They constitute the promise to go outside the system and not lose touch, to court isolation as a privileged epistemological position without cutting oneself off from the object of one's observations.

What this means for the themes of conspiracy and paranoia in postmodern American fiction at this point is difficult to assess. It seems significant that both texts do not see themselves transformed from this outside position into something other than what they already are. Dr. Pepper's exemplary fiction of "the paranoid man's ultimate fear"--the single fully developed example of "latent history" in the whole text--retells the novels plot in terms of a conspiracy story, which means that the novel *Great Jones Street* itself cannot be a conspiracy story. Consequently, Pepper's narrative is not really a conspiracy story because it does not claim full authenticity. Consequently, no thing is really fully identical with itself.

This last option plays of course into the notion of the "split" running through a schizophrenic text that this reading has been entertaining all along. Within a novel like *Great Jones Street*, which conceives of its own narrative model as objectionable yet wishes to retain its authenticity and strength, the only way to serve both purposes is to split itself and incorporate the split into its conceptual and organizational framework. Whenever nostalgia fails to recall the conspiracy story and hold it at a safe distance, the utopian impulse can project the model's desirable qualities into a text which then can be viewed as advanced beyond the state of the material which it had to incorporate.

The same strategic indecisiveness, so to speak, applies to *Ancient History* as well. Although the narrative goes to some extent to emphasize the artificiality of its rhetorical constructs, which somehow try to approximate a reality whose complexity goes beyond binary oppositions (the topographical metaphor, the alphabetical arrangement of first names, the coincidences and doublings, and so forth), it never steps outside of its own bounds to rebuild itself as "paraphase." Its objective should not be confused with a simple projection of the imaginary onto the future; the hope that things will get better some distant day. On the contrary, the question here is exactly "how can you stay equidistant from something that's cut itself loose from the foreseeable future?"[29] Some of its rhetorical devices emphasize this desire of the novel to be simultaneously itself and the "Other." There is, to mention but one example, the incessant play on neologisms where morphology and etymology are being broken down and reassembled to go beyond expression as mere recognition.[30]

The notion of historicity, however, which is at the root of what both novels are finally "about," is not without problems. The manipulation of certain aspects of the conspiracy novel is legitimized by pointing out that what is fair game for intervention must, therefore, have been based on conditions which are historically obsolete anyway. The argument of historic progress necessitates an increasing amount of textual evidence; a process that is logically reversed, but tends to produce an ever-accelerating process of innovation and deviation from the norm. What the utopian impulse accomplishes in this context is to legitimize experiment while maintaining a firm grasp on tradition.

Notes

[1] Don DeLillo, *Great Jones Street* (Boston: Houghton Mifflin, 1973); Joseph McElroy, *Ancient History: A Paraphase* (New York: Alfred A. Knopf, 1971).

[2] *Great Jones Street* 138.

[3] *Great Jones Street* 10.

[4] *Great Jones Street* 186.

[5] *Great Jones Street* 264.

[6] Anthony DeCurtis, "The Product: Bucky Wunderlick, Rock'n Roll, and Don DeLillo's *Great Jones Street*," *Introducing Don DeLillo*, Ed. Frank Lentricchia (Durham: Duke UP, 1991) 136.

[7] The background for this remark is the chapter on *Running Dog* and *Hind's Kidnap*, in which a more in-depth treatment of the tension between these two terms is attempted.

[8] *Great Jones Street* 16/17.

[9] *Great Jones Street* 57.

[10] According to Tom LeClair, the novel's "characters seem quite familiar now that the music and drug culture of the 60s has revealed itself in its 80s memoirs." The critical perspective here has to be removed by a decade to be able to see the unmentioned intermediate decade as the antithesis against which something like "the 60s" can be defined. See Tom LeClair, "Crowds, Power, and Force," *In the Loop; Don DeLillo and the Systems Novel* (Urbana: University of Illinois Press, 1987) 94.

[11] The description Bohack eventually gives Bucky phrases the split in terms of a spatial metaphor ("the lunatic fringe") which implicitly construes the distinction not in time or as a result of process or development, but as an inherent structural feature. This rhetoric places the commune in a kind of perpetual present.

[12] *Great Jones Street* 193.

[13] *Great Jones Street* 36.

[14] *Great Jones Street* 16.

[15] Transparanoia and its affiliates are described in terms of a parent-child relationship by Globke. As much as this trope may hold a potential for being transformed or extended into a historical vision, Globke's rhetoric suggests a more ahistorical, almost psychoanalytical view.

[16] Fredric Jameson, *The Political Unconscious: Narrative as a Socially Symbolic Act* (Ithaca: Cornell UP, 1981) 22.

[17] Tom LeClair, "An Interview with Joseph McElroy," *Anything Can Happen: Interviews with Contemporary American Novelists*. Ed. Tom LeClair and Larry McCaffery (Champaign: University of Illinois Press, 1983) 237.

[18] *Ancient History* 260.

[19] *Ancient History* 123.

[20] In its combination of psychological arbitrariness and "literal-mindedness," this is a typical decision for one of McElroy's protagonists, reminiscent of Jack Hind's decision to de-kidnap objects and places in *Hind's Kidnap*. In order to establish a semantically and metaphorically coherent and meaningful structure, McElroy has been willing to go to these extremes throughout all of his work.

[21] The reference to Mailer is examined in more detail in Joseph Tabbi's article ""The Generous Paranoia of Those Who Pursue Themselves": McElroy, Mailer, and *Ancient History*," *Review of Contemporary Fiction* 10.1 (Spring 1990) 86-94. Springing from an encounter between Mailer and McElroy when Mailer was lecturing to McElroy's students at Queen's College, Tabbi contends that Dom is a fictive representation of Mailer. Tabbi reads the novel primarily as an effort to reconcile the private with the public self and to alleviate the paranoid fears arising from this fragmentation of personal identity. Another interpretation of this constellation between the two personalities has been suggested by Tom LeClair in his article "Opening Up Joseph McElroy's *Letter Left To Me*," in which he argues that in McElroy's struggle with father figures the reader witnesses a kind of Bloomian Oedipal struggle between "good" and "bad" writing, i.e. writing that is or is not faithful to the father's standards. I have quoted this article in more detail in my own chapter on *White Noise* and *The Letter Left To Me*.

[22] *Great Jones Street* 75.

[23] *Great Jones Street* 76.

[24] *Great Jones Street* 254.

[25] In his essay on *Great Jones Street*, Tom LeClair suggests that Chess may actually *be* Dr. Pepper. Similarly, he extends the range of conspiratorial speculation to include "US Guv," which could have planted the drug and masterminded the Commune's activities that obviously exceed its own potential. Besides the fact that there is little textual evidence to distrust Chess's statement that he is not Pepper, the nature of Chess's monologue as a speculation, as the following through of a hypothetical situation, remains unaffected by the speaker's identity. The passage in LeClair's analysis shows, however, how the paranoid text imposes its structure on the reader's effort to achieve coherence and closure. See Tom LeClair, "Crowds, Power, and Force," 100-101.

[26] *Ancient History* 139.

[27] Tabbi 91.

[28] ". . . if the ideological function of mass culture is understood as a process whereby otherwise dangerous and protopolitical impulses are "managed" and defused . . . then some preliminary step must also be theorized in which these same impulses . . . are initially awakened within the very text that seeks to still them. If the function of the mass cultural text is meanwhile seen rather as the production of false consciousness and the symbolic reaffirmation of this or that legitimizing strategy, [then it] must necessarily

involve a complex strategy of rhetorical persuasion in which substantial incentives are offered for ideological adherence." Jameson, *The Political Unconscious,* 287.

[29] *Ancient History* 155.

[30] A metaphor like "Vectoral Dystrophy" (260) offers a link between the paraphase with its inherent tendency toward abstraction and the "live dichotomy" (244) of reality. If perception is located in the brain, and the brain can be mapped into functional sectors, then even perception is a question of space; just as the muscle's exercise exerts pressure by contracting, i.e. altering spatial relations. This attempt to sketch out the body-metaphor as a link between the abstract and the concrete or between the paraphase and the phase, also suggests that the Utopian impulse must somehow accommodate the human body as an essential condition, or even location, for historical change.

5. The Names *and* Lookout Cartridge*: The Representation of Space*

The shift from Modernism to Postmodernism is accompanied by a shift of other historical dominants: away from the processes of cognition and toward articulation, away from the question of how we can know, to the question of how we construct what we know through how we communicate, to others and ourselves. The intense preoccupation of such canonical "high" Modernists as Woolf, Proust, or Joyce with the workings of the individual consciousness, which already allows for the idea that the mind constructs by other means than the purely sensory, eventually gives way to a conception of consciousness which is less monadic, inward, or monologic. This shift toward Bakhtinian heteroglossia is reflected in the move from Freudian to Lacanian psychoanalysis which calls into question the possibility of drawing clear demarcation lines between what is inside and what is outside the individual consciousness. The concept of consciousness itself, from a postmodern point of view, is opened to a more dialogic interaction between what used to be so unproblematically called "the individual" and its environment. Eschewing all binary pairings, postmodernist versions of the Western founding myth of presence, identity, or centrality challenge the essentialist Freudian claim to the ego so that the problem of articulation is always already inscribed in the problem of cognition.[1]

This reinscription of a cognitive into an articulatory discourse, or reformulation of a problem of perception into a problem of communication, inevitably raises the all kinds of questions about the validity of "individual" experience, the mechanisms of mediation between sensory data and conceptual patterns, the claims to truthfulness and authority that any speaker can legitimately make, and so forth. As complex as the consequences of this change of paradigms between modernism and its successor may be in any given case, its one major result which is relevant to the development of this argument is the shift toward a conception of experience as collective, dialogic, and mediated.

Thus, representing space in postmodern fiction becomes a formal problem which is inevitably enmeshed in politics, since space, obviously, is mute and cannot represent itself.[2] Filtering the experience of space, as it branches out into the themes of travel, tourism, exotism, colonialism, and so forth, through the individual consciousness of a narrator or protagonist automatically becomes more than a reflection of this individual's disposition or character. Its account must take in the cultural background that is already inscribed into this space, as well as the political practices, the distribution of power, the forms of social organization, and so on. This is, of course, nothing new, as the work of Kipling, Conrad, or other Western authors easily demonstrates who are commonly associated with the subject of colonialism. The significant shift in the treatment of this and related thematic complexes that occurs with postmodernism, however, transfers the interpersonal background to the level of intertextuality, where it can be manipulated as a more self-conscious strategy of representation than its purely thematic predecessor.

In Joseph McElroy's *Lookout Cartridge* and Don DeLillo's *The Names*,[3] the development from a cognitive to an expressive metaphor outlined above is re-enacted as the two narrators' experiences of the foreign or the exotic. DeLillo's protagonist in *The Names*, James Axton, works as a political risk analyst, gathering data and creating regional and national profiles for what, to his own surprise, turns out to be the American Intelligence Community. The reader and Axton himself are led to believe for the longest time that an American conglomerate, affectionately called "the parent," is Axton's employer. His profession accounts both for his living abroad, away from America, and for his incessant travels all over the Middle East and the Mediterranean, although his private interest in the *ta onomata* conspiracy soon replaces the professional obligation as the motivation for his travels. The scope of locations, which the narrative introduces as potential settings for the conspiracy, is further increased through secondary characters, such as Owen Brademas. Owen's travels, again in semi-professional capacities, bring into consideration places and cultures outside of Axton's own range, which is centered on Athens and, within it, the Acropolis. Interlacing strands of narrative in flashback, conversation, anecdote, handbook entry, and travel guide, the novel foregrounds Axton's centrality as the mediator between the space in which the narrative enfolds and the reader who must, together with the protagonist, bring locations together to create a coherent narrative. The investigation of the cult and its conspiratorial activities, as well as the uncovering of the CIA's involvement in "the Parent's" activities, give the spatial narrative a pattern to follow in which itinerary and conspiracy are equally responsible for generating the plot.

A similar pattern of conspiracies superimposed upon the reading of space lays the epistemological groundwork for Joseph McElroy's *Lookout Cartridge*. The narrator, Cartwright, freelances as a consultant, scouting out innovative technologies for a firm in New York. Together with a childhood friend he also moonlights as an independent filmmaker. In both functions, he travels primarily in between his home in Highgate, London, and New York. Not unlike the double conspiracies in *The Names*, Cartwright's narrative accounts cover the investigation of the conspiracy that leads to the destruction of a film the two friends have shot, and the uncovering of the subsequent conspiracy trying to cover up the destruction itself. The novel consists of the competitive movement of disparate narrative forces revolving around the binary pairing of covering and uncovering, cohesion and fragmentation. Straying from the axis London-New York in an attempt to revisit, metaphorically and literally, the locations where the film was originally shot, Cartwright's investigations integrate an even wider variety of locations into the narrative.

The conceptual shift away from the authenticity of experience manifests itself in DeLillo's and McElroy's concern with America as their novels' absent center. In both cases, the narrative develops around a geographical center, Athens in one case, the axis London/New York in the other. With a generous sweep, it then gathers a host of scattered locations around this center. As frayed and fragmented as this model of center versus periphery in itself might be, its significance for the narrators and for the total shape of the narratives lies in its essential eccentricity in relation to "the cool theme of America itself."[4]

Accordingly, both narrators' musings revolve around the question of America, which itself is construed as a powerful absence and ironic reversal in *The Names*, or as an entity without presence outside the dichotomy between Old World and New World in *Lookout Cartridge*. For McElroy, America constitutes one problematic half of a schizophrenically split global culture.[5] It becomes a point of reference for characters who rely on the "Yankee dollar," knowing that ultimately ". . . you measure the pound by it. You rely on the American connections."[6] Still, America itself tends to remain so invisible that the two friends, in planning their film project, do not expect to have any problems when they aim "to find visions intermingling England and America so you wouldn't be able to tell."[7] The questions what America means and what it means to be American are therefore implicated in the narrators' attempt to solve the riddle of the conspiracies surrounding them, which, in turn, are inscribed into the narrativization of space. Both novels are American novels, firmly anchored within the complex and provisional abstraction "America," as numerous critics have recognized.[8]

It is as tempting as it is misleading to assume that foreign culture itself, together with its inscription into landscape or space, appears as a manifestation of conspiracy. Even though the incomprehensible, exclusive, and collective Other of the foreign culture undoubtedly displays features conforming, at least on the surface, to the paranoid view for the Western spectator--an argument that has been made most convincingly by Edward Said in *Orientalism*[9]--the characteristic feature of the conspiracies in both novels is clearly their conceptual dependence on America itself as an absent center. Although the narrative depicting "first contact" and the conspiracy story are similarly concerned with issues of cognition and the process of familiarizing the exotic through the act of naming, it would still be difficult to construe a close thematic association between both themes. First contact stories commonly reveal "the Other" as a reflection of oneself, whereas the conspiracy story is primarily concerned with preserving the essential distinction between the individual and the collective.

Not surprisingly, then, the tropes applied to the mediation of both narrators' experience are inextricably linked to America and not to the countries that provide the experience that is later recounted as the novels' plots. Instead of a cognitive metaphor, which in itself would insinuate that the ideological construct "America" can somehow be experienced without mediation or is accessible to some ideal apparatus of sensual apprehension, the novels chose a literary metaphor, inserting themselves strategically into a field of cultural production and a specific tradition that will then intervene between the narrators' highly idiosyncratic and individualized experience and the foreign landscape resisting or deflating interpretation.

For the purpose of this intervention, *The Names* reaches back to the theme of the expatriate in American literature, presided over by such iconic figures as Hemingway, Lowry, or Bowles. With these cultural icons DeLillo's characters share the melancholic rootlessness, the existential *Geworfensein*, and the frantic covering up of their sickness unto death through incessant change of location and activity and a kaleidoscopic succession of rapidly forming and dissolving social bonds. Tirelessly talking about and thus thematizing their situation, DeLillo's Americans differ from their literary forefathers only in their relative degree of self-consciousness about being historical late-comers, actors impersonating what was once authentic. They are too blasé to be innocent whenever they are abroad. Axton himself realizes that

> Americans used to come to places like this to write and paint and study, to find deeper textures. Now we do business.[10]

Unlike Paul Bowles' travellers, however, DeLillo's expatriate Americans are never really at risk to "go native." Thinking of themselves as a unique "subculture," they are simultaneously actors and audience to themselves and others. This painful self-consciousness prevents the loss of an identity that is not constituted within oneself any more, but rather in the relational network and the mutual reaffirmation of the artificial community around.

Because DeLillo's and McElroy's protagonist travel mainly to do business, their experience of the exotic is also mediated through a peculiar split within the source of their alienation. Since Axton works as a risk-analyst and Cartwright as a stringer for new technologies, they both are involved in the production of cultural representations. That is to say, they participate in the appropriation, reformulation, and dissemination of images of the exotic and therefore contribute to the cultural machinery that intervenes in their own unmediated experience. What they do as tourists is not significantly different from what they do as professionals. What they do as tourists and/or professionals brings them into little contact with the culture whose surface they happen to be skimming at any given moment. The modernist notion of alienated labor is reprocessed through this conflation of labor and leisure and emptied of all conventional content. The modernist gesture of heroic search for the self, which underlies the loss of identity in the threatening vision of the American gone native, is made equally impossible by this move.[11]

Having thus fragmented the notion of consciousness, the postmodernist twist to this already slightly defamiliarized narrative is the emphasis on the construction of space itself as text. All characters, reprocessing themselves through the trope of the expatriate, are also self-conscious readers of the signs they encounter along their travels through the pre-processed, always already experienced text of the foreign lands. Corresponding to the overt theme of *The Names*--the politics of representations and writing in particular--Axton states categorically that

> [all] these places were one-sentence stories to us. Someone would turn up, utter a sentence about foot-long lizards in his hotel room in Niamey, and this became the solid matter of the place, the means we used to fix it in our minds . . . The sense of things was different in such a way that we could only register the edges of some elaborate secret . . . There was no equivalent core.[12]

As the place itself is condensed and depreciated by its aphoristic description, the speaker has placed himself in a culturally predefined context rather than in relation to a radically new experience. One sentence is enough to replace the immediate experience for the listener.

McElroy, on the other hand, goes back to the beginning of the modernist period, providing protagonist and reader with the conflict between New World innocence and Old World sophistication as a trope for the compromised nature of experience. The "International Theme" is a complex, heterogeneous trope that involves subjects, narrative strategies, and ideological presuppositions which, even preceding Henry James, firmly belong to the standard inventory of American literary history. Cartwright's travels, which take him back and forth between London, where he lives, and New York, where he does most of his business, follow the traces of cultural inheritance, colonial dependence, and political power in the global economy between the Old and the New World. Carrying small change in both currencies in his pockets, the novel's protagonist defines himself either ironically as "an untrustworthy merchant adventurer named Cartwright,"[13] or, somewhat oxymoronically, as "the domestic male expatriate."[14] In his recurring associations for both London and New York, the latter is conceptualized as "the city's grid,"[15] while the former figures as "villages, almost."[16] The contrast between the Old World with its cozy neighborhoods and the New World with its abstract grids is ironically reversed in the narrator's mind by associating his childhood in Brooklyn Heights with the metaphor that, in the present moment, is reserved for London. By the same token, London becomes a metaphorical antidote superseding New York as an "anesthetic TNT to soften New York into a mere *remembrance* of what the future used to seem."[17]

Even though the narrative, with its loops and jolts, veers time and again from the straight transatlantic line, it still remains centered around it. "Unfortunately," Cartwright muses in regard to his peculiar state of consciousness, "to be between does not necessitate being constantly connected with what one is between."[18] Lack of connection is being explored as a source of insight and as philosophically unstable grounds for acting upon one's insights, as accurate as they may be.[19]

Corresponding to the postmodern twist in DeLillo's narrative, *Lookout Cartridge* goes beyond the conceptual boundaries of the international theme in exactly this emphasis of in-betweenness as a state of privileged insight but limited power. While the international theme remains anchored in the opposition between Europe and America, its postmodernist variant strives for the dissolution of the pairing and the delimitation of its constitutive categories. McElroy's protagonist, in spite of his concern with cultural and individual origins and identities, is truly at home only in a place halfway between the two cultures.[20]

In outlining and describing the two major strategies with which the notions of "experience" and "consciousness" are being redefined insofar as they apply to the experience of space, I have systematically omitted the question of functional use. What is the pragmatic, if not ideological, gain of intervening in concepts which are considered basic or irreducible, fundamentally true or epistemologically sound? In order to answer these questions, I want to go back to the beginning of my argument and recast the story it tells one more time; this time, however, attempting to trace the ideological inscriptions left by both authors in the previously discussed ontological and epistemological adjustment.

By using the term "intervention" to describe the mechanisms processing experience for the postmodern consciousness, any strategy mentioned above is seen and judged only for its capacity to sever rather than connect. But since these cultural mechanisms do function both ways--what stands in between the old and the new separates *and* connects-- the question arises what the ideological implications would be if they were instead appreciated for their complementary capacity. Suddenly, the fact that the protagonists of both novels are White Western Males ceases to be a metaphorical sign representing "consciousness" and takes on a more specific meaning.

The essential passivity of space, its need to be articulated through a voice which is not its own, follows Western traditions of the split between subject and object.[21] Commonly, this duality assigns the dominant role to the observer who must appropriate the world according to his own agenda. Even the field of popular anthropological journalism, which includes such dramatically different approaches to space as Bruce Chatwin's in *The Songlines* or William Least Heat-Moon's in *PrairyErth*,[22] has mostly caught up with the problems that such an act of conceptual appropriation creates. Chatwin's or Moon's cultural models for articulating space are already well aware of how their narrators function as amateur anthropologists who mediate and interpret what they observe. Therefore, DeLillo's and McElroy's choice of a Western white male as protagonist places both novels at the center of all plots in a postcolonial world. Here, conspiracies play into the fears and fantasies of those holding power, individually and collectively, and who consequently see their power redefined, lessened, and rerouted in the process of political change. McElroy is clearly aware of America's global role; *Lookout Cartridge* tells of draft-dodging during the Vietnam war, the presence of American first-strike bases on Corsica, and the establishment of an American commune in Chile by an American and an English university. Similarly, DeLillo's Middle East is a place of American overt and covert, military and economic intervention. What both texts have in common is that the conspiratorial activities originating in marginal groups (McElroy's terrorist network, DeLillo's cult of social outcasts) aim to restructure power in their own idiosyncratic interests. The conspiracies pertaining to "the mainstream" (McElroy's implicating Dagger DiGorro in the plot to destroy the film, DeLillo placing the CIA at the center of Axton's activities) pursue clandestine objectives that compromise the protagonists' integrity by making them accomplices in the plot they are trying to uncover.

Space itself, in the light of these conflicting interests, ceases to be the neutral abstraction as which it had initially appeared and starts to occupy ideologically more concrete sites. Space in *The Names* appears as the dichotomy of rural/urban whenever the narrative integrates experiences pertaining to Athens into the conceptual totality of Greece. Space figures as the dichotomy of industrialized/pre-industrial whenever the narrative recounts conceptual shifts between "back home" and "out here." And spatial relations are inscribed into the dichotomy exotic/familiar whenever the novel dramatizes the experience of displacement, awe, or the inability to attach one's experience to an abstract sense of location. *Lookout Cartridge* plots not only America and England against each other, but also both America *and* England against culturally more marginal places like Corsica, the Outer Hebrides, or the Bahamas. The lines along which these antinomies are being developed and interrogated correspond, at least partly, to those in *The Names* (industrial/agrarian, colonial/postcolonial, and so on).

In this context, the novels' insistence on absent centers is somewhat problematic. It re-enacts the power relations between America and the exotic outposts of civilization, which both texts are supposedly *really* about. It is still the exotic locations which, simultaneously and somewhat paradoxically, occupy the conceptual margins and the narrative center of Axton's and Cartwright's global perspective. In accord with the all-too familiar representational politics of colonialism, everything *but* America continues to serve as a mirror image in which America only sees itself. Aside from their function as tools for American narcissism, these countries are invisible, inarticulate, insubstantial. Their invisibility is caused exactly by the fact that they are channels of power and not places where power resides.[23]

This power, however, is being exercised with the help of technologies that are crucial to both texts' ideological concerns. Aside from DeLillo's obvious preoccupation with written and spoken language, *The Names* is also about surveillance and its visual technologies. One of the minor characters in *The Names*, Frank Volterra, is an American film-maker who tries to locate the cult in order to record one of their ritual killings on film. This record would have the same epistemological value as Cartwright's and DiGorro's amateur film, which accidentally preserves the images of some members of the terrorist network. Both films are recording illegal activities and thus have the potential to become incriminating evidence, producing irrefutable proof of certain individuals' location in time and space. They lend themselves, seemingly by some intrinsic nature of the medium itself, to the purpose of surveillance and control, supervision and indictment. Not by coincidence does Cartwright, for example, observe upon handling a gun that it "had a moment of weight at the end of my bent arm like our damned camera."[24] Camera and gun are the icons of the explorer's technology. As much as both authors present the issue of the media and the medium as one of epistemology, its political significance keeps insinuating itself through the ideological inscriptions by which it is already surrounded. The question of truthful representation, of authenticity and ontology, must be reformulated in more political terms once representation becomes a function of technology: who controls the technology? Who points the camera at whom? In what ways are both camera and gun alike? Whose gaze, through the lens or along the barrel, is being given the power over life and death?

Language itself must certainly be included in this discussion of technology. Film and film-diary are played against each other by McElroy, who goes so far as to identify the narrator himself with a recording and replaying technology, the title's "lookout cartridge." Since "film, diary, memory, and the novel itself are all politically dangerous technologies of representation,"[25] McElroy places a great deal of emphasizes on how access to them is controlled and regulated, and how they themselves intervene in human communication. Language in its written form is another technology necessary to produce, record, disseminate, or erase the spoken word in the multilingual deliberations of *The Names*. Critic Paula Bryant, in commenting on the plot of the novel, concludes that

> Jim [Axton] has gone from despising language as timeless, pure abstract, and thus limited, to seeing its potential as dynamic medium, irrational, immediate, expressive, although impure (because reworked and reworkable).[26]

Reworkable like a tool, language is no longer exclusively part of human nature; instead it is seen as a physically manipulable object with the ability to manipulate human nature and nature in general. Language ceases to be natural; it becomes a piece of technology.

The pattern of metaphorical resonances thickens even more if one considers the basic physical facts on which film depends to achieve the illusion of animation and continuous motion. Relying on the persistence of the human eye, sequential animation is created by lining up static images in a steady and continuously spaced sequence. These images in themselves are nothing but spaces, their diagonal width measured in millimeters according to an international industrial standard. The trope of "plot" in both senses of the word and in its reliance on the principle of *post hoc ergo propter hoc* is therefore highly reminiscent of the technological principle of film. It also reflects the pattern of travel, the constant succession of spaces into which a particular moment is inscribed each and which, perceived in sequence, create the impression of logical and temporal coherence and narrative validity.

Commonly, space in narrative is either a function of depth or of "that strongest thing of all, surface."[27] Both aspects have been explored extensively by critics who are trying to determine how the perception of space has changed over time. Preceding the postmodern conceptions discussed here, Henri Lefebvre has located depth in the cultural layers that have accumulated around space.

> Each network or sequence of links--and thus each space--serves exchange and use in specific ways. Each is produced--and serves a purpose; and each wears out and is consumed, sometimes unproductively, sometimes productively.[28]

Unless space could be consumed through narrative without "using it up," the narrativization of space can only add another layer of cultural inscription to obscure nature underneath. Characterized by the nostalgia for a moment before space was fully mapped out and utilized, Lefebvre's account nevertheless points the way toward discourses that are less appropriative of their object. William Least Heat-Moon, for example, outlines a model of depth in *PrairyErth* which he calls a "deep map" and which is reminiscent of what anthropologists like Clifford Geertz have called "thick description." At the other end of the spectrum, Bruce Chatwin describes the Australian aboriginal notion of the "dreaming" in

The Songlines, which provides a narrative concept based on sequential perception and syntagmatic arrangement of experience. Both writers are trying to undo the postmodern perspective while maintaining the readability of space; an effort similar to that of the protagonist in *Hind's Kidnap* who tries to "de-kidnap" all those implied in his theories.

The conspiracies inscribed into space by DeLillo and McElroy make such a reading practically impossible. Conspiracies in *The Names* and *Lookout Cartridge* either create a kind of knot in the flow of information, or they thin out or dilute this flow, at times to the degree of a complete standstill. Thus, clues leading to the discovery of the conspiracy are either scattered so that no single perspective is removed far enough to encompass them all at once; or they are clustered in one location so that, through their extreme proximity, they cancel each other out, overlap, or create enough distracting noise to render themselves virtually illegible. A passage like the following, quoted from *The Names*, recreates the sense of depth that even the most callous and experienced of DeLillo's tourists experience with a sense of awe.

> Along the intricate and twisting paths, among the broken towers, I began to wonder if this might all be one structure, the whole village, a complex formation whose parts were joined by arches, walls, the lower rooms that smelled of animals and forage. There seemed no clear and single separation between the front and back ends of the village, between this oblong tower and that. It was their place, I was sure . . . All the buildings joined. One mind, one madness.[29]

Here, the association of place or location with the cult and their conspiratorial activities is raised to the conscious level of both reader and protagonist. The village is "their place." The description provides a comprehensive inventory of the rhetoric of conspiracy and paranoia: the trope of hyperbole is reflected in the all-including nature of the artifice; the play on the difference between appearance and reality is articulated in the juxtaposition of structural integrity and outward collapse; the labyrinthine floorplan corresponds to the inscrutability and Byzantine complexity of conspiracies, and so on. For good measure, it seems, the author also adds a dash of symbolism by pointing out that animal nature is, of course, confined to the lowest level of the structure, or by providing the biblical image of the broken tower as a reminder that the novel incessantly revolves around issues of multiculturalism and language. On the whole, the passage, which in its multifacetedness produces the kind of interpretive frenzy or delirium Baudrillard and Jameson identify as one of the characteristic marks of postmodernism, poses the question whether this specific setting is still legible as landscape/text, or whether it deliberately produces a depth in which signs cancel each other out through their proximity and density. Considering what a superb stylist DeLillo is, it seems unlikely that the passage is simply overwritten.[30]

Surface, on the other hand, comes into play through the particular positioning of the narrator toward the landscape. The traveller is much more a postmodernist tourist than a modernist expatriate. The character of Reid, for example, another American abroad in *Lookout Cartridge,*

> spoke of London with that tone of the American who's had a year maybe and knows the ropes and will tell you a few tricks and will get off a remark about English laziness or the future of the Labour Party . . . [31]

The notion of superficiality in this passage, of a kind of discursive *ennui,* so to speak, is reinforced by the steady paratactic rhythm of the repeated "and"s between the syntactic units of the sentence. Reid's attitude is characterized as one of pragmatic rather than in-depth knowledge and of profound indifference toward another culture as long as he must acknowledge that it is a phenomenon independent of himself. These notions constitute an approach which is more interested in surface than depth, more preoccupied with the syntagmatic spread of information rather than its layering in an ever-increasing thickness.

Sites like the mysterious village in *The Names* appear in the pages of *Lookout Cartridge* as well. They are usually connected to a particular sense of historic depth or prehistoric, almost magical, mythic resonance, like Stonehenge or the Callanish Stones. It is safe to assume that the insertion of these sites, which are simultaneously overcoded and inarticulate (just as the narrator himself is "overcommitted and underconnected"), into the smooth postmodern surface of spatial experience constitutes an overriding concern within the newly emerging paradigm. Apart from the interpretive frenzy or euphoria, which brings minor characters in McElroy's novel to associate a place like Stonehenge with obscurist notions like the "practical mysticism of the land,"[32] and despite the commonsense realization that "Stonehenge was a rather typical American tourist stop and all the mystery had gone out of it with the car park and the souvenir stand,"[33] Cartwright himself describes the same sense of awe as DeLillo's narrator when faced with a place like Stonehenge. Touched, Cartwright muses that "[what] I found was a ground so old and powerful it could not be lessened by others' relation to it."[34] Not surprisingly then, this moment of recognition is at its strongest when the artifact of Stonehenge is stripped of its textuality. "I let myself feel at peace touching [the rock surface] ," Cartwright admits, "where there were no initials to be seen."

Ironically, this sense of mystery is reinforced by the fact that the only killing for which Cartwright himself is responsible occurs right here, among the stones of Stonehenge. Cartwright himself states that

> there are times when your sense of being between here and there, between people, between one
> thing and another, fades not even into absurdity but into something else, death or revelation,
> more likely death.[35]

Beyond the interpretive categories of multiple readings, economic reality, and semantic overcoding, the place insists on an additional quality that cannot be articulated within any of the categories that the texts themselves provide. Death functions as the emblematic revelatory experience that defies any effort of textualization. Certain places seem to shatter the predominantly relational perception that governs the narrator's sense of the world and insist on a presence that cannot be captured by all the self's sophisticated strategies outlined so far. Cartwright's epistemological and conceptual maneuvers may be sufficient for recuperating the aspect of surface in a place like Stonehenge. As long as there is another dimension to escape to, then surface itself is not threatening. The blank space on the rock does not stand in the way of experiencing a sense of the sublime in the presence of true mystery. But all strategies are bound to fail when confronted with something that defies both dimensions, depth and surface, and disrupts their relational play. What is being recuperated by the strategic move of designing places that are unreadable as both surface and depth--even at the cost of accepting the mysterious, obscure, or mystical--is a space of authenticity in which the postmodern dilemma of knowledge versus action can be resolved.

Accordingly, both novels, which open with scenes of travel or transportation, that is to say, movement between different points on the postmodern global map, achieve some degree of narrative resolution in the end.[36] This sense of resolution translates the metaphor of space, through the intervention of conspiracy as its narrative medium, into a response to what Fredric Jameson calls

> the two fundamental logical choices in the face of this dilemma [i.e. a completely
> postmodernized world]: totalization by fiat, in a situation in which lived totalization is
> impossible; and life among the unlinked fragments of the same untotalizable world.[37]

In both *The Names* and *Lookout Cartridge*, the response to Jameson's epistemological and ontological challenge consists of a refusal to accept the categories that constitute the dilemma in the first place. After a symbolic act of defiance--throwing a TV set out of an apartment window--McElroy's protagonist admits that "I was not sure what I had seen but I knew what we had done."[38] Acknowledging the tension between cognition and action, the passage shifts emphasis toward the act with all its implications. All the while it expands the isolated "I" of cognition into the communal "we" of concrete action. The consequence of this act seems not so much to produce a blueprint for some kind of blind political activism, but rather to send a signal calling for collective action, for the removal, literally and metaphorically, of the mediating representational technology, and the liberation of self-consciousness from its preoccupation with cognition.

The Names first provides the reader with a similarly optimistic sense of closure in the segment entitled "The Desert," but then goes on to offer a second ending in "The Prairie." This alternative ending comments directly on the preceding affirmation of communication and heterogeneous discourse. Communication is "worse than a retched nightmare. It [is] the nightmare of real things, the fallen wonder of the world."[39] After the violent outcome of the two competing conspiracies--the cult murders and the assassination attempt in the park--anything situated outside of discourse, "the nightmare of real things," is tainted by this violence. Not unlike Lookout Cartridge, direct exposure to violence also disrupts discourse retrospectively, creating the same feeling of unease or awe as the experience itself. As long as Andreas Eliades, a potential conspirator in The Names, merely mentions American military intervention in Greece, for example, his remarks are safely absorbed into the heteroglossic flow of chatter among the American expatriates. Only upon looking back, the misdirected attempt to assassinate Axton adds an ominous, dangerous significance to Eliades' words.

As far as the reader can tell at this point, only violence can break the smooth postmodern discursive surface. In this sense, violence would be refuting Jameson's categories that insist on the impossibility to create a space that is not immediately compromised by the impossible conditions of its existence.[40] Assuming that critic Dennis Foster is correct in observing that "society can live with violence--or rather could not survive without it--so long as it is rationalized, represented within a myth and a technology,"[41] then it is DeLillo's and McElroy's particular accomplishment to recuperate violence from its consoling myths and technologies and give it a proper space within the postmodernist topography.

Notes

[1] This challenge to "experience" as a self-evident conceptual category becomes politically more pertinent when applied to a more concrete situation. Donna Haraway states that "'experience,' like 'consciousness' is an intentional construction, an artefact of the first importance. Experience may also be *re*-constructed, re-membered, re-articulated. One powerful means to do so is the reading and re-reading of fiction in such a way as to create the effect of having access to another's life and consciousness, whether that other is an individual or a collective person with the lifetime called history." Feminist discourse would, for instance, take this statement as a starting-point for asking questions about the formation of identity through "experience," or its validation or legitimization. See Donna J. Haraway, "Reading Buchi Emecheta: Contests for 'Women's Experience' in Women's Studies," *Simians, Cyborgs, and Women: The Reinvention of Nature* (New York: Routledge, 1991) 113.

[2] For the theoretical groundwork on which this analysis is based, see Henri Lefebvre, *The Production of Space* (Oxford: Blackwell, 1991).

[3] Joseph McElroy, *Lookout Cartridge* (New York: Carroll & Graf, 1974), and Don DeLillo, *The Names* (New York: Alfred A. Knopf, 1982).

[4] *Lookout Cartridge* 181.

[5] Ironically, both novels reverse the connotations of the Old World/New World dichotomy. Jim Axton's *American* employer, for example, whose economic and clandestine interventions manipulate politics in the entire Middle East, including Greece--the cradle of Western Civilization--is ironically called "the parent."

[6] *Lookout Cartridge* 17.

[7] *Lookout Cartridge* 26.

[8] Critic Matthew Morris, for example, establishes *The Names* as a text that can only indirectly address its geographical center. In his article "Murdering Words: Language in Action in Don DeLillo's *The Names*," *Contemporary Literature* 30.1 (1989), Morris' argues that the displacement of America as a central concern "depends on the assumption that other people are either quite familiar or entirely alien,"(127) which allows for a perspective on America as either a presence latent in everything exotic, or as a threatening absence from the exotic. In either case, America itself functions as an essentially inaccessible point of reference.

[9] Edward Said's argument in *Orientalism* (New York: Pantheon, 1978), however, is more concerned with unmasking the Western construction of what is experienced as exotic with an emphasis on

mechanisms of psychological projection and scholarly appropriation. As in any story about cultural contact, the generic markers of conspiracy are conspicuously absent from Said's account.

10 *The Names* 6.

11 see Leonard Wilcox, "Baudrillard, DeLillo's *White Noise* and the End of Heroic Narrative," *Contemporary Literature* 32.3 (1991). Wilcox argues that, with postmodernism, the modernist notions underlying the great Western narratives of individual, heroic struggle are starting to fade. As notions based on the works of Freud or Marx, which used to be enabling devices for certain narrative patterns (the quest, "silence, exile, cunning," the expatriate, etc.), are becoming increasingly obsolete, contemporary fiction responds with such strategies of ideological "emptying out" as, for example, pastiche or the use of simulacra.

12 *The Names* 94.

13 *Lookout Cartridge* 31.

14 *Lookout Cartridge* 23.

15 *Lookout Cartridge* 3.

16 *Lookout Cartridge* 114.

17 *Lookout Cartridge* 247 [italics my emphasis]. The quotation probably echoes Gertrude Stein's famous dictum that America is the oldest nation because it has been in the twentieth century for the longest time. The allusion to Stein could very well cast her as an icon for the international theme as manifested in such categories as "life" or "biography".

18 *Lookout Cartridge* 59.

19 *Lookout Cartridge* 512. ". . . my post-Terminal sense that I'm at the center but overcommitted and underconnected;" and "You will not have both power and the understanding of it," 504.

20 The novels themselves are certainly richer in their strategies to displace the privileged position of the individual consciousness than this reading allows for. A critic like Gregor Campbell, for example, points out that the technological metaphors in *Lookout Cartridge* play an important part in re-defining the relation between the individual observer and the collective interventions in the interpretation of data. The technological metaphor of the narrator as a "lookout cartridge," which "will provide a kind of privileged, inner access to the systematic functioning of power," interrogates notions of authenticity from a different angle than the argument presented here. Campbell's reservation that "information is generated by a lookout cartridge, but it must be processed by a human observer" indicates that technology is ultimately of lesser importance for the critic than perhaps for the author. See Gregor Campbell, "Processing *Lookout Cartridge*," *The Review of Contemporary Fiction* 10.1 (Spring 1990) 113.

21 This theme ties in with the novels' broader concerns with colonialism and postcolonial strategies of resistance to more subtle forms of foreign domination. For further information on this line of

interpretation, see Edward Soja, *Postmodern Geographies: The Reassertion of Space in Critical Social Theory* (London: Verso, 1989).

[22] William Least Heat-Moon, *PrairyErth (a deep map)* (Boston: Houghton Mifflin, 1991), and Bruce Chatwin, *The Songlines* (New York: Viking, 1987).

[23] This view is being corroborated by several critical studies of both novels; see Robert Buckeye, "*Lookout Cartridge*: Plans, Maps, Programs, Designs, Outlines", John O'Brien (ed.), *The Review of Contemporary Fiction*, 10.1 (Spring 1990). Buckeye argues that the novel reflects America's unwillingness to face itself in the 60s: "In this reading of the text, Cartwright's failure is also a failure of national collective will. At the last, America did not want to know about itself," 122. See also McElroy's description of the flow of power in *Lookout Cartridge*: "Power shown being acquired from sources where it had momentum but not clarity . . . Preying on power. Saving power from itself." 77.

[24] *Lookout Cartridge* 409.

[25] Campbell, "Processing *Lookout Cartridge*," 112.

[26] Paula Bryant, "Discussing the Untellable: Don DeLillo's *The Names*," *Critique: Studies in Modern Fiction* 29.1 (Fall 1987) 28.

[27] *Lookout Cartridge* 228.

[28] Lefebvre 403.

[29] *The Names* 196.

[30] The phenomenon has been called "ecstasy of communication" by Baudrillard, who associates a feeling of euphoria with the postmodern condition. Baudrillard's description is even more significant for providing a corrective to the existential unease that is commonly associated with postmodernism.

[31] *Lookout Cartridge* 116.

[32] *Lookout Cartridge* 351.

[33] *Lookout Cartridge* 342.

[34] *Lookout Cartridge* 182.

[35] *Lookout Cartridge* 144.

[36] *Lookout Cartridge* opens in a helicopter hovering over New York, from where the narrator observes, far removed from the actual event, an explosion down in the city's grid. Eventually, this event will be tied in with the conspiracies that already envelop him. DeLillo begins every one of the major segments of *The Names*, which are all named after landscape formations, with a similar moment of physical motion: "The Island" opens in a car moving through Athens, "The Mountain" in an aircraft taxiing on the runway, "The Desert" in an airport terminal. As these beginnings move from literal to symbolical motion, the last segment,"The Prairie," finally brings this movement to a halt by showing the central character in the middle of a crowd.

6. Mao II, Players, *and* Lookout Cartridge: *The Politics of Power*

As if to corroborate Richard Hofstadter's famous dictum about the ubiquity and flexibility of conspiracy theory, recent historical events have lead to a renewed interest in the kind of conspiracy theories characteristic of American culture since the 1960s.[1] Since an earlier version of this essay was drafted, geared primarily toward a reading of contemporary American conspiracy fiction from the early 1960s on, the bombing of the World Trade Center on February 26, 1993 and subsequent police activities leading to arrests and further speculation on the dangers of religious fundamentalist dissent from within the American political landscape have refocused public attention on conspiratorial activities from an international to a domestic setting. To the observer of the subtle changes in the dominant paradigms of political rhetoric ever since the end of the Gulf War and the preceding movements of postcolonial empowerment through Islamic fundamentalism, both the acts of terrorist violence and the official response they have elicited seem almost inevitable. They appear to be retrospective justification of somewhat vague conspiratorial fears and concrete manifestations of exactly the kind of conflict that these fears have been, legitimately or not, based upon.

Conspiracy theory, and its steady recurrence as a theme in contemporary fiction, has reflected these changes from the so-called "End of the Cold War" on, demonstrating its enduring usefulness in a climate of shifting political alliances by rearranging its discursive strategies to suit new needs and new political realities. Unlike the ominous threat of the "Evil Empire" during the Reagan years, contemporary conspiratorial fears have brought the object of fear home, placing The Other in our midst as a danger that needs to be combatted with steadily increasing budgets for surveillance, legislature enabling government agencies to go about their business more efficiently, and public support organized around implementing these strategies as legitimate means by which "we" protects ourselves from "them"--terrorists, religious fundamentalists, crazed fanatics, and other subversive elements. Even though American intervention in the international political arena has frequently attempted to implement a rhetoric that blurs the distinction between domestic and foreign affairs altogether, the main target of recent conspiracy theory has shifted clearly toward matters of internal security over the last few years; a change that has brought the figure of the terrorist back to the center of both political attention and collective imagination.

The other aspect of the change that conspiracy theory has undergone in the "New World Order" is the fragmentation of the sense of centrality that used to govern America's conception of its position toward global politics, not so much as the intrusion and intertwining of local into global conflict, which has been part of the collective experience since the Vietnam War, but rather as the bewildering multiplicity of local conflicts that, despite their global consequences, seem to lack increasingly the symbolic subtext of the larger conflict they had come to represent for so long. Not only has the violence suddenly been carried from the exotic locations we were used to seeing it in into a place we thought of as safe--a conceptual reversal that in itself constitutes a scandal--but the sources of this violence are also harder to pinpoint, more heterogeneous. We find ourselves confronted with a phenomenon of many shapes and multiple origins. Faced with the challenge, posed by the figure of the terrorist, to the state's structurally, legally, and historically legitimized monopoly on violence, and with an increasingly uncomfortable sense of the structural disjunction of global political conflict, it almost seems as if current conspiracy theories are trying to reassure us that the politically motivated violence we are supposed to fear can ultimately be understood in the same conceptual categories we have learned to live with for so many years.

Reigning in that heterogeneity and reinstating the logic of "us versus them," conspiracy theory generally tends to trace power to a distinct origin, an evil presence. It personalizes and allegorizes conflict, opening it to the specific ideological inscriptions of any given culture, and thereby makes it tenable. It allows us to reduce politics to personal hostility and, in the process, conceptualize one form of political conflict by utilizing an outmoded earlier form. Whereas conspiracy theory structures, familiarizes, and naturalizes this bewildering diversity, imposing an order that recreates the Manichaean simplicity of good versus evil against all better and more rational political judgement, conspiracy fiction, on the other hand, attempts to undermine and subvert the unchallenged assumptions of these theories, expose their political objectives for what they are, and reflect the role they play in the complex networks of cultural and social practices. Picking up on the historical transformations over the last three decades, conspiracy fiction has addressed 1960s "counterculture" in such novels as Pynchon's *The Crying of Lot 49* or Joseph McElroy's *Lookout Cartridge*, the American fear of "international terrorism," ranging from the 1972 Olympic Games in Munich to the escalation of open hostility between the US and Libya in the mid-80s, as reflected in such novels as Don DeLillo's *Players* or *Mao II*, up to the current economic and political fears about the end of the "American century", the demise of global American economic and cultural hegemony, as thematized in such novels as Michael Crichton's controversial best-seller *Rising Sun*. In all cases, it might seem as if the fear of conspiracy serves the purpose of reaffirming a sense of collective identity by emphasizing its intrinsic and extrinsic counterforces, whereas the fiction dealing with conspiracy and paranoia reconfigures the dichotomy of fragmentation and integration as a conflict of competing forces within the same discursive and political field; in other words, by dissolving the concept of the binary distinction between us/them, inside/outside, familiar/foreign, civilized/savage, and so on, conspiracy fiction makes conspiracy theory accessible to a cultural critique by restoring its status as rhetoric, and, in the process, renders cultural paranoia visible as an instrument of power on the same ontological level as the conspiratorial threat it conjures up in the hands of skilled demagogues and concerned politicians.

In trying to trace these patterns of conflict, the intersections of power and opposition, institution and subversion, in three novels--Joseph McElroy's *Lookout Cartridge,* and Don DeLillo's *Players* and *Mao II*--readers are, again and again, confronted with the figure of the terrorist as a consistently ambivalent, yet infinitely adaptable trope of conspiratorial violence.[2] In *Lookout Cartridge,* for example, American businessman and expatriate Cartwright is confronted with an underground network of terrorists, to whose illicit activities--smuggling draft-dodgers across the border and committing random acts of violence--he becomes an involuntary witness, as some footage of a film he is working on with a longtime friend accidentally captures some of the conspirators and their doings. Pursuing his own line of inquiry, Cartwright becomes entangled in their politics, which themselves touch upon other conspiratorial terrorist networks, such as the separatist movements in Scotland, Wales, and on Corsica. Finally, Cartwright ends up acting, partly by accident, partly by design, as the agent of the central conspiracy's "dis-covery." The same ambivalence about getting involved in and resisting a terrorist conspiracy is at the center of Don DeLillo's *Players,* in which a yuppie stockbroker allows himself to be implicated into the underworld of terrorists and informers to escape the terminal *ennui* plaguing his private and professional life. *Mao II*, DeLillo's latest novel, introduces a publicity-shy novelist, who, through his literary agent, becomes involved in the labyrinthine politics of US-Middle Eastern relations. His presence and active intervention are supposed to lead to the release of a Swiss UN worker and amateur poet held hostage in Beirut.

Despite the unique elements that set these three novels apart from each other, one of the paradigms defining the field in which they all operate is the depiction of the terrorist as a prolific and charismatic, yet unreliable and inauthentic source of discourse. In *Mao II*, for example, the terrorist leader Abu Rashid holds forth on the political objectives of his taking of Western hostages.

> "We teach them [i.e. teenagers] identity, sense of purpose. They are all children of Abu
> Rashid. All men one man . . . We teach that our children belong to something strong and self-
> reliant. They are not an invention of Europe . . . No martyrs here. The image of Rashid is
> their identity."[3]

However, the admittedly legitimate claim to self-determination and its link to the mechanisms of representation as means of creating and sustaining identity are ironically and paradoxically undercut by Rashid's claim that identity is supposed to derive from self-effacement and erasure in some protofascist submission to a messianic leader. He himself demands this Oedipal surrender to an omnipotent paternal entity to maintain his leadership. The group's trading of hostages ". . . like drugs, like weapons, like jewelry, like a Rolex or a BMW"[4] is further indication of the ambiguity of Rashid's theoretical statement. Its emphasis on a postcolonial identity and the political means of defining it is undercut by the fact that the commodities listed are all Western products and therefore signifiers of the colonial heritage and his country's symbolic as well as economic dependency. Images of both international entrepreneur and radical subversive are tightly interwoven, rendering the figure unreadable for any interpretive approach attempting to recuperate it for either side's political agenda.

Similar strategies of simultaneously introducing the terrorist as a theoretician and intellectual and withdrawing or undermining his credibility by contrasting it with his equally ambiguous actions are also used in the other two novels. The group allowing American draft dodgers to flee the country during the Vietnam War in *Lookout Cartridge* is fronted by a figure who proceeds with the same keen insight into the link between economic and representational power as Rashid. Somebody like Paul, who is willing to consider the use of "a symbolic war on children waged against school buses,"[5] is obviously willing to consider all forms of violence, even those he allegedly opposes, as legitimate means for the anti-war protest in the US. As Paul and his group are engaging society in violent conflict, they realize that, instead of providing a valid policy of opposition, their function may be merely restorative or, at best, cathartic. Ultimately, they may supply their culture with an escapist and politically affirmative genre that functions very well within the confines they were hoping to break out of. Exasperatedly exclaiming "God save us from bourgeois adventure,"[6] John, one member of Paul's group, actually verbalizes this precarious and ambivalent position, which the novel goes on to examine primarily in terms of its epistemological consequences. How can you act in good conscience, McElroy asks, and be of any political use if ". . . you will not have both power and the understanding of it?"[7] Similarly, Rafael Vilar, the spokesman of the terrorist network in *Players*, legitimizes his cell's planned attempt on the New York Stock Exchange with a logic that is as compelling as it is revealing of the group's duplicitous nature. In trying to break the inhumanity of power translated into electronic data, they plan to attack the Exchange as a symbolic site of this abstract power. Because this attack constitutes in itself a symbolic gesture, the group's politics is always already caught up in the free *exchange* of one abstract code for another across enemy lines. An attack on the New York Stock Exchange, the bombing of a school bus, or the abduction of a Swiss UN worker are calculated acts of violence that make little sense unless one believes that politics is grounded in symbolic action, one might even say ritual.

While both authors consistently refuse to address the pragmatic value of conspiracy in this context, they do agree that this swirl of signifiers requires some form of counterbalance. Terrorists are perpetrating acts of violence. To reduce these acts to mere problems of political encoding would mean to embrace a form of postmodern *jouissance* that is clearly not appropriate here. By acknowledging the immediate reality of the body, the three novels take this dilemma that the terrorist figure itself creates into consideration. *Lookout Cartridge* revolves around several grisly acts of murder, *Players* ends with a nameless immobilized body in a motel room, and *Mao II*, almost fondly, reproduces its protagonist's obsessively compiled lists of bodily waste products. Physical degradation or violation appears to break with the problems of encoding that the terrorist raises and can therefore be considered a strategy of subversion. Yet even this form of subversion must answer to power on its own terms and, in the process, compromise itself. The aggressive control over the victim's body in which the terrorist asserts his power over that of another remains ultimately a political act. Even if such an act of violence is deemed random, its significance can only be determined by refiguring it as a statement, i.e. as a form of representation. The recurring pattern emerging from this dialogue between power and resistance is characterized by a metaphorical operation in which antagonistic sides become aspects of each other. This goes so far that, at times, they are virtually indistinguishable from one another. They communicate in the same symbolic language and trade off casualties with comparable brutality.

Critics like Robin Morgan have traced the terrorist's cultural lineage back to problems of psychosexual fixation and projection.[8] Diane Johnson follows this line of argument but pushes its implications beyond the point of purely personal involvement. Johnson points out that the free exchange of properties across enemy lines constitutes a structural mechanism which transforms the demarcation line between establishment and underground, licit and illicit. The line becomes simultaneously a challenge to define the difference between the two and a temptation to cross over. In other words, it turns into a symbolic testing ground for an Oedipal struggle in which more than personal power is at stake. In this struggle,

> each side resembles the other in its assumptions, in its respect for Jesuitical reasoning and
> certain rules . . . Terrorist action is not so much an example of lawlessness as a comment on
> the rules, an aspect of the structure itself.[9]

The element of seduction that is so essential to Morgan's psychosexual definition of the terrorist's function within the cultural semantics is presented here as the temptation to defy confining categories, switch identities, and exploit structural homologies for one's own purposes. According to Johnson, the terrorist therefore occupies the position of the clown, trickster, fool, or holy man, who is straddling the ideological fence separating the charlatan from the "spokesman of authority."[10] Depending on the individual reader's preconception, the terrorist's lack of accountability and refusal to submit to a procedural legitimization of power can therefore be read two ways. It is either an inability to participate properly in society's institutionalized rules of exchange, in which case the terrorist appears as an incompetent amateur or dangerous, maladjusted loner. Or it is a deliberate refusal to play by these rules altogether, which would then make him into a self-serving opportunist or, last but not least, into a figure of legitimate political dissent. More than his marginality, it is this "dangerously" appealing ability to cross literal and metaphorical borders, to make oneself "unreadable" within a symbolic language established to create safe identities, that challenges established notions of presence and authenticity. Foregrounding not only radical forms of ambiguity, but also the process of signification itself, the terrorist has become a cherished figure of postmodernist transgression, his conceptual makeup and strategic value closely related to that of, for example, Donna Haraway's "cyborg."[11]

For that same reason, the passages quoted above do not depict the terrorist first and foremost as a figure of violent resistance to official power, a disruptive force like Conrad's or Dostoyevski's anarchists, or as someone who is "out of the loop" of power like Pynchon's Preterite. Rather, the terrorist's predominant feature is his ability to produce discourse. He is the one who speaks, rants and raves, theoretizes, argues, monologizes, and lectures. A prolific source of language rather than action, he is immersed more deeply in discursive or rhetorical than ethical contradictions and ambiguities. Despite the seriousness with which all three novels treat the issue of physical violence, the actual confrontation with the reality of terrorist action tends to be a matter of "parenthetic" epistemological status, consistently removed from the narrative's immediate access. Thus, the explosion of the van in the opening sequence of *Lookout Cartridge* appears to Cartwright as the abstract phenomenon of "a light without sound" in the "city's grid"[12] far below. Just as Lyle Wynant never experiences the shooting of George Sedbauer on the trading floor of the Stock Exchange firsthand in *Players*, what first appears as the experiences of the hostage in *Mao II* turns out to be the account of writer Bill Gray's intellectual exercise in trying to capture the stranger's experience and overcome his own creative impotence. While violence itself, in all three novels, is muted by being kept at a safe distance, however, its perpetrators, the terrorists, are given ample opportunity to talk.

As Morgan and Johnson have pointed out, one of the essential features of the terrorist, together with his ability to cross over between enemy lines, is his significance in foregrounding the process of signification by which the conceptual map of the territory in which these conflicts take place is being produced. In this sense, the terrorist is the author of a text that, in turn, requires a reader, an accomplice, in order to complete the act of communication. The conspiratorial act, as Fredric Jameson has pointed out in his analysis of conspiracy in contemporary American film, "as an empirical event, a unique occurrence in that particular latitude and longitude, on that particular date in the calendar . . . must also be *made* to mean its meaning: it must in short be *allegorized.*"[13] Since this allegorization is a process that, particularly in the kind of discourse that is already highly self-referential, does not originate from one source only, but is created through the dialogic interplay of heterogeneous elements, the conspiracy novel usually supplies a reader function alongside that of the author. An agency functioning in the role of detective, whether individual or collective, becomes the author of a competing narrative, which tries to establish certainty over ambiguity, resolve all textual riddles, and reinstate the order disturbed by the conspiracy.[14] Making the text of conspiracy mean something, therefore, becomes an object of contention and competition, a process of continuous writing and rewriting in order to establish a version of events that asserts itself as the authoritative statement capable of closing the narrative. How this competitive dialogue between reader(s) and writer(s) is being constructed, rather than who is victorious in it, becomes an indication of what conspiracy fiction is really about. To understand the significance of the terrorist fully, it is therefore necessary to examine how the trope is being assembled through dialogue and contrast; that is to say, we must examine the figure of the detective who functions as the complimentary, or rather supplementary force to that of the terrorist.

Together with the reader of *Lookout Cartridge*, who is trying to make sense of the continuous growth and increasing depth of information, the novel's protagonist is involved in the act of reading the clues and writing the story that integrates these clues into one convincing narrative. The allusion to cartography in Cartwright's name already points to his profession, which is to read the unexplored, uncharted territories of technology. At the same time, he is the author of reports that expertly assess the future market value of these new discoveries. In his function as an accidental observer, a detective who reluctantly acknowledges that he has been "inserted into a situation,"[15] Cartwright's reading skills are paradoxically deficient. Though they are sophisticated enough to prevail against most obstacles, natural and human-made, they also lack in discipline to an extent that the appetite with which Cartwright accumulates information keeps him from determining the right measure of how much he can and must know. The terrorist conspiracy, against which, among other things, Cartwright's quest for knowledge is plotted, functions as the source for the inexhaustible proliferation and confusing heterogeneity of the text he is trying to decode. Imposing one authoritative version onto this splendid chaos becomes impossible for someone so conscientious, so aware of the fact that what is ultimately at stake is not only a purely epistemological riddle but the capacity to make pragmatic as well as ethical decisions.

But solving these riddles takes on greater significance for the reader than acquiring the means to structure and close the narrative. The question is not only 'What is the solution to the mystery?' but also "What will you have in your hand if you do get to the bottom of your film mystery?"[16] McElroy's question clearly indicates that something grander, metaphysically more valid is to be gained by getting to "the bottom" of things. Cartwright's disposition as a reader reaffirms this metaphysical presupposition about the solution to the mystery. His intellectual appreciation and sensual enjoyment of the density and richness of clues, as well as the hermeneutical apparatus with which he confronts the multiple texts in which he finds himself enmeshed, both characterize Cartwright as a reader whose attitudes philosophically predate the text he himself is producing. Not unlike other detective figures in contemporary conspiracy fiction, such as Oedipa Maas in Thomas Pynchon's *The Crying of Lot 49*, McElroy's protagonist affirms the possibility that the moment of denouement, which remains eternally delayed and projected outside of the novel itself, carries such great significance that metaphysical transcendence is actually possible. The novel, as radically postmodern as its textual politics might be otherwise, breaks with its own paradigmatic structure by reaffirming an ultimate signified outside of its own textual play.

In DeLillo's *Players* the protagonist, Lyle Wynant, is attempting to recuperate exactly this form of transcendence by searching for a significant link between his own private life and the greater, political scope of the terrorist conspiracy he is "inserted into." Like Cartwright's, the text of his own life--work, marriage, leisure--intersects accidentally and only marginally with the text of the conspiracy. Terrorist figures like A. J. Kinnear, "possible terrorist, possible informer, probable double agent,"[17] promise to open doors into an alluring new territory. They suggest something that at first glance appears as an alternative to the dreary routines of Pammy's and Lyle's lives. The difference between Lyle's and Cartwright's degree of influence in establishing their own reading over that of the terrorist's, however, is reminiscent of Roland Barthes' distinction between "readerly" and "writerly" text. Since there is no significant difference between the empty routines of his private life and the cliché-ridden, petty, and ultimately futile machinations of the terrorist plot, Lyle's decision to get involved in the conspiracy denies the realm of terrorism the special status that it may have laid claim to on the basis of its willingness to resort to physical violence, its intrinsic persuasiveness, or the sheer appeal of its metaphysical nostalgia. Lyle's strategies of participating in terrorism as a political option are not those of a reader who would expect some form of transcendence or conceptual breakthrough from solving the puzzle. Instead, his actions are those of the "entertainment consumer,"[18] whose attitude toward the world is passive and affirmative and whose primary function is to make choices in order to attain instant gratification, thereby erasing all ontological differences between the items he chooses from. Stripped of their potential intrinsic and individual value, objects, human relations, and social roles matter only insofar as they are instantly attainable, easy to be discarded, and contextualized in an environment of plenitude, choice, and relative ontological demotion. Although, as LeClair concedes, the author is "showing the causes of societal game-playing; not attacking play as self-indulgence, but illustrating its necessity for the human organism,"[19] DeLillo's notion of play involves an ontological detachment that affirms the rules of any game by emphasizing the systemic condition of disinterest caused by the ability to move on to another game at will. When the narrative of *Players* splits into two strands, both of which depict the efforts of Pam and Lyle to escape from their routines, the terrorist conspiracy begins to emerge as a choice of "lifestyle" and a re-enactment of the popular genre of the thriller. By inviting us to identify the correspondences between characters in the narrative and figures in the film presented in the novel's opening sequence, DeLillo suggests that, as consumers of the cinematic and literary artifact, we can enter into any prefabricated cultural text with limited commitment, just as the characters in the novel itself.

Unlike Cartwright, for whom some metaphysical "bottom" of the mystery still beckons with the promise of genuine epiphany, Lyle's participation in the conspiratorial networks of terrorism and counter-terrorism merely traces, and thereby doubles, the patterns whose existence precede his own involvement. His contribution to solving the conspiracy merely reproduces the given text, creating a simulacra that, as LeClair pointed out, may serve all kinds of therapeutic, cathartic, or provocative purposes for Lyle himself and for the reader. What this strategy does not accomplish, however, is to generate a truly dialogic situation which might produce a shared text that, in exceeding the sum of its parts, aims for something beyond the smooth surface of its own postmodernized environment. Lyle's acceptance, even encouragement of double-bonds, as he betrays and switches between both sides of the law, only imitates a genuine violation of the rules by which the game of conspiracy is structured. Double agents, moles, renegades, and traitors are merely extensions of the text, increasing its possible degree of complexity and density, yet still adhering strictly to its rules.

Whereas *Players'* presents the smooth, seamless surfaces of a monolithic postmodernized environment in which the potentially subversive process of "reading conspiracy" is being assimilated into the complacency of commodity consumption, *Mao II* appears less pessimistic in its depiction of how conspirator and detective and the text they create together can function as a viable model for rethinking and restructuring reigning cultural and political paradigms. What is at stake for DeLillo, more than a decade after *Players*, is the possibility of claiming a position from which the complicity between the terrorist conspiracy and the structures it pretends to attack can be opposed or fractured. Is it possible to introduce an element of contention, opposition, or subversion into the fabric of the conspiracy novel when narrative and ideological traditions urge readers to perceive the links between detective and conspiracy to be unassailable, either because terrorists are less clearly the enemy than we would like to believe, or because detectives are less capable of reinstating the world to its preconspiratorial state? As compromised and deeply ambiguous as the model for subversive and creative interference at these critical points in *Mao II* may appear, it still constitutes, in my opinion, a valid ideological option, an insightful provocation, and a valuable contribution to the expanding vocabulary of the genre.

Unlike his earlier incarnations in *Lookout Cartridge* and *Players*, the detective in *Mao II* is actively involved in rewriting the postmodern conspiratorial narrative from the perspective of dissent. Reclusive writer Bill Gray, whose paranoid anxieties about maintaining his isolation from the communities of fans, readers, publishers, colleagues, and political allies that his work has created, and about committing to a gesture of closure for his current book, becomes the icon of this alternative narrative position. Combining the modernist stance of "silence, exile, cunning" with the perpetual process of painstaking refinement, Gray is remaking himself in the image of Joyce and Flaubert in an attempt to construct an image of high modernism as a gesture of resistance to what Cartwright calls his "hypothetical field of multiple impingements."[20] Unsuccessfully trying to outmaneuver the complicity between detective and conspiracy, very much like his generic predecessors, Gray occupies a position of hesitant involvement and passive resistance. From several sides, he is being urged into the intrigue, a seduction that ceases to intrigue him as soon as he realizes how deeply his own cherished position is being compromised. To the small degree that he initially allows himself to be implicated into the plots revolving around the hostage, he himself becomes a victim just like the young Swiss, stripped of the carefully assembled defense of his individuality and exposed to the world of "crowds and power."[21] Eclectically raiding the realm of modernist iconography, DeLillo draws a portrait of Gray that consists of aspects from different manifestations of modernism. Consequently, the figure becomes an idiosyncratic hybrid, emphasizing quite poignantly the author's concern with plotting heterogeneity against the monolithic power of postmodern culture. Unable to produce neither the *Gesamtkunstwerk* of life and work seamlessly merged, nor the book to end all books (Joyce's *Finnegan's Wake*, Flaubert's "book about nothing," or Mallarmé's *Livre*), Gray, instead, manages to disappear and erase himself successfully, endowing the work with the aura that, he suspects, it is incapable of maintaining on its own.

Although DeLillo returns with *Mao II* to the motif of close association between the conspiratorial text and the sphere of consumerism, it is only in the context of *Players* that a strategy of splendid isolation would suffice as a gesture of resistance. Gray's case demonstrates dramatically that the author's absence from the public eye and prolonged silence have fueled, rather than atrophied a publicity machinery that has elevated the his claim to privacy to the rank of "a local symptom of God's famous reluctance to appear"[22] and keeps marketing him, no matter if he produces or not. Since the power of this machinery is geared toward textual and commodity production, just as the author himself, isolation and silence alone are not sufficient means of throwing sand into its gears. Rather, silence and absence open up a space which remains a potentiality, a site that remains, as of yet, uncolonized until it is noticed and taken advantage of. In the absence of prior claims, postmodern culture will attempt to invade that space by staging the author as celebrity. It will extend its range by textualizing the absence of what "the author" is about, that is, textual production itself. Silence as a viable strategy becomes self-defeating when its agent is not in control of the circumstances under which he functions as a signifier or as a signified; that is, when "his" discourse ceases to be private property by virtue of some notion of metaphysical presence and becomes public property. As long as he does not fill the space his silence has opened with specific content, his own intentions are overridden as soon as he himself becomes the product. Through a series of strategically placed oppositions, the novel unmistakably outlines a postmodern environment that Gray, and perhaps DeLillo himself, perceive as a force to be resisted. In filling Gray's private space with a modernist iconography, the novel restructures the central conflict between textual production and textual consumption along the conflict between cultural paradigms: crowds versus individuals, photography versus writing, Andy Warhol versus Bill Gray, terrorists versus artists.

Unlike the other two types of postmodernist detectives--the old-fashioned reader and the consumer--Bill Gray displays an obstinate refusal to yield a version of himself that could be considered as properly postmodernized. Readers may be willing to disagree with my interpretation on the grounds that, in fact, Bill Gray's resistance is merely a futile, even pathetic gesture of resistance to the extent that he is already integrated into the system he tries to oppose. Operating within the larger sphere of discursive practices, the notion of

Literature, practiced by Gray, as privileged access to knowledge and power seems absurd. Literature has already become a subsystem of the dominant cultural paradigm of, for instance, the free play of celebrity media coverage and the industrial replicability of photographic representation. Whether or not Literature does, in fact, give access to some form of supreme knowledge, it remains primarily a social institution and a business. As soon as Gray turns his powers outward, beyond the confines of his small, jealously guarded space, in an effort to break the bounds of his own range of influence and transplant (or "smuggle" or "insert," to use McElroy's terminology) his ideology into the system into which his own subsystem is embedded, he fails miserably. The revisionary stance of attempting to rewrite the text of conspiracy by inscribing subversive messages into its very fabric quickly loses its confrontational element. Instead of conflict through engagement, Gray retreats to a position in which he can construct an alternative narrative but remain at a safe distance.

It is not the writer then, but Brita, the photographer, who has the last word in the novel. Its closing sequence is set in Beirut, where, to the light of a flash unit, the endless recuperation of cultural space as palimpsest is being celebrated through the image of "an old Soviet T-34, some scarred and cruddy ancient, sold and stolen two dozen times, changing sides and systems and religions."[23] Even Bill's two disciples Scott and Karen, who faithfully carry on his project of keeping his work in a perpetual state of unreadability and preserving its creator's status as *deus absconditus*, have made their decision in favor of limited power in the small function allocated to them by the task of managing Gray's estate. Gray's death, under these circumstances, appears therefore as an indication of not only his personal failure, but the co-optation of the position he represents. His anonymous and unrecognized death is a symptom of the hopeless imbalance of ideological powers in favor of postmodern society.

What remains are certain ambiguities with which DeLillo endows the writer's position in order to point toward possible paths of resistance. These ambiguities can be read as either a form of heroic failure in the face of overwhelming opposition, or as a kind of maliciously stubborn success that becomes a challenge to the integrity of the whole modernist iconography in the service of ideological subversion. From a purely pragmatic perspective, it is not too significant whether Gray's perception of himself as a distinct stronghold of resistance is pathetically deluded or, in fact, accurate. Significant is, however, that DeLillo allows Gray to inscribe the kind of closure into his text--his own, self-determined death and disappearance into perfect anonymity, as well as his book's perpetual incompleteness--that functions within his own ideology rather than that of its competitor. Wanting "devoutly to be forgotten"[24] and stripped of all papers that could serve as means of identification, even the ones tying him to his adopted name and public persona, Gray dies in a scenario of almost mythical transfiguration--in transit, peacefully, on a ship sailing into the rising sun. Heroic or foolish, he has the last word in his own story, playing for integrity and making the game where it can still be won.

The differences between the political agenda of these three samples of contemporary American conspiracy fiction and that of conspiracy theory of comparable complexity could not be more obvious. Despite the indisputable origins of the genre in the classic detective story, contemporary conspiracy fiction is only marginally concerned with the clash between the conspiratorial forces, represented here by the figure of the terrorist, and the agency of the detective. It shows a certain degree of indifference toward the binary distinctions regulating almost all varieties of conspiracy theory. Some readers' ideological apprehensions about the tendency of the genre to construe the re-establishment of law and order as its ultimate narrative goal--a fundamentally conservative, at times even reactionary political stance--is therefore not justified. Reinstating the world to its prelapsarian innocence is not at stake here, just as these narratives concern themselves only marginally with the more metaphysical inventory of the detective story (truth, guilt, justice, and so on). Permeated with the ambiguities arising from the corrosion of these binary distinctions, conspiracy fiction of the type discussed here is more intelligently, maturely, and comprehensively engaged in the critical project of exposing the schisms within discursive formations we are willing to accept as seamless. It points out the, at times, disconcerting correspondences between systems we have learned to think about as diametrically opposed, or, at least, as distinct. Which are, for instance, the conflicts that have been suppressed by a Cold War rhetoric that has, for over four decades, regulated public discourse on global politics? How much of a historical paradigm shift is, in fact, the so-called "End of the Cold War?" Considering the increasing tensions and the subsequent militarization of localized conflicts worldwide (Afghanistan, Somalia, the former Yugoslavia, to mention but a few), in what ways do religious fundamentalists and their claims to power on the one hand, and the forces of political resistance mobilized against them on the other actually correspond to each other?

Instead of advising its reader which side of these dichotomies to come down on, most of contemporary conspiracy fiction proposes that conspiracy theory must be simultaneously resisted and embraced, putting the reader into a kind of interpretive impasse. It must be resisted because it is a manipulative form of ideological and pragmatic discourse, yet it can be embraced because it provides a legitimate and effective strategy of subversion. As trickster or cyborg, charlatan or court jester, the terrorist challenges the assumptions that any valid political strategy in this context can extricate itself from the culture in which it is formulated, and that its options are merely to chose from what it already finds in the political culture. In *Players*, conspiracy fiction denies the instant gratification of the consumerist choice that underlies all forms of activism. In *Mao II*, it deconstructs the double-bind situations, encouraged by the terrorist perspective, that arise from the strategic disadvantage of localized political engagement. And in *Lookout Cartridge*, it questions the problematic status of a position dependent on leverage from outside the political system.

Now that the conflict between the superpowers during the Cold War has ceased to function as the key metaphor for the global political system, and religious fundamentalism seems to be gradually replacing the antagonistic half of this metaphor, the theme of conspiracy has taken on the additional function of organizing the conceptual framework for this historical shift. Fredric Jameson's reading of

> the figuration of conspiracy as an attempt . . . to think a system so vast that it cannot be encompassed by the naturally and historically developed categories of perception with which human beings normally orient themselves,[25]

accounts more for conspiracy theory and its conceptual rigidity, or for more conspicuously "ideological" or propagandist works of fiction, than it does for the kind of novels I have discussed here. Obviously, the construction of specific, historically determined conceptual categories when faced with the necessity of getting a grasp on something that defies conceptualization is a process geared toward both the understanding and the co-optation of that mysterious phenomenon. Mapping the uncharted territory for systematic ideological colonization--whether in fiction or in political rhetoric, whether as Jameson's "cognitive mapping" or as a more aggressive act of appropriation--is therefore always caught up in the trappings of "bourgeois adventure." For its own benefit, recent conspiracy fiction has started to pay more attention to the consequences of its deconstruction of oppositional politics and to its complicity with genres of literary and extraliterary escapist discourse. Texts like the ones discussed here can, at best, interfere with the rhetoric of conspiracy theory. They cannot make something *not* happen, but what they can accomplish is to make something not happen invisibly or inconspicuously. If they are capable of serving as strategic disturbances at a time when newly emerging economies of power are starting to settle in on a global scale, then we must, in fact, give them credit for doing a good job in saving us from "bourgeois adventure."

Notes

[1] see Richard Hofstadter, *The Paranoid Style in American Politics and Other Essays* (Chicago: University of Chicago Press, 1979). Perhaps *the* most influential definition of conspiracy theory and its significance in American cultural discourse, Hofstadter's notion of a "paranoid style" indicates the spread of its rhetoric across all ideological barriers. In the course of my further argument, I am greatly indebted to the conceptual framework laid out in this seminal article.

[2] Don DeLillo, *Players* (New York: Alfred A. Knopf, 1977); *Mao II* (New York: Viking, 1992), and Joseph McElroy, *Lookout Cartridge* (New York: Alfred A. Knopf, 1974).

[3] *Mao II* 233.

[4] *Mao II* 235.

[5] *Lookout Cartridge* 406.

[6] *Lookout Cartridge* 484.

[7] *Lookout Cartridge* 405.

[8] Robin Morgan, *The Demon Lover: On the Sexuality of Terrorism* (New York/London: Norton, 1989), particularly Chapter 2, "The Deadly Hero: The Oldest Profession," 51-85.

[9] Diane Johnson, "Terrorists As Moralists: Don DeLillo," *Terrorists and Novelists* (New York: Alfred A. Knopf, 1982) 109.

[10] Johnson 105.

[11] Arguing from a different context, Donna J. Haraway has presented the cyborg in several of her highly influential essays as such a figure of ontological confusion and undecidability. To expand on the characteristics implied in my own discussion of the terrorist, see Haraway's essay "A Cyborg Manifesto," *Simians, Cyborgs, and Women* (London: Routledge, 1989) 149-183.

[12] *Lookout Cartridge* 3.

[13] Fredric Jameson, *The Geopolitical Aesthetic: Cinema and Space in the World System* (Bloomington: University of Indiana Press, 1992) 45.

[14] see the specific application of Bakhtinian notions of reading and writing to the genre of detective fiction in Peter Hühn's "The Detective as Reader: Narrativity and Reading Concepts in Detective Fiction" *Modern Fiction Studies* 33.3 (Autumn 1987) 451-466.

[15] *Lookout Cartridge* 11.

[16] *Lookout Cartridge* 176.

[17] Tom LeClair, *In The Loop: Don DeLillo and the Systems Novel* (Urbana: University of Illinois Press, 1987) 153.

[18] LeClair, *In the Loop*, 149.

147

[19] LeClair, *In the Loop*, 150.

[20] *Lookout Cartridge* 439.

[21] Since the novel insinuates that, what initially appears to be the omniscient narrator's account of the hostage's ordeal is actually Gray's artistic reconstruction, an attempt to imagine and write what he cannot know firsthand, the identification of both figures is extended to a degree that everything the hostage lives through becomes a dramatized and stylized reflection and projection of Bill Gray himself.

[21] Jameson, *The Geopolitical Aesthetic*, 1-2.

[22] *Mao II* 36.

[23] *Mao II* 239.

[24] *Mao II* 216.

7. Libra *and* Women and Men: *The Representation of History*

Whenever conspiracy fiction self-consciously addresses the question of history, its objective is to defamiliarize, and thus fictionalize, stories which we have all come to accept as truthful accounts of what happened in the past. Instead of providing roots, history becomes, as one of DeLillo's characters calls it, "the sum total of all the things they aren't telling us."[1] Simultaneously, conspiracy fiction has commonly attempted to project a view of history that is capable of encompassing "history" as a totality. At a time when the reigning paradigm of historiography constructs its object as a multiplicity of coexisting histories, writing a comprehensive "secret history" must pose a challenge to historians in a number of ways. First of all, conspiratorial histories undermine the notion of special histories by projecting a unified secret history with only one objective, clearly definable shape, and a finite number of distinct agents. This imposition of one single history onto a multitude of histories is clearly at odds with the larger cultural paradigm of cultural diversity within which historiography is just one isolated discipline.

At the same time, however, conspiratorial history also manages to antagonize the opposing ideological camp, whose advocates, though they may agree in principle with the idea of heterogeneous histories, place greater emphasis on the common themes that run through all of the individual voices and tie them into a larger master-narrative. Incompatible with this version of diverse histories conforming to one master-narrative is conspiracy theory's insistence that the plot of history is always and inevitably identical, no matter what the circumstances and conditions may look like from one case to another. Because the narrative and ideological patterns of conspiratorial history are so immutable and inflexible, they tend to erase the cultural and political specificity of any given historical event in order to integrate it into its own grand narrative. This narrative is foregrounding its connotations as a rhetorical genre. Its methodology may be rooted in the conventions of scholarly inquiry, but its ideological objective and structural appearance are clearly grounded in fictional narrative. Both of these qualities make it not only problematic as a serious method of historical epistemology, but also as an instrument for the writing of any history that tries to emphasize how uniquely different one national experience is from another.

Since contemporary historians place so much emphasis on the heterogeneity of histories, absolute truth is not what is primarily at stake in the challenge that conspiracy fiction poses to historiography. Fictional conspiracies take their place among other allegorical representations of a historical object that is always and necessarily dispersed among multiple authors. Conspiracy theory engages historiography on its own thematic and methodological grounds, struggling to construct a convincing alternative reading to historical events whose authenticity is grounded primarily in some form of communal consensus (among historians, among witnesses and sources, among authors of all kinds). Conspiracy fiction, however, avoids competing for a supreme historical narrative, be it that of serious historians or that of conspiracy theorists. Ideally, it does not indulge in the nostalgia of recuperating a lost sense of coherence. Instead it aims at deconstructing both the narratives used to accomplish that goal and the motivations behind the attempt.

Perhaps the most prominent of all conspiratorial histories, in both fiction and theory, is the vast conspiracy that can be traced back to the beginning of time and commonly unfolds on a global scale. History as we know it is only a misleading, arbitrary manifestation of this hyperbolic trope. In respect to this particular narrative premise, the correspondences between stories that claim to be fiction and stories that claim to be fact are remarkable in their similarity. Both "serious" alternative histories and novels such as Umberto Eco's *Foucault's Pendulum*, Ishmael Reed's *Mumbo Jumbo*, or Robert Shea's and Anthony Wilson's *Illuminatus Trilogy* are based on the assumption that, according to Reed, "beneath or behind all political and cultural warfare lies a struggle between secret societies."[2] Yet none of these novels even remotely suggest that there could be any factual or historical accuracy to their speculations. However, the sum of their ideas, methods, and conclusions constitutes a significant percentage of the political and historical theories developed and fiercely defended by groups on both ends of the political spectrum, such as, for example, the John Birch Society or the Black Panthers.[3] Furthermore, the notion of a vast conspiracy itself constitutes the subject of a long-standing discursive tradition that goes back as far as the French and the American Revolution. Charles Brockden Brown's *Wieland, or The Transformation* or the German *Geheimbundroman* are examples of this tradition, which eventually becomes part of the theme itself by reflecting the historical rootedness of both the theory and its subject. Neither the tradition nor the structure of the idea therefore suggests that there is anything inherent in the subject matter itself which predisposes it toward fact or fiction. Obviously, what is truth to some are merely crazed ravings to others. As many historians would agree, facts require interpretations to make sense, and confusing the fact with its interpretation means taking someone at their word without knowing their intentions.

Clearly, the differences between fictional and factual conspiracy narratives are merely gradual and cover a variety of options for deciding whether any given story is credible or not. The way readers determine where exactly in this continuum of credibility any individual narrative is located depends mostly on the degree of cultural consensus that society has already established for the historical event in question. Against this consensus readers can measure if the element of conspiracy appears as an artificial imposition upon the historical truth. Even if they are willing to concede their relative ignorance of what really happened, readers are still sufficiently familiar with what constitutes the prevailing notion of truth. They can recognize the dominant paradigm, if not even the central variations within this paradigm. One extreme on this scale of gradual variations between truth and fiction is what can be called "the fantastic," that is to say, all narrative options that require readers to make frequent and drastic changes in the ontological ground rules that the text itself establishes. The other end of the spectrum is constituted by what can be called "the realistic," which would encompass the narrative options that are structured most consistently within one set of ontological ground rules and play out their premises in the most consistent manner.[4]

This method of distinguishing factual from fictional conspiracies attempts to take into account the problem that historical truth has increasingly been redefined as a socially and historically situated construct. What has largely been dismissed is the view that history is the sum of all facts, uncompromised by intentionality and interests and readily accessible across historical boundaries. To insist that any notion of what is fictional can be defined by comparing it to "reality" implies that within any society there is a shared reality which equally applies to every member, whatever his or her gender, social status, and ethnicity may be. Undoubtedly, such a totality does exist, but every literal account of it must necessarily remain incomplete and remain reduced to an ideologically motivated effort at representation. Any historical narrative that pretends to represent the social and historical totality, especially at the current moment when the complexity and scope of this totality have increased beyond all historical precedent, is therefore likely to mystify its readers about its own limitations.[5] Historiographical epistemology in all its contemporary variations has become too self-conscious to continue operating with the positivistic assumption that new data can be measured against the truth within stable and clearly definable horizons of inquiry. Instead, historians have taken on the project of tracing Bakhtinian heteroglossic histories and their interrelations, demoting the ideal of a recuperable social and historical totality to the status of a utopian, conflict-free, and perhaps dangerously reactionary fantasy that has little to do with the theory and nothing to do with the practice of history.

Since all fiction takes place in history and is, to some extent, determined by its forces, it may be necessary to discuss briefly the distinction between the kind of historical fictions addressed here and the universal historicity of all forms of discourse, particularly that of the novel. The distinction that appears most useful in this context is based on the transformation that history has to undergo in order to enter into a work of fiction. In all novels that depict history by applying the formal strategies of literary realism (metonymy rather than metaphor, social type rather than symbol, mimesis rather than allegory, to name but a few key-elements) the theme of conspiracy occupies an ambiguous and complex intermediary position between signifier and signified. Commonly the approach of the conspiracy novel is rooted in the conventions and traditions of the Romance.[6] That is to say, the conspiracy novel has a predisposition toward the self-conscious dramatization and allegorization of its subject. The aesthetic of the Romance is therefore too consistent with that of conspiracy fiction for a comparison of individual texts on the basis of relative representational accuracy. All those narratives that relate to their historical intertext in a conspicuously allegorical manner would therefore be of lesser interest. Sinclair Lewis' *It Can't Happen Here*, Finney's *Invasion of the Body Snatchers* or Condon's *Manchurian Candidate*--relevant as they may be for their position on fascist tendencies in American conservativism, the McCarthy Era, and the Cold War--can be read in a straightforward manner as allegories of history proper.

The idea of a spectrum of conspiracy fiction, which would organize individual texts according to their degree of fantastic versus realistic elements, allows for a comparison of how deeply novels defamiliarize historical truth, based not on an absolute but on a relative scale. Starting with the least degree of the fantastic, we would find narratives that locate the fictional premise in the past, cover the period afterwards with a realistic account of how this event could have been kept secret up to the present day, and integrate this hybrid history into the readers' experience of their own present. Such conspiracy novels would include Frederick Forsyth's *Day of the Jackal*, in which the historical detail that has been altered in order to generate the narrative's factual appeal is relatively small and insignificant. It would also apply to alternative histories that require a more drastic intervention into official history, such as, for instance, Kim Newman's *Bad Dreams* or Dan Simmon's *Children of Night*. Like most other fantastic fiction following in the tradition of the Lovecraftian alternative history, these texts make it necessary to accommodate a science-fictional element into the ontological framework of the novel.

Narratives of this kind usually confront the reader with a gesture of dramatic disclosure. True history, which has been written and/or concealed by an elite group of insiders, is being revealed to the public and a new, revised version of what really happened is instated in the place of the preceding undemocratic cover-up. Further to the fantastic end of the spectrum, readers would find stories that require a more fundamental suspension of disbelief, which tends to make the distinction between factual and fictional conspiracies more easily recognizable. These would be narratives that concede the workings of conspiracies within a history that is already unfamiliar due to a change in the past, such as, for example, the implementation of a paradigmatic scientific breakthrough before its actual historical occurrence, as in Gibson's and Sterling's *The Difference Engine*. In Robert Harris' *Fatherland* or Philip K. Dick's *The Man in the High Castle*, the conspiracies, though not clearly successful in their outcome, are geared toward reinstating the reader's official history to the status of alternative history. In a reversal of fictional and factual histories, both Harris and Dick presuppose that Germany and Japan have won WW II. The resulting political realities would call for a conspiracy to establish and disseminate an alternative history which would be truthful for the readers but of course be nothing but a piece of subversive fiction within the ontological framework of the novel. By reversing not only the positions of winner and loser in the outcome of WW II and then extrapolating the consequences, but also by reversing the function of conspiracy in this altered ontological framework, these novels introduce an element of autoreferentiality to the genre that increases the degree of their fantastic nature. Therefore they would appear on the further end of the spectrum, as far from Forsyth and the conventional thriller as possible.

In between the two extremes we would find texts that subscribe to a more differentiated view of history as a totality and therefore thematize conspiracy as a historical phenomenon of much more specific consequences. In this group of novels are Coover's *The Public Burning*, all the major novels by Pynchon, Don DeLillo's *Libra* and Joseph McElroy's *Women and Men*, but also E.L. Doctorow's *Ragtime*, Richard Powers' *Three Farmers on their Way to a Dance* as well as Powers' *Prisoner's Dilemma*. By placing historical next to fictional characters, mixing imaginary with more or less well-known historical events, and exploring the ambiguities and complexities created by this strategy, these texts occupy a position in the middle of the continuum. Marginally, they participate in the two more extreme forms of conspiracy fiction discussed before. Most likely, their unique inherent heterogeneity makes defining them more difficult; yet it also allows for a more complex stance on the question of historical totality and its representation.

According to Frank Lentricchia, these novels also occupy a middle position within the American cultural mainstream. Based on their refusal to uphold the clear distinction between fictional and factual, between the concrete individual experience and the social and historical categories in which this experience takes place, they can address the crucial dilemma of individualism in a mass society. They succeed in creating a narrative that constructs a dialectic relationship between individual and collective.[7] Judging by their rhetorical devices and the ideological weight they carry, as well as the powerful tradition these texts are grounded in, the intermediary position on our imaginary scale is even more revealing when it is filled by works that combine Lentricchia's historical fictions with the conspiracy novel. What novels like Pynchon's *Gravity's Rainbow* or Coover's *The Public*

Burning can accomplish like no other kind of writing is to undercut official history by opening up a rich discursive field that allows for all varieties of dissent. With Coover and Pynchon, this dissent is satiric, exposing the violence and cynicism with which one history is enforced at the expense of another. With Doctorow and Powers, it is nostalgic, a reminder of possible but suppressed histories. Where exactly DeLillo and McElroy are located on this secret map of alternative histories is best determined by a closer look at two of their most conspicuously "historical" novels.

The most striking feature of both *Libra* and *Women and Men*[8] is their preoccupation with events that seem hardly worthwhile as targets of defamiliarization, whether through the imposition of a conspiratorial subtext or any other method. The assassination of John F. Kennedy, as well as US covert intervention in South American politics, are chapters in the history books which are already synonymous with conspiracy in American popular culture. From the staggering amount of conspiracy theory about the assassination to such books on covert US activities in South America as Bob Woodward's *Veil* or the work of Noam Chomsky,[9] the two subjects are well established as "an area of research marked by ambiguity and error, by political bias, systematic fantasy."[10] Unlike authors who select a historical subject to which conspiracy is an afterthought or superimposition, DeLillo and McElroy have decided on material that is acknowledged territory of conspiracy theory and fiction. That is to say, in these specific cases it is unlikely that both novels' conspiratorial subtext serves the function of introducing a defamiliarizing element into an otherwise well researched field of knowledge. One cannot fictionalize what is already fictionalized.

However, neither *Women and Men* nor Libra are simple retellings of familiar stories whose elements of conspiracy, players, and plot twists are already well established and commonly accepted. That the novels do not simply reaffirm some murky scholarly consensus of "what really happened" for the cultural mainstream becomes obvious when we consider for a moment the rejection and critical resistance that particularly *Libra* has met with upon its first publication.[11] In some way, both novels transgress the borderlines separating the kind of story that promises to reveal some hidden truth from the story that promises to reaffirm the existence of a secret we already knew existed. The choice of subject matter is hardly coincidental here; it does raise the question why both authors are determined to pick a historical subject that is "pre-fictionalized," so to speak. Is it in order to fictionalize it even further? Why reaffirm the existence of conspiracy in a context which already presupposes its existence in one way or another? In order to determine the aesthetic objective of this second turn of the screw, it is necessary to backtrack for a moment and reconsider how exactly conspiracy contaminates any context it is placed in with the element of fiction. In what way does conspiracy fictionalize history, and how does it function in a narrative that openly admits to its own status as fiction?

One crucial function of conspiracy, in theory and in fiction, is to impose order, structure, narrative goals, and functions of agency. Conspiracy narratives inevitably revolve around issues of cognition and revelation. Their goal is the naming of conspirators and the reformulation of relationships through this act of naming. Their characters are functions of these narrative presuppositions, and so on. When this pattern is applied to history, it suggests a number of features that are potentially not inherent in the historical events themselves: historical figures, for example, are commonly more complex and ambiguous in their behavior and decisions than the restraining narrative function of detective, renegade, or conspirator permits. Coincidence is ruled out and intentionality becomes the ubiquitous force behind all historical progression. Nobody denies the existence of conspiracies in history, but all evidence of what historians consider an appropriate account of past events points back to the difference between fact and interpretation. Historical events in themselves, though they are open to interpretation, have no sense of teleology. They simply occur, and only afterwards and through a process of hermeneutical reasoning is it possible to determine their direction, meaning, and outcome. For a Christian fundamentalist or a UFO buff, history incorporates a grand teleological narrative which is sometimes concealed but always accessible through informed interpretation. As historians like Hayden White have argued, any form of narrativity is a means of structuring. Narrative carries its own set of ideological premises and is therefore always already an act of implicit interpretation. Conspiracy necessarily foregrounds its own artificiality as such a device of structuring. It fictionalizes because it narrativizes.[12]

The preceding remarks about the relationship between history and conspiracy apply most of all to the kind of history to which, according to common consensus, conspiracy is an extrinsic force or imposition. What about the kind of history, however, that is already inscribed with a conspiratorial subtext from the very beginning and has, like the Kennedy assassination, become synonymous with conspiracy per se? For all cases in which conspiracy has been established as part of what really happened beyond the shadow of a doubt historians or politicians can only speak because the conspiracy has failed, its secrecy has been dismantled, and its efforts have been thwarted. In other words, following the implications of conspiracy to their extreme, no successful conspiracy has ever been recorded in the history books; in other words, the most powerful and insidious conspiracies are those that have maintained their secrecy and have therefore most likely achieved their goals.

This infinite argumentative regress leads to a notion of history which presupposes that, even in the historical conspiracies that have been exposed and aborted, there will always remain a kind of residual indeterminacy. This element of unresolvedness can, at best, be minimized to the degree of insignificance. The effect of conspiracy in all cases in which it is intrinsic to the historical event is consequently to render history residually unknowable and impenetrable. The fact that, for example, any gesture of authoritative closure is structurally impossible within the rhetoric of conspiracy is reminiscent of the way in which all writing which does not lay claims to reality the way historiography does generates its meaning. Through conspiracy, real or fictitious, history takes on the epistemological status of fiction, as defined by poststructuralist and deconstructionist criticism. Its meanings have now been transferred from the sheer facts to their interpretation-- things must be made to mean, they must be allegorized. The meaning of any text remains essentially unstable and ambiguous. Its conflicts remain unresolvable, and its value becomes relative and strategic. Contemporary historians may have eventually come around to the position conspiracy theorists have taken all along. From the moment they started thinking about the sum of historical events as texts, conspiratorial or otherwise, the act of interpretation itself became more significant, while the prospect of determining these texts' ultimate meaning became increasingly more irrelevant.

In fiction, the appeal of conspiracy is more narrowly defined. Since fiction is already and by definition a narrative form, conspiracy only enhances that effect through connotative signals that function within fiction's indigenous codes. Traditionally grounded in the conventions of the Romance, conspiracy undercuts the claims of conventional realism. It introduces an element of the fantastic, as Eric Rabkin uses the term, into text which themselves signal their commitment to another, more realistic genre. Usually, paranoid delusions display forms of hermeneutical overdetermination; suspicions feed off the urge to generate more evidence, which they themselves produce, entrapping the paranoiac in increasingly convincing and tightly argued convictions. Their utter lack of persuasiveness for somebody outside the paranoid framework is due to the argument's adherence to a specific code which recognizes its own prescribed rules and justifies its existence and results through procedural accuracy. In other words, conspiracy fictionalizes because it constitutes a genre. Merging an aesthetic code that is inimical to mimesis and instead prefers hyperbole, melodrama, and allegory with a text grounded in the conventions of literary realism raises this text's level of autoreferentiality and thus increases the fictitiousness of the events depicted.

Based on these observations, Fredric Jameson has argued that the murder of John F. Kennedy might very well be "the paradigmatic political assassination in (Western) modern times,"[13] primarily for its relevance to problems of postmodern representation, mass media, and political iconography. It is exactly this interpenetration of historical event and cultural appropriation that Don DeLillo is focusing on in *Libra*. In order to represent history as a text that is always already read and interpreted, the novel incorporates literally a number of characters who enact possible models of response to the events surrounding the assassination of both Kennedy and Oswald for us.[14] Incidentally, we are to glimpse a schoolbook behind Oswald in the book depository entitled "Ten Rolling Readers;" an ironic reminder that nothing is left to coincidence in conspiracy fiction. Most prominent among the novel's iconic readers is Nicholas Branch, "a retired senior analyst of the Central Intelligence Agency, hired on contract to write the secret history of the assassination of President Kennedy."[15] Confined to a small enclosed space and surrounded by the monumental records of the event, Branch's efforts rely on the cooperation of an anonymous Curator who is controlling the flow of data and, together with it, the outcome of Branch's own interpretation. The curator tends to supply Branch with more information than any single reader can possibly process. Wondering whether he is writing "a history no one will read,"[16] Branch occupies a position that is defined by historical posteriority, which confers a state of impotence and insecurity upon him. As a postmodern historian, he rejects closing the case and instead opts for creating a state of prolonged indeterminacy. Branch "has decided it is premature to make a serious effort to turn these notes into coherent history."[17]

How problematic Branch's position is becomes clear when we compare it to that of Beryl Parmenter, the wife of one of the conspirators responsible for the killing. Watching the footage of Oswald being shot by Ruby on television over and over again, Beryl finds a way of reconciling herself with an unknowable history. Unlike Branch, who is concerned with establishing factual truth, Beryl's hard-earned response is that of collective moral responsibility. Beryl resists the mind-numbing pull of the medium of television, which itself "only deepened and prolonged the horror"[18] through the technological capacity to replay the images endlessly and thus strip them of all immediate impact. She finally realizes "that it was cowardly to hide" and instead manages to return Oswald's final and impenetrable look into the camera.[19] The moment is even more significant because it breaks up one of the central images of conspiracy, the infinite regress of knowledge which eventually forces every reader into a state of paralysis. Instead of wondering what it was that Oswald knew at that final moment, Beryl decides to break out of the regressive loop and accept the perhaps unsettling consequences of having been inserted into another system, that of personal, ethical responsibility.

The third reader is Oswald's mother Marguerite. She is given the opportunity to construct a response in her monologue at the end of the novel which differs significantly from those of the other readers because of its sincere pathos. Having been assigned the position of an outsider to her son's public and private life, Marguerite's response is the one least caught up in the concern for posterity and the problems of representation. Instead, she construct small, fragmentary narratives that attempt to recuperate Lee from history and return him to a human, understandable dimension. Portraying Lee as a boy with a dog, a Christ figure, or a good son, Marguerite confronts the code of history with stories of domesticity, religious and secular mythology, or family tragedy in an attempt to fragment a narrative of totality. In reducing this inhuman narrative to its small, comprehensible components, Marguerite tries to rescue Lee from becoming his public persona, now that he himself cannot resist the narratives that others construct about him any more.

Somewhere else I have commented on the incorporation of iconic figures into novels conforming to the new paradigm emerging in conspiracy fiction. These iconic figures are made to represent, preserve, and reify elements of the preceding paradigm which have been relegated to a secondary status in the text without disappearing completely. Similar to this strategy of creating heterogeneity through the preservation of historically demoted features, the three readers in *Libra* function as iconic representations of a heterogeneous discursive field surrounding the actual historical event. Aside from the specific ethical and narrative choices that they offer, they signify both the intertwining of fact and interpretation and the posteriority of the act of reading in relation to the occurrence itself. Taken together, these iconic readers represent a way of constructing meaning that can be associated with the kind of reader response criticism practiced by critics like Hans Robert Jauss or Stanley Fish. They employ a methodology, primarily geared toward literary studies, that approaches the individual text as a phenomenon mediated through and inseparable from the history of its reception. As an augmentation to the "horizon of expectation," a notion derived from more conventional hermeneutics, reader response criticism concedes the crucial importance of mutually impinging cultural intertexts rather than persisting in the problematic binary distinction between text and context.

The self-conscious intertextuality of *Libra* manifests itself in a series of tropes centered around the notion of transgression, spill, or shift of category. Recurring as a topological metaphor, the theme is played out in the description of Nicholas Branch's workspace. What first appears as a distinct entity, "the room of documents, the room of theories and dreams,"[20] which Branch has added to his house when commissioned for his work by the Agency, soon ceases to be separate and starts invading the house itself. "Paper is beginning to slide out of the room and across the doorway to the house proper."[21] The separation of both spaces proves impossible; what came afterwards penetrates what preceded it. Just as the space representing conspiracy, politics, and the public cannot be kept separate from the space representing domesticity, family, and privacy, the categories separating history and fiction start to slide into each other.[22]

Working through the documents trailing behind the assassination, Branch realizes that a common rhetoric unites what first appear as distinct ways of knowing. Thus, the Warren Report, the epitome of factuality, becomes the

> megaton novel James Joyce would have written if he'd moved to Iowa City and lived to be a
> hundred . . . This is the Joycean Book of America, remember--the novel in which nothing is
> left out.[23]

Factuality, like the overdetermination of the paranoiac's argument, starts to resemble fiction the more its principles are being pushed to the extreme. Oswald's wish to enter history, which forms perhaps the most stable feature of his otherwise rather indistinct personality as a fictional character, is basically the wish to enter textuality and become subject to the rhetorical rules regulating discourse, be it in tabloid journalism, romantic fiction, or serious scholarly historiography. The transformations that his name undergoes in the course of the narrative are an example of the steady progression of rhetorical variations that lead to the final goal of him becoming *the* Lee Harvey Oswald of official history. He has accomplished the task of becoming a fictional character at the moment he himself is being assassinated.

What *Libra* makes uncompromisingly clear with this rhetorical turn is that an event like the Kennedy assassination is not once, but twice fictionalized before the trope of conspiracy even enters the picture. Thomas Carmichael, who argues that "belatedness and self-reflexiveness are the inescapable conditions of political violence"[24] in all of DeLillo's fiction, sees this double defamiliarization not exclusively as a feature of the writing's aesthetic and ideological presuppositions, but more as an expression of the cultural paradigm in which DeLillo's work has to find its place.

> DeLillo's fiction also invites us to read a prior text not as suppressing its instability, nor as
> site of textual authority to be subverted, but as representative of the very instability his
> fiction portrays as the generalized context of the postmodern condition.[25]

Despite the fact that Joseph McElroy's presentation of conspiratorial history in his monumental novel *Women and Men* utilizes a similar approach of reflecting autoreferentiality and historical belatedness both as a general cultural paradigm and as a personal aesthetic choice, the author's decision to address Chilean history seems motivated by a different rationale than the one behind *Libra*. Covert US participation in the overthrow of the Allende regime and the institution of the military dictatorship under Pinochet can hardly compare, in its traumatic impact on the collective imagination and the ability to incite rich and varied discourse, to what DeLillo calls "the seven seconds that broke the back of the American century."[26] Unlike the Kennedy assassination, Chilean domestic and foreign politics--"the Chilean Connection," as critic Gene Frumkin calls it, alluding to yet another well-known conspiracy story[27]--is a subject which has hardly generated an equal density of analysis and elaboration. If at all, then Chile provides a kind of textbook example of American foreign politics in what used to be called "the Third World" and is now, somewhat euphemistically, referred to as "Developing Countries." The fate of socialism in Chile is one detail in the complex interplay of global politics, in which the United States are involved to one degree or another. Yet its ranking on the political, historical, and cultural agenda of the American collective imagination is clearly not one of high priority. Still, the highly publicized hearings in the Iran-Contra Affair may have provided a background against which Chile suddenly appears as a more significant case study in American imperialist politics. Since *Women and Men* must have been in the writing long before Iran-Contra became subject of public discussion, it is unlikely that McElroy expected the reader to perceive the Chilean plot through the filter of the other event, which in itself carries all the elements of great conspiracy narratives. Whether the historical correspondences are purely accidental, or whether *Women and Men* proves to be attuned more closely to the realities of US foreign politics from the 1970s to the end of the 1980s, remains to be decided by the individual reader.

Considering how McElroy has structured the vast body of narrative in *Women and Men*, the traumatic political coup which leads to the installment of the military dictatorship in Chile seems to send a ripple through the fabric of the novel which fades as it leads readers further and further from the event itself. McElroy subverts the conspiratorial narrative in two steps. First, he superimposes the conspiracy upon the struggle to overcome colonial domination and achieve self-determination in Chile, and then discusses the coup indirectly by concentrating almost exclusively on Chilean undercover activities in the US, directed against exiles and political enemies. As the infringement upon national sovereignty, which was committed originally by the CIA, is redirected toward the former aggressor in what is still a direct consequence of the original coup, the relationship between conspirator and victim is being reversed. Not unlike the concept of international conspiracy in *Lookout Cartridge*, America is suddenly deprived of its role as agent and reduced to that of setting, where somebody else's "political terrorism and its quiet linguistic routines" are being resolved.[28] Like America itself in novels dealing with international terrorism, such as

Mao II or *Players*, the dense urban fabric of New York becomes a mere metaphor for the actual site of conflict.

Distancing the reader from the cause of all this plotting and counterplotting is as much an aesthetic device as it is a means of disabling a reading strategy that allows the reader to perceive the colonial subtext as a straightforward homogeneous history from which valuable lessons can be learned. The novel's stance of insisting on political involvement on the basis of ambiguity corresponds to its aesthetic efforts of subverting the relationship between signifier and signified. The indirect depiction of the Chilean coup d'état serves both as a concrete political, historical, and personal reality and as metaphor for other narratives of similar diversity. As "the cloak-&-dagger mystification narrows to a domestic point," critic Gene Frumkin argues, "a woman [is] concerned about her body's welfare in her mind."[29] Readers are faced with the ambiguity of a signifier that suggests simultaneously a literal and metaphorical reading. "Pinochet's persecution of alternatives" becomes, in turn, the concrete expression of the violent suppression of that same ambiguity. Implementing an aggressive strategy of disambiguation--political, personal, historical, social, and so on--becomes one hallmark of a fascism that is inherent in any conspiratorial history. Reinstating ambiguity therefore becomes one of the major targets of the novel's deconstruction of conspiracy as narrative and ideological code.

Although the narrative in *Libra* encompasses Oswald's entire lifetime, the "seven seconds" in Dealy Plaza compact his lifetime into an infinitely small metaphorical space. Compared to this temporal and geographic perspective, *Women and Men* tells a number of stories that reach well beyond one lifetime or the bounds of the earth itself. Still, both novels share one conspicuous absence. Just like in *Libra*, McElroy's readers are only confronted with the aftershocks of an upheaval. The trauma itself remains outside the grasp of the novel. This exclusion occurs even despite the fact that *Women and Men* addresses history long before 1972 and takes place in a geography much more exotic than South America. Its readers are either too late or perpetually in the wrong place. Whereas the coup itself remains inaccessible, we are confronted with a host of characters whose relative position toward this initial cause defines the shape and structure of the conspiracies it has generated.

Up close the reader will find characters like the economist Mackenna or the diva, who are both Chilean citizens living in New York and act either actively or passively in opposition to the Pinochet regime. The diva's position is the more precarious of the two because her lover deTalca is a member of the Chilean military and may be involved in the confinement of her father back in Chile. Connected to these central figures are friends and relatives, who take a personal or political interest in their struggles. They become implicated into the affairs of both the exile-Chilean community in the US and the covert operations of the Chilean authorities aimed at infiltrating this community. One step further are journalists like Spence or James Mayn. Mayn's interest in Chile is also of a more personal nature because of his friendship to the woman Mayga, who was presumably murdered by the Chilean military. Finally, there are all the characters who are connected to these conspiratorial activities through either another, closer character (such as, for example, the bicycle messengers whose contacts are established through the senders and recipients of the messages they deliver), or through random, coincidental intersections with the sphere of conspiratorial politics (the other members of Grace Kimball's workshop, which Mackenna's wife happens to be attending, for instance).

As the novel abounds with other conspiratorial plots, the central event of the Chilean coup d'état starts to spill over, metaphorically as well as historically, into the larger fabric of the novel. To accomplish this proliferation of the event, the characters themselves do not need to serve as messengers. The correspondences that connect these historical plots are sometimes based on structural homologies, sometimes on a more metaphorical transfer of properties. Conceptualized as a late twentieth-century colonial narrative, the Chilean plot is being projected specifically onto the economic exploitation of New Mexico, the westward expansion of European immigration into Native American tribal cultures, and the ideologies of exotism that have accompanied this economic exploitation. The ambiguous postcolonial reality of New Mexico, as McElroy's narrator explains, is that it is "more outside-controlled than any other state, yet in itself more foreign, magically foreign."[30] As a melodramatic event befitting the aesthetic language of opera, the coup becomes the catastrophe that separates families (the diva and her father), lovers (the diva and DeTalca), and friends (Mayn and Mayga). Literally, the conspiracies instigated by American-Chilean politics may have enabled convicts to break out of the prison where Foley has been confined all along--another case of spill, crossover, or transgression. Similarly, in the chapter on Mayn's friend Larry and his studies in economics, McElroy suggests that certain economic theories which pretend to describe economic processes objectively are, in fact, the result of political co-optation and suppression; that is, they are constructed upon the aggressive invasion of one conceptual category into another. In all of these cases, Chile functions as a crucial reference point for "the Great American Question *Who was here first?*"[31]

Since readers are positioned closest to James Mayn and Grace Kimball, and since the novel's double protagonist is itself located in the more marginal sphere of the concentric circles of characters surrounding the Chilean coup, most of the crucial information regarding the center of this model has been mediated, reworked, and manipulated before it reaches the reader. The compromised nature of information positions readers at the exact libration point, to use the novel's own imagery, between certainty and the responsibility it bestows, and ambiguity and the caution it requires. At this exact remove, knowledge is sufficiently available to make the reader an accomplice, yet power is so elusive that active participation remains largely impossible. Typical of McElroy's preoccupation with determining the exact manner in which knowledge predisposes action, this threshold reflects quite poignantly the position of Americans toward the political and military activities of their government. The historical events retain a residual indeterminacy: to what degree was the CIA involved in overthrowing a foreign democratically elected government? How much did American politicians know? How active are Chilean undercover operations in the wake of the overthrow, and so on?

Although this ambiguity is grounded more firmly in the conspiratorial subtext of the novel than in the impenetrability of the historical text itself, its consequences are more significant for the reading of history than the reading of fiction. Ambiguity is constructed in a manner which denies readers the possibility of opting out of historic responsibility because all available information is unreliable and any course of action is therefore deeply compromised--a path reminiscent of the one Beryl Parmenter decides on in *Libra*. At the same time, it precludes the convenient path of activism that considers itself beyond reproach for believing itself in possession of the totality of historical truth, which may very well be the path taken by DeLillo's conspirators. Far from immobilizing its characters, as well as the historical subject, by putting them in this undecidable situation, however, *Women and Men* charts a course of action that embraces this same ambiguity.

Libra was presenting historical truth as dispersed through one single hegemonic cultural discourse. This discourse generates heterogeneity only because the ideological objectives of the makers of cultural consensus tend to change over time. The result is a history that, like conspiracy, projects heterogeneity, but is secretly homogeneous. This constitutes the universal cultural paradigm which also happens to apply to the reading and writing of history: the secret history is unified, and only on the surface does it project diversity. *Women and Men*, however, presents the cultural discourse itself--Robert Jauss' history of reception with its multitude of successive and simultaneous readers--as a heterogeneous discursive formation in which conspiracy has to compete for dominance like any other narrative or fictional claim to truth. There is no single history in *Women and Men*, not because its authenticity is lost through mediation, but because "history" itself is an object of perception that is created by the epistemological and ideological presuppositions of any given discipline. Sciences and scholarly inquiry create rather than discover their subject. Their imposition of patterns and limitations, something McElroy calls the "gridthink of territorial plot"[32] constitutes an object of study that would otherwise remain infinitely connected and disseminated through its intertexts. Together with this reconceptualization comes the open acknowledgement of any number of such preliminary, strategic definitions. Rather than admitting that historiography can never get to the bottom of things because conspiracy creates unresolvable residues of undecideability, historians would be inclined to point to other disciplines as a more effective access to the more mysterious aspects of their own subject. The discipline itself changes as it enters a history of its own. True interdisciplinary inquiry into the nature of the world, rather than positivist historiography, is what *Women and Men* is attempting to create and integrate into the discourse of conspiratorial fiction.

Unlike Thomas Pynchon, DeLillo and McElroy construct conspiracy as a cultural text that needs to be balanced, counteracted, and augmented by a force from the outside. What *Gravity's Rainbow* refers to as the "They System," a synonym for the all-encompassing conspiracy, will, according to Pynchon, eventually generate a "We System," that is, a "counterforce" to the corrosive and paralyzing power of conspiracy which derives its impetus from a reversal of paranoia's distinctive features. Indeterminacy turns into freedom from restrictions; claustrophobic fears of persecution turn into an appreciation for occupying a central position in the grand scheme of world history, and the apprehensions about rigid structures turn into a constructive use of structure for the purpose of imposing order upon chaos. This possibility of embracing conspiracy and paranoia, which figures prominently in such novels as *The Crying of Lot 49,* where it is explicitly presented as the conceptual groundwork for a politics of radical dissent, does not apply unconditionally to conspiracy novels operating within the new paradigm. After Pynchon, authors tend to apply textual strategies which locate the grounds of alternative histories not within, but outside of conspiracy. They call into question Pynchon's ideological conceit that infiltration and temporary appropriation of opposing political positions constitutes a viable political strategy.

At first glance, however, *Libra* seems to share Pynchon's optimistic assumptions about stepping out of the cultural mainstream. DeLillo shows some of the fascination with non-scientific methods of conceptualizing experience that are so prominent in *Gravity's Rainbow.*[33] Emanating primarily from the figure of David Ferrie is a string of images and discussions revolving around astrology and superstition, premonition and predetermination, which is highly reminiscent of the séances and metaphysical pseudoscience that *Gravity's Rainbow* returns to time and again. Marginal characters in *Libra*, like Jack Ruby's strippers Lynette and Baby LeGrand, subscribe to astrology, just as the homosexual scene in New Orleans, into which Ferrie introduces Lee, seems to entertain a strong relationship with the irrational. With the sharp contrast between Clay Shaw's world and the suburban middle-class environment of conspirators like Everett or Parmenter, as well as the insistence on an intuitive affinity between non-scientific thinking and socially marginal groups, DeLillo places astrology both on a social and epistemological map. Touching upon "the truth at the edge of human affairs,"[34] astrology exposes a historical narrative waiting to be made visible. Significantly enough, this narrative is primarily hidden from those who figure most prominently as its agents. As Ferrie himself puts it, "Librans never notice references to themselves."[35]

As ambivalent as the history leading up to the assassination might be, the novel continuously points to the "pattern in things."[36] This suspected pattern justifies a reading of history which sees order but refuses to believe that it is the result of conspiracy. The validity of this interpretation is backed mostly by two strategies. First, an overwhelming amount of circumstantial evidence is being presented by those who subscribe to this somewhat unconventional reading. Coincidences that are just too good to be true confirm the conspirators' suspicions that things may come out as planned, yet not because they are planned at all. These are coincidences that the characters have no control over. Secondly, the truth contained in these pieces of evidence is more aesthetically than epistemologically appealing. Oswald's biography with its inconsistencies, incompatible opposites, and random extremes appears as a perfect illustration of Ferrie's dictum that Librans are characters who tend to be in a state of balance that makes them susceptible to be influenced either way, possibly in a manner that is inconsistent with their "usual" character. Even if this means that astrology gives access to these random patterns, it still does not say anything about whether they are significant in the first place.

Whenever *Libra* does not give a voice to astrology as a form of metaphysics, it presents the reader with coincidence and randomness. The element of chance function as the secular manifestation of that same effort to construct a pattern of meaning against conspiracy that otherwise resorts to astrology. This complex of themes is most strongly associated with Nicholas Branch and Win Everett, but, as with Dave Ferrie's interest in astrology, it permeates the entire novel on a more fundamental level. As consistently as DeLillo utilizes the familiar trope of infinite regress, which suggests that coincidence might very well be the most sophisticated disguise for premeditation and planning, *Libra* does take a stand in favor of an element of mystery, uncalculability, and unpredictability. While most supposedly random incidents can be interpreted as carefully plotted by one of the competing plots, the novel's single most crucial scene is almost completely exempt from this ambivalence. When Oswald walks into Guy Bannister's office in New Orleans, after having been ingeniously set up without his knowledge, and tries to apply for undercover work, there is no indication that his action is determined by anything but his free will; no manipulation is at work.[37] The conspirators themselves are baffled and, consistent with their character, suspect foul play. Since this scene also describes the first and therefore most important intersection of the novels' two plotlines--one biographical and personal, dispersed over chapters named after places; the other political and collective, alternating chapters named after moments in time--it constitutes the one narrative detail which is irreplaceable and essential in whichever one of the readings of historical facts the reader selects. This scene places coincidence at the center of the novel, and with it everything that escapes the pull of conspiracy and paranoia. In a text that so vitally relies on plotting in both senses of the word, there would be no history without this incalculable coincidence.

Like *Libra*, *Women and Men* is structured around a key-trope that implies a sense of balance, of corresponding and ultimately complementing halves. This metaphor is, in part, expressed in Harry Mathews' statement that the novel performs

a generalized reduction and destruction of dualities, separations, distinctions, hierarchies: in history, in physics, in ethics, in the uses of language and literature.[38]

However, the specific image of balance presented in Women *and Men*--that of breathing and of "con-spiring," that is, breathing-together, which also manifests itself in more marginal images as, for example, the libration point between two planets--aims at recalibrating dualities rather than abolishing them altogether. A destruction of dualities can occur when both halves are set apart from each other. The image of systolic and diastolic movement, however, reminds readers that both halves are distinct yet complimentary entities. *Women and Men* does not show that dualities are constructed out of unrelated phenomena, but that they are constructions that subdivide what belongs together. Only by reading the deconstruction of dualities as a process that focuses on complementarity rather than distinctiveness can Mathews therefore arrive at the conclusion that

the way everything is linked to everything else makes talking about separate bits of subject matter difficult: a discussion of almost any detail will lead to another and eventually involve the whole book.[39]

Breathing imagery is everywhere in the novel. The long and formally most dazzling chapters in *Women and Men* are entitled "Breathers," just as the novel starts out with a human being drawing in its first breath. In tracing the etymology of the term "conspiracy," the implication of breathing-together becomes even more strikingly significant as McElroy creates an endlessly shifting, yet always clearly discernible collective omniscient narrator who is, not entirely facetiously, referred to as "angels." In following this imagery of organic, rather than mechanistic, movement and countermovement, conspiracy could very well be seen as a drawing in of breath, a gathering of strength and concentration, a focusing and collecting. It then calls for a complimentary move that would fragment, refract, disperse, scatter, and relax all of these forces so that the cycle could begin anew. As dissimilar as the two complexes of images may be otherwise, both the scales of the Libra and the alternating inhaling and exhaling imply that the novels might have to offer an alternative or counterbalance to their own conspiratorial narrative.

Not surprisingly then,*Women and Men* shares *Libra*'s preoccupation with alternative ways of generating knowledge about the world. Whereas DeLillo addresses primarily the discourses of astrology and coincidence, McElroy aims for alternative sciences in all their confusing variety, as would be appropriate for an encyclopedic novel. Recuperating even the previously mentioned image of the grid, his protagonist

> will take legend and geological report, and . . . it's history as common in the invisible slow violence of the land's change as in the cities of the sky invented upon high mesas by the four-dimensional grid of mind.[40]

Similar to the notion that history must be constituted by a self-consciously defined discipline, knowledge is being recuperated from an essentialist philosophy and transformed into the construct, or rather, the series of constructs, created by the specific ways of knowing and the endless potential of metaphoric proliferation of information. Science appears in the form of meteorology, geology, biology, and so on. Non-, or pre-scientific ways of defining and encoding knowledge manifest themselves in such diverse methods as Navaho sand painting, the Blessing Way, or the Ghost Dance Movement. These alternative sciences find their equivalent in the latter day methods of individual healing and political consciousness-raising practiced and taught in Grace Kimball's workshop. While one could argue that McElroy is being ironic in depicting Grace and her exuberant and occasionally very "American" convictions, he is, without doubt, seriously engaged in all the practices that are somewhat less eclectic and culturally more consistently indigenous.

This distinction between scientific and non-scientific practices is, yet again, transformed into, and projected onto, the practice of history. While one half of the book's hemispheres strives to write a historical narrative of political and economic struggle, the other half balances this enterprise, which is firmly rooted in Western philosophical practices and conventions, by presenting a mythological counternarrative. At times, Chile makes an appearance as the land of Choor when the novel recounts the stories of Mayn's grandmother Margaret. In these elaborate stories, Margaret herself appears sometimes as the Navaho Princess. Her suicidal daughter, James' mother Sarah, figures as a character whose demonic possession can be cured by creating an opening in her head. These narratives with their conspicuous correspondences tie together geological with meteorological history, global history with family history, and personal history with mythology into one glorious inextricable tangle. If conspiracy has entered this complex network of systems anywhere, then it must have permeated all of it to some degree.

The discussion of these alternative ways of knowing and how they are integrated into a rewriting of history brings the argument back to the beginning. In the prefatory remarks to this chapter, I mentioned the tendency in contemporary historiography to consider history as a heterogeneous text, written by a multitude of different authors, upon which one or the other master-narrative, among them conspiracy, can be superimposed. Keeping this model in mind, it must appear as if novels like *Libra* or *Women and Men* are belaboring the obvious, attempting to reveal an epistemological presupposition in fiction that historians have already firmly established in the mind of the reader through changes in their own field. To point out that history is, in fact, neither the eschatological plot of religious or metaphysical speculation, nor the grand narrative of literary realism or, for instance, the Victorian novel, seems to revive an outmoded philosophy of history only to abolish it or declare it as irrelevant by the same token.

However, the history that is relevant here is not written by historians or journalists. It is a history that writers like DeLillo and McElroy inherit from Thomas Pynchon and his predecessors working in a literary and therefore primarily rhetorical tradition. Consequently, the objective of novels like *Libra* or *Women and Men* is not to dismantle a particular, crucial concept in general historiography, but to reformulate that concept wherever it surfaces in literary discourse and redefine, in the process, the tradition's relationship with other discourses, such as historiography itself, sociology, psychology, and so forth.

For convenience sake, I have associated this tradition of conspiracy fiction mostly with Thomas Pynchon, but it also includes other writers and their subgenres, such as William Gibson or Bruce Sterling, for whom the insistence on an outmoded paradigm may be a more significant historical atavism since their work is commonly considered to be on the cutting edge. Like Gibson's and Sterling's, "Pynchon's Paranoid History"[41] is still accessible in its totality through the means of allegory. History can be represented as a totality insofar as its underlying conspiratorial plot figures as the allegory that pulls even the most disparate historical events together, supplying the connections across geographical and ideological space. Needless to mention that this allegory itself is based on the trope of hyperbole, which also falls away at the moment the new paradigm starts taking hold.

In order to formulate a position of resistance to this totality--resistance to the conspiracy itself, and with it, resistance to the overwhelming and incomprehensible forces of history--the historical subject has no other option than to embrace history first. This is, after all, not about getting out of history, but about getting a foothold in it. In Pynchon, this embrace is construed as the necessary precondition of subversion; all other efforts are doomed to fail simply due to the hopeless imbalance of power. Once characters have resigned themselves to the inescapability of history, they can turn its forces against itself: out of the impersonal and threatening "They" arises the affirming, almost humanistic concept of the "We System." In Gibson and Sterling, the affirmation of history as totality leads to the notion that, only by finding a niche in society that is unobserved, overlooked, or low on "Their" priority list, is it possible to exist undisturbed and write a history of one's own. Spatially, these are the abandoned warehouses, the enclaves between surveillance zones, and the back alleys of *Neuromancer* or *Count Zero*. Historically, these are the tribal rituals, the cargo cults, and the eclectic religions in *Islands in the Net* or *Schismatrix*. Like the microscopic societies of Thanatoids and anarchists in Pynchon's *Vineland*, characters survive by remaining inconspicuous. Burrowing deep into federal witness protection programs, they are tolerated behind enemy lines because their powers are widely dispersed though the vast information networks.

Despite the fact that *Libra* or *Women and Men* fall back on conspiracy as a structuring mechanism of historical totality, they oppose the notion that history, even conspiratorial history, constitutes a totality that is ultimately unrepresentable, even though it may still be meaningful. In McElroy's words, history can be understood as "an articulate structure accommodating a multiplicity of small-scale units."[42] *Libra* accomplishes this by asserting that there is a counterforce to balance conspiracy, which is located within the system but constitutes a gray area that resists systematic integration.*Women and Men* suggests that there is no essential core of truth to the notion of history; that its existence is always based on the epistemological and ideological presuppositions with which any given discipline approaches it. The lacunae that the old paradigm constructs inside the totality and by which it reaffirms that same totality are now transferred to the subtext (i.e. conspiracy theory) by which this totality was created in the first place. Conspiracy ceases to be the grand narrative which bestows order on historical facts and makes them intelligible. Instead, it becomes incomplete and unrepresentable without another narrative that would accomplish for conspiracy what conspiracy used to accomplish for history.

To some degree, this development in conspiracy fiction reflects the paradigmatic changes historians have already made in their discipline some time ago. It reflects the same sense of fragmentation of a central master-narrative into a number of smaller, distinct histories, each endowed with a latent sense of the whole. This fragmentation is nothing new, considering that, for example, Jean-Francois Lyotard has discussed this phenomenon for scientific thought some time ago and, in the process, defined it as one of the crucial elements of postmodernity.[43] Postmodern fiction seems to have taken its time to catch up with an already postmodernized historiography, playing out its strategy of fragmentation in its main discourse first before finally transferring the paradigmatic shift onto the level of its meta-discourse, like other disciplines that focus on models of historical thinking before it. On the level where the discourse reflects back upon itself, conspiratorial histories have been stripped of their claim to totality. They can no longer function as "meta-histories," to utilize Hayden White's expression, that reconcile the historical subject with a history beyond the individual's grasp. Fredric Jameson may be right in assuming that part of the postmodern condition is to feel incapable of conceptualizing and representing the social and historical totality. All familiar narratives with which we used to be able to represent this totality are failing since they cannot encompass any more what has grown in size and complexity beyond all historical precedent. Even allegorical representations have been rendered ineffective in the light of these developments; though they have always been marked as incomplete, they could at least perform their task with a sense of optimism. However, conspiracy novels like *Libra* or *Women and Men* seem to indicate that it is the claim to totality itself that we have to relinquish in order to alleviate the feeling of helplessness whenever we are confronted with the inadequacy of our conceptual tools.

Notes

[1] Don DeLillo, *Libra* (New York: Viking, 1988) 321.

[2] Ishmael Reed, *Mumbo Jumbo* (New York: Macmillan, 1972) 18.

[3] for both the variety of groups subscribing to conspiracy theories and the structural and argumentative similarity between their theories, see David Brion Davis, *The Fear of Conspiracy* (Ithaca: Cornell UP, 1971), or Sanford Pinsker, "America's Conspiratorial Imagination," *The Virginia Quarterly Review* 68.4 (Autumn 1992) 605-625.

[4] The layout of this conceptual model was suggested by Eric Rabkin's model of the fantastic in *The Fantastic in Literature* (Princeton: Princeton UP, 1976), especially the discussion of the reversal of ontological ground rules in Chapter 1 ("The Fantastic and Fantasy") 12.

[5] see *The Geopolitical Aesthetic: Cinema and Space in the World System* (Bloomington: Indiana UP, 1992) where Jameson argues that the effort to conceptualize this totality has motivated the application of the trope of conspiracy in order to encompass the threatening, mystifying aspect of what cannot be grasped with conventional metaphoric means any more.

[6] see Robert Levine, *"Introduction"* in *Conspiracy and Romance: Studies in Brockden Brown, Cooper, Hawthorne, and Melville* (Cambridge: Cambridge UP, 1989).

[7] Frank Lentricchia, "Don DeLillo." *Raritan: A Quarterly Review* 8:1, 29 (Spring 1989) 4-6.

[8] Joseph McElroy, *Women and Men* (New York: Alfred A. Knopf, 1987).

[9] Bob Woodward, *Veil: The Secret Wars of the CIA: 1981-1987* (New York: Simon & Schuster, 1987); Noam Chomsky, *The Noam Chomsky Reader*, James Peck, ed. (New York: Pantheon, 1987).

[10] *Libra* 15.

[11] Most prominently, the rejection of the novel by Jonathan Yardley in his review in the *Washington Post*; see Lentricchia, "Don DeLillo."

[12] Hayden White, "The Question of Narrative in Contemporary Historical Narrative," *The Content of the Form: Narrative Discourse and Historical Representation* (Baltimore: Johns Hopkins UP, 1987) 48.

[13] Jameson, *The Geopolitical Aesthetic*, 47.

[14] Since the conspiracy theme requires a constant oscillation of characters between the functions of reader and author, these figures are deliberately exempt from the conspiratorial plotline; Marguerite because she has bonds to Lee which exceed the merely pragmatic and functional; Beryl because she is unaware of her husband's activities, which adds a certain sense of dramatic irony to the fact that she takes on this important role of transcending conspiracy; and Branch simply because he is writing long after the events have taken place.

[15] *Libra* 15.

[16] *Libra* 60.

[17] *Libra* 301.

[18] *Libra* 446.

[19] *Libra* 447.

[20] *Libra* 14.

[21] *Libra* 378.

[22] Thomas Carmichael has made a similar argument about the significance of topography in *Libra* in his essay "Buffalo/Baltimore, Athens/Thomas: John Barth, Don DeLillo, and the Cities of Postmodernism," *Canadian Review of American Studies* 22.2 (Fall 1991). Carmichael extends the analysis of significant space to the larger geography of the novel, which moves toward Dallas for its cataclysmic moment. Here, the city stands for the "double-coded condition" of postmodernism, serving both as an icon for "the desertification of America" and as "figural image of the scene of replenishment." 248. Carmichael's image of "double-coding" corresponds to the decline of clearly defined perceptual categories that I was discussing above.

[23] *Libra* 181/182.

[24] Thomas Carmichael, "Lee Harvey Oswald and the Postmodern Subject: History and Intertextuality in Don DeLillo's *Libra*, *The Names*, and *Mao II*," *Contemporary Literature* 34.2 (Summer 1993) 213.

[25] Carmichael, "Lee Harvey Oswald and the Postmodern Subject," 204.

[26] *Libra* 181.

[27] Gene Frumkin, "A Reader's Voice: Inside *Women and Men*," *The Review of Contemporary Fiction* 10.1 (Spring 1990) 252.

[28] *Women and Men* 579.

[29] Frumkin, "A Reader's Voice," 253.

[30] *Women and Men* 252.

[31] *Women and Men* 266.

[32] *Women and Men* 320.

[33] see Joseph Tabbi, "Pynchon's Dreams of Engineers," *Novel* (Winter 1992) 160-180.

[34] *Libra* 175.

[35] *Libra* 339.

[36] *Libra* 330.

[37] *Libra* 129-130.

[38] Harry Mathews, "*We for One: An Introduction to Joseph McElroy's* Women and Men," *The Review of Contemporary Fiction* 10.1 (Spring 1990) 199.

[39] Mathews, "We for One," 221.

[40] *Women and Men* 334.

[41] Scott Sanders, "Pynchon's Paranoid History," *Twentieth Century Literature* 21.2 (May 1975) 177-192.

[42] Women and Men 322.

[43] One of the key-positions in the discussion on postmodernism, Lyotard's argument hardly requires any further comment; for specific reference, see Jean-Francois Lyotard, *The Postmodern Condition: A Report on Knowledge* (Minneapolis: University of Minnesota Press, 1984).

III. Conclusion

In the introduction to his multi-volume inquiry into *The History of Sexuality*, Michel Foucault outlines a concept of power which seems to corroborate the dictum that opened this entire discussion on conspiracy fiction; that postmodernism is at its most paranoid when it turns the anthropological gaze inward. Typified by Clifford Geertz on the one hand and Roland Barthes on the other, the gaze of Western scientific traditions is always inextricably tied to the issue of power. For Barthes, it is the power to replace the hidden truth about the world we live in with the subject's affirmation of autonomy. This call for individual empowerment, counterbalanced by Geertz's comparably modest request for a better understanding of ourselves through the encounter with another culture, can be heard as a faint echo in Foucault's writing whenever he addresses the insidiousness and ubiquity of power.[1]

Although Foucault's model of power is based, as the title of the unfinished series of studies indicates, on an analysis of sexuality rather than the more specific social and discursive practices of conspiracy fiction, it seems to share one fundamental notion about conspiracy with all fiction discussed in the preceding pages. Sexuality, like conspiracy, is as ubiquitous as narrative itself. At first glance, both sexuality and conspiracy appear safely removed from the more "sane," "mainstream," or "normal" discursive practices revolving around the facilitation of power, such as the discourses on politics, medicine, law, economics, historiography, and so forth. When sexuality and conspiracy cross over into the arena of power it happens rather inconspicuously. Their modest claim to power is a virtue that makes them less vulnerable to conscious control and surveillance, as Freudian psychoanalysis and conspiracy theory have taught us. The question alone why we should care about fictitious conspiracies when we are confronted with historical ones which affect our lives so much more immediately is reminiscent of the aftertaste, associated with sexuality, of the pathological, the perverse, or the scandalous. Conspiracy fiction is basically gratuitous and irrelevant. These are indications that we are entering territory where, by token of taboo or marginalization, power is both more *and* less in the consciousness of those experiencing it. It insinuates itself persistently from the corner of their eyes although it never becomes fully visible.

Before I start outlining Foucault's model of power, a brief prefatory remark on his notion of historical change may be called for. As in so much of his work preceding the *History of Sexuality*, Foucault sets a crucial historical threshold at the epistemic watershed moment marked by the arrival of the Enlightenment, at some point in the course of the seventeenth century. Running through both periods before and after this moment and "despite the differences in epochs and objectives," is "a representation of power" which, according to Foucault, "has remained under the spell of monarchy."[2] In the exercise of the law, the administration of punishment, and the legitimization of violence, this conception of power is focused on a distinct origin of truth and power, "even if the latter is questioned insofar as it is personified in a collective being and no longer a sovereign individual."[3] Opposed to this monarchist, anthropomorphic model is the Machiavellian concept of power, which, to the present day, is perceived as "cynical" or scandalous. It has retained its power to provoke because it breaks away from some fundamental truth holding together the relationship between the subject and the object of power, between sovereign and subject, government and citizen, and so forth. Machiavelli, "who conceived the power of the Prince in terms of force relationships,"[4] breaks with this anthropomorphization and individualization of power, announcing a paradigm shift whose result still determines contemporary political thinking to a large extent.

Looking back upon the personified models of power from a contemporary position, a certain degree of ideological distortion is inevitable as long as their political philosophy is to remain intact. Contemporary readers of conspiracy fiction may think of themselves as advanced beyond the stage of centrist models of power, but, according to Foucault, they are still secretly caught up in their conceptual categories. With its hero worship, cult of personality, and "rugged individualism," American culture is most prone to reject the re-formulation of its anthropomorphic notions of power into those suggested by Foucault. Nothing could be more alien to the mainstream of American culture than to think of power as "force relation."

According to *The History of Sexuality*, power is continuously in process, negotiated, and contested for. It is not an imposition from the outside, but resides in its inscription into other type of relationships. Its basic nature is contractual or communicative and therefore its effects are felt not only in interdiction but also in incitement and encouragement. The intentionality animating and directing power recuperates its objective existence from pure subjectivity and structures its movements according to tactical considerations. Its heterogeneity is the source of its functional efficiency and provides simultaneously the opening for its revolutionary restructuring.

This brief outline of Foucault's model of power is highly reminiscent of the power that conspiracy fiction assigns to the agency of the conspiracy itself, rather than to the agency of the detective. Foucault's notion of power, as it permeates a particular political or cultural entity, is determined by an inescapable ubiquity, which other cultural critics like Geertz would probably object to. Geertz is convinced that no culture or its anthropological account is "so coherent as a paranoid's delusion or a swindler's story."[5] Compared to this point of view, Foucault's grasp for a conceptual totality must come across as the infusion of political totalitarianism into any system of social or political organization. Clearly Foucault is predisposed to a perception, not unlike that of Tony Tanner, that tends to identify culture with collective power and thus ultimately associates it with conspiracy. Foucault's effort at "discovering the Continent of Meaning and mapping out its bodiless landscape,"[6] as Geertz might paraphrase the ideological thrust of *The History of Sexuality*, insinuates the existence of a descriptive and conceptual totality, ready to be accessed or invaded from the outside. This act of appropriation is far from being ideologically neutral, particularly since we are all inhabiting this continent already. Sheltered from the disturbing political implications of his rhetoric by a lack of self-referentiality--after all, the anthropologist is commonly dealing with foreign cultures--Geertz is a good example of the kind of power Foucault addresses.[7] It is exactly the evasiveness (process), flexibility (heterogeneity), secrecy (inscriptiveness), and cynicism (strategy) of conspiracy that make it a suitable representation for staging the appearance of power. The detective becomes a mere supplement to power; the agent by which we would like to see power heal itself.

Although Foucault's concept of power has never managed to invade American mainstream culture on a broad base, writers of conspiracy fiction like Pynchon, Gaddis, Coover, and others, must have been listening attentively. Foucault's model, though designed with a different purpose and objective in mind, still provides an accurate description of the facilitation of power in these postmodernist writers' work. Most of all, American novelists under the influence of Pynchon seemed to have shared Foucault's somewhat sombre and pessimistic outlook regarding the individual's possibilities to understand the world and become an active participant in it. Despite the conciliatory nod toward revolutionary politics, Foucault insists that there is no escape from power. Any movement in either direction will always be caught up in its mechanisms.[8]

The trope that comes to mind, both in reading Foucault and in reading, for instance, Pynchon, is that of the grid. Permitting the unfolding of "force relations," the grid is without center or periphery. The sites it organizes are all of equal value. On a grid, it is possible to determine the relative position of one site in regard to another. Yet it becomes impossible to determine the value of both sites by reference to a center or privileged point of reference (the King, the government, the inner circle of the conspiracy, the criminal master-mind, and so on). As a non-hierarchical form of abstraction, the grid largely provides the paradigm of postmodern spatial experience.

It is in regard to the Foucaultian grid of power relations that the newly emerging paradigm of American conspiracy fiction sets itself apart from its inherited traditions. At first glance, McElroy's and DeLillo's writing seems to be concerned with the same subject as Pynchon's. But *Lookout Cartridge* opens with a scene in which the protagonist looks down upon "the city's grid;" Jack Hind in *Hind's Kidnap* is always aware of his position in the grid of the city and the surrounding landscape, and a character in *Women and Men* even plans to break out of the "gridthink of territorial plot." Similarly, characters in DeLillo's *The Names* travel across a globe so thoroughly mapped that any place is comparable to any other place while all places are basically alike. Reaching out into contemporary conspiracy fiction, one could easily extend the list; the body as an openly structured, i.e. polymorphously perverse, grid for the inscription of messages in Richard Powers' *The Gold Bug Variations*, the intricately and infinitely layered con-games in David Mamet's *House of Games*, the patterns of surveillance and the "consensual hallucination" of Gibson's cyberspace, and so forth.

Conspiracy itself has been the narrative that has aided postmodern fiction in formulating the idea of the grid. As one of Peter Hühn's authorial agents, conspiracy remains impossible to grasp because it disseminates its messages among its members in a perfect recreation of Derridean *différance*. As long as power continues to circulate, no single point on the grid can be attacked or even just approached with violent intentions. It is this strategic evasiveness that conspiracy fiction, from Kafka to Marge Piercy, has always responded to most strongly, particularly when it masqueraded as one or the other form of twentieth-century bureaucracy. Before Pynchon, the image of the grid must have carried positive connotations because it did put an end to the outmoded anthropomorphic models of power. Here was a concept that would help getting rid of the monarch. The grid is a trope of democracy, equality, conformity. For Pynchon and others like him, however, these positive connotations have quickly been reversed. Postwar American culture has demonstrated that collective and impersonal forms of political domination can be just as daunting as the centralized power of the State. The image of the grid, and with it the perception of postmodern culture as being both violent and elusive, leaves few options but to surrender to that culture's impervious power.

Unlike most fiction preceding postmodernism, Pynchon's fiction for the most part has already made the transition from the anthropomorphic model to the model of interlocking force relations. While popular fiction still elaborates on conspiracies centered around mastermind criminals, Pynchon's conspiracies have always been the equivalent of what Geoffrey Hartmann calls "whodonuts," i.e. potentially non-hierarchic collectives constructed around absent centers. The fact that, on these decentralized grids, power flows from no distinct source, in all directions simultaneously, and toward no stable site, has been the reason for Gaddis', Pynchon's, or Gibson's detective figures to cherish their marginality. To find the blind spot on the grid, to fall through the cracks in the system, to make oneself as inconspicuous as Oedipa Maas in the closing scene of *The Crying of Lot 49*, waiting silently for the mystery to reveal itself--this used to be the source of power for those who are trying to put up resistance to the collective forces around them. Marginality confers power; or, at least, it used to.

When Joseph McElroy's protagonist in *Ancient History* wishes for a "paraphase," or when figures in Don DeLillo's *Great Jones Street* try to imagine a "latent history," they are aware that they move on the same grids of power as Pynchon's Preterites or Gibson's hustlers and punks. As marginal figures, however, they know that the same grid by which Oedipa Maas' power is being disseminated and channelled away from her is also *re*-cycling power, circulating it, and eventually bringing it full circle. Every non-hierarchical conspiracy is simultaneously isolating the individual from and connecting it with the power it facilitates. Any strategy that aims to infiltrate power is therefore meaningless, since its undercover agents already inhabit the same space as the conspiracy they are trying to invade. To be inconspicuous means being overlooked by institutionalized power. But at the same time it also means being isolated from the kind of power that is emanating elsewhere and could be received and used for one's own purposes. This attitude is not identical with embracing the overwhelmingly superior concentration of power through some emulation of Pynchon's "positive paranoia." If accumulating, hoarding, or retaining power is impossible, one can at least channel and facilitate it. The technologies necessary for this participatory subversion are readily available and waiting to be used for filling in the global grid. An entire branch of the politics of subversion or infiltration, in fiction as well as in real-life politics, becomes questionable with this paradigmatic shift.

One could speculate on the historical changes that have influenced conspiracy fiction and its paradigms in this manner. DeLillo's writing, and to some degree McElroy's as well, suggest that the political strategies grounded in the 1960s have become obsolete. Most of the time DeLillo's characters seem revisit the same ideological landscape with a sense of profound nostalgia in which Pynchon's characters used to be genuinely at home. It becomes doubtful if, for example, surveillance has not yet reached a state of sheer technological perfection that makes it impossible to pursue a Pynchonesque strategy of invisibility, even as a "tourist" returning to a familiar place.[9] Pynchon imagines such scenarios in the Reagan years, yet for the 90s, in his most recent novel *Vineland*. The description, however, of the remnants of 1960s counterculture turns revealingly into an indictment of its political gullibility and co-optation, at times sliding into an almost parodistic display of stereotypes and oddities. For writers like McElroy and DeLillo, whose most significant works were written from the 1970s on, the fiction of marginality as a means of empowerment has already lost most of its appeal.

Unlike the earlier transition from anthropomorphic tropes of power to the trope of the postmodern grid, the newly emerging paradigm of contemporary American conspiracy fiction does not constitute a radical break with the tradition. There is a sense of careful consideration, re-evaluation, and constructive subversion about this shift of paradigms that makes it more difficult to discern, though no less significant in its effects. It must steer its course past the highly popular "postmodernist potboilers," such as, for example Umberto Eco's *The Name of the Rose* or Lawrence Norfolk's *Lempriére's Dictionary*; novels whose commercial success indicates that the kind of fiction that used to be on the cutting edge has become a form of popular entertainment. Each in his way, Eco and Norfolk profit from a nostalgia for grand conspiracy narratives that highbrow fiction has increasingly abandoned over the last twenty years and that occasionally surfaces in the new conspiracy fiction when one or the other marginal character reminisces about a time when plots were tight and existential despair was good for a laugh. In a way, popular fiction has pursued its goals more consistently and without the self-conscious apprehension of writers like Paul Auster or Eco. Though formulaic, the treatment that writers of horror and science fiction have given the theme of conspiracy has been a vital source of inspiration for the more academic writing, as the influence of science fiction writers like Gibson on such by-now canonical postmodernists like Kathy Acker has demonstrated. Nostalgia, however, is out of place in any of these interfaces. The "gridthink of territorial plot" would prefer to keep diverse phenomena separate and uphold the notion of a perfectly elusive power. The new conspiracy fiction, however, is reminding its readers that the dreaded postmodern lack of depth is concealed by surfaces on which the detectives move as effortlessly as the conspiracies.

Notes

[1] Michel Foucault, *The History of Sexuality: An Introduction* (New York: Random House, 1978).

[2] Foucault 88.

[3] Foucault 89.

[4] Foucault 97.

[5] Geertz 18.

[6] Geertz 20. The metaphor is even more significant in this context because it corresponds to the depiction of space in such novels as *The Names* or *Lookout Cartridge*.

[7] Not only is Geertz' rhetoric permeated by a colonialist discourse that links knowledge to conquest, but it also has sexist overtones that conceptualize the act of gaining knowledge in terms of an aggressive penetration. Whether Geertz himself realizes it or not, both subtexts are heavily charged with the issue of power.

[8] This specific reading of Foucault may overlook some and emphasize other qualities that were, in these proportions, not the author's main concern. However, the specific instances of interpretive misprision committed here (such as, for example, the systematic downplaying of revolutionary politics) are revealing because of their political and historical contexts.

[9] For examples from urban planning and development, see Mike Davis' description of surveillance, population control, and space management in *City of Quartz: Excavating the Future in Los Angeles* (New York: Random House, 1990); for a more abstract discussion of postmodern space, see Edward Soja, *Postmodern Geographies: The Reassertion of Space in Critical Social Theory* (London: Verso, 1989).

Works Consulted

Aaron, Daniel. "How to Read Don DeLillo." *Introducing Don DeLillo.* Ed. Frank Lentricchia. Durham/London: Duke University Press, 1991. 67-83.

Aldridge, John. *The American Novel and the Way We Live Now.* New York: Oxford University Press, 1983. 53-59.

Asimov, Isaac. *Foundation.* New York: Ballantine, 1951.

Barthes, Roland. *S/Z.* New York: Hill & Wang, 1974.

---. *Mythologies.* New York: The Noonday Press, 1972.

Barton Fink. Writ. Joel and Ethan Cohen. Dir. Joel Cohen. Prod. Ethan Cohen. With John Turturro, John Goodman, and Judy Davis. Twentieth Century Fox. 1991.

Baudrillard, Jean. *Simulations.* New York: Semiotext(e), 1983.

Bawer, Bruce. "Don DeLillo's America." *The New Criterion.* 3. 8 (April 1985): 34-42.

Bersani, Leo. "Pynchon, Paranoia, and Literature." *Representations* 25 (Winter 1989): 99-119.

Blaylock, James. *The Paper Grail.* New York: Ace, 1991.

Bloom, Allan. *The Closing of the American Mind: How Higher Education Has Failed Democracy and Impoverished The Souls Of Today's Students.* New York: Simon & Schuster, 1987.

Brandt, Bruce E. "Reflections of "The Paranoid Style" in the Current Suspense Novel." *Clues: A Journal of Detection* 3. 1 (Spring/Summer 1982): 62-69.

Braudy, Leo. "Providence, Paranoia, and the Novel." *Native Informant.* Baltimore: Johns Hopkins University Press, 1981. 619-637.

Brockden Brown, Charles. *Memoirs of Carwin, the Biloquist.* Orlando: Harcourt Brace Jovanovich, 1926.

Brooke-Rose, Christine. "The New Science Fiction--Joseph McElroy: *Plus.*" *A Rhetoric of the Unreal: Studies in narrative and structure, especially of he fantastic.* Cambridge/New York: Cambridge University Press, 1981: 268-288.

Bryant, Paula. "Extending the Fabulative Continuum: DeLillo, Mooney, Federman." *Extrapolations.* 30.2 (1989): 156-165.

---. "Discussing The Untellable: Don DeLillo's *The Names.*" *Critique: Studies in Modern Fiction* 29.1 (Fall 1987): 16-29.

Buckeye, Robert. "*Lookout Cartridge*: Plans, Maps, Programs, Designs, Outlines." *The Review of Contemporary Fiction* 10.1 (Spring 1990): 119-126.

Bywater, William. "The Paranoia of Postmodernism." *Philosophy and Literature* 14. 1 (April 1990): 79-84.

Cain, William. "Making Meaningful Worlds: Self and History in *Libra*." *Michigan Quarterly Review* 29. 2 (Spring 1990): 275-287.

Campbell, Gregor. "Processing *Lookout Cartridge*." *The Review of Contemporary Fiction* 10.1 (Spring 1990): 112-118.

Canetti, Elias. "Herrschaft und Paranoia: Der Fall Schreber, Erster Teil." *Masse und Macht*. Vol. 2. Regensburg: Hanser, 1960. 179-213.

Cantor, Paul A. ""Adolf, We Hardly Knew You."" *New Essays on* White Noise. Ed. Frank Lentricchia. Cambridge: Cambridge University Press, 1991. 39-62.

Caramello, Charles. *Silverless Mirrors: Book, Self, and Postmodern American Fiction*. Tallahassee: University of Florida Press, 1983.

Carmichael, Thomas. "Buffalo/Baltimore, Athens/Thomas: John Barth, Don DeLillo, and the Cities of Postmodernism." *Canadian Review of American Studies* 22.2 (Fall 1991): 241-49.

---. "Lee Harvey Oswald and the Postmodern Subject: History and Intertextuality in Don DeLillo's *Libra, The Names*, and *Mao II*." *Contemporary Literature* 34.2 (1993): 204-218.

Cawelti, John. *Adventure, Mystery, and Romance: Formula Stories as Art and Popular Culture*. Chicago: University of Chicago Press, 1976.

---, and Bruce Rosenberg. *The Spy Story*. Chicago: University of Chicago Press, 1987.

Champigny, Robert. *What Will Have Happened: A Philosophical and Technical Essay on Mystery Stories*. Bloomington: Indiana University Press, 1977.

Chatwin, Bruce. *The Songlines*. New York: Viking, 1987.

Chesterton, G.K. *The Man Who Was Thursday*. London: Dodd, Mead, & Company, 1908.

Chomsky, Noam. *The Noam Chomsky Reader*. Ed. James Peck. New York: Pantheon, 1987.

Colby, Kenneth Mark. *Artificial Paranoia: A Computer Simulation of Paranoid Processes*. New York: Pergamon Press, 1975. 12-13.

Condon, Richard. *The Manchurian Candidate*. New York: Mc Graw & Hill, 1959.

Coover, Robert. *The Public Burning*. New York: Viking, 1977.

Cowart, David. "Attenuated Postmodernism: Pynchon's *Vineland*." *Critique: Studies in Contemporary Fiction* 32.2 (Winter 1990): 67-76.

Crichton, Michael. *Rising Sun*. New York: Alfred A. Knopf, 1992.

Crowley, John. *Little Big*. New York: Bantam, 1983.

---. *Aegypt*. New York: Bantam, 1987.

Crowther, Hal. "Clinging to the Rock: A Novelist's Choices in the New
Mediocracy."*Introducing Don DeLillo*. Ed. Frank Lentricchia. Durham/London:
Duke University Press, 1991. 83-99.

Davis, David Brion, ed. *The Fear of Conspiracy*. Ithaca: Cornell University Press, 1971.

Davis, Mike. *City of Quartz: Excavating the Future in Los Angeles*. New York: Random
House, 1990.

DeCurtis, Anthony. ""An Outsider in This Society": An Interview With Don DeLillo."
Introducing Don DeLillo. Ed. Frank Lentricchia. Durham/London: Duke
University Press, 1991. 43-67.

---. "The Product: Bucky Wunderlick, Rock'n Roll and Don DeLillo's *Great Jones Street*.
"*Introducing Don DeLillo*. Ed. Frank Lentricchia. Durham/London: Duke
University Press, 1991. 131-143.

Delaney, Samuel. *Dhalgren*. New York: Bantam, 1975.

DeLillo, Don. *Americana*. Boston: Houghton Mifflin, 1971.

---. *Great Jones Street*. Boston: Houghton Mifflin, 1973.

---. *Ratner's Star*. New York: Alfred A. Knopf, 1976.

---. *Players*. New York: Alfred A. Knopf, 1977.

---. *Running Dog*. New York: Alfred A. Knopf, 1978.

---. *The Names*. New York: Alfred A. Knopf, 1982.

---. "Human Moments in World War III." *Esquire*, July 1983: 118-126.

---. *White Noise*. New York: Viking, 1985.

---. *Libra*. New York: Viking, 1988.

---. *Mao II*. New York: Viking, 1991.

Dick, Philip K. *The Man in the High Castle*. Boston: Gregg Press, 1979.

---. *A Scanner Darkly*. New York: Ballantine, 1977.

Doctorow, E.L. *Ragtime*. New York: Random House, 1975.

---. *The Book of Daniel*. New York: Random House, 1971.

Donaldson-Evans, Lance. "Conspiracy, Betrayal, and the Popularity of a Genre: Ludlum,
Forsyth, Gerard de Villiers and the Spy Novel Format." *Clues: A Journal of
Detection* 4.2 (Fall/Winter 1983): 92-114.

Eco, Umberto. *The Name of the Rose*. San Diego: Harcourt Brace Jovanovich, 1983.

---. *Foucault's Pendulum*. San Diego: Harcourt Brace Jovanovich, 1989.

The Element of Crime. Dir. Lars von Trier. With Michael Elphick and Esmond Knight.
1988.

183

Elkin, Stanley. "Joe Mc Elroy Introduction." *The Review of Contemporary Fiction* 10.1
    (Spring 1990): 7-9.
---. *The MacGuffin.* New York: Viking, 1991.
Ferraro, Thomas J. "Whole Families Shopping at Night." *New Essays on* White Noise.
    Ed. Frank Lentricchia. Cambridge: Cambridge University Press, 1991: 15-38.
Finney, Jack. *Invasion of the Body Snatchers.* New York: Dell, 1954.
Foster, Dennis. "Alphabetic Pleasures: *The Names.*" *Introducing Don DeLillo.*   Ed.
    Frank Lentricchia. Durham/London: Duke University Press, 1991: 157-175.
Foucault, Michel. *The History of Sexuality: An Introduction.* New York: Random House,
    1978.
Freedman, Carl. "Towards a Theory of Paranoia: The SF of Philip K. Dick." *Science
    Fiction Studies* 11 (1984): 15-24.
Freud, Sigmund. "Psycho-Analytic Notes on an Autobiographical Account of a Case of
    Paranoia." Vol. 12 of *The Standard Edition of the Complete Psychological Works of
    Sigmund Freud.* London: The Hogarth Press, 1958: 9-85.
---. "A Case of Paranoia Running Counter to the Psycho-Analytic Theory of the Disease."
    Vol. 14 of *The Standard Edition of the Complete Psychological Works of Sigmund
    Freud.* London: The Hogarth Press, 1958: 261-273.
Frow, John. *Marxism and Literary History.* Cambridge: Harvard University Press, 1986.
    138-147.
---. "The Last Things Before the Last: Notes on *White Noise.*" *Introducing Don DeLillo.*
    Ed. Frank Lentricchia. Durham/London: Duke University Press, 1991. 175-191.
Frumkin, Gene. "A Reader's Voice: Inside *Women and Men.*" *The Review of
    Contemporary Fiction* 10.1 (Spring 1990): 248-257.
Fulcher, James. "American Conspiracy: Formula in Popular Fiction." *Midwest Quarterly:
    A Journal of Contemporary Thought* 24.2 (Winter 1983): 152-164.
Gaddis, William. *The Recognitions.* New York: Harcourt Brace, 1955.
---. *JR.* New York: Alfred A. Knopf, 1975.
---. *Carpenter's Gothic.* New York: Viking, 1985.
Geertz, Clifford. "Thick Description: Toward an Interpretive Theory of Culture." *The
    Interpretation of Cultures: Selected Essays.* New York: Basic Books, 1973. 3-33.
Gibson, William. *Neuromancer.* New York: Ace, 1984.
---. *Count Zero.* New York: Ace, 1986.
---. *Mona Lisa Overdrive.* New York: Bantam, 1989.
---, and Bruce Sterling. *The Difference Engine.* New York: Bantam, 1991.

184

Ginzburg, Carlo. "Clues: Roots of an Evidential Paradigm." *Clues, Myths, and the Historical Method*. Baltimore: Johns Hopkins University Press, 1989. 96-126.

Goodheart, Eugene. "Some Speculations on Don DeLillo and the Cinematic Real." *Introducing Don DeLillo*. Ed. Frank Lentricchia. Durham/London: Duke University Press, 1991. 117-131.

Grace, Sherrill. "Fritz Lang and the 'Paracinematic Lives' of *Gravity's Rainbow*." *Modern Fiction Studies* 29.4 (Winter 1983): 655-670.

Graff, Gerald. *Literature Against Itself: Literary Ideas in Modern Society*. Chicago: University of Chicago Press, 1979.

Graumann, Carl, and Serge Moscovici. *Changing Conceptions of Conspiracy*. New York: Springer, 1987.

Groh, Dieter. "The Temptation of Conspiracy Theory, or: Why Do Bad Things Happen to Good People? Part I: Preliminary Draft of a Theory of Conspiracy Theories." *Changing Conceptions of Conspiracy*. Eds. Carl Graumann and Serge Moscovici. New York: Springer, 1987. 1-13.

Hall, Stephen. "Transcendental Meteorology and Umbrella Days: A Fan's Notes." *The Review of Contemporary Fiction* 10.1 (Spring 1990): 275-282.

Haraway, Donna. *Simians, Cyborgs, and Women: The Reinvention of Nature*. New York: Routledge, 1991.

Harris, Robert. *Fatherland*. New York: Harper Collins, 1992.

Hartmann. Geoffrey. "Literature High and Low: The Case of the Mystery Story." *The Fate of Reading and Other Essays*. Chicago: University of Chicago Press, 1975. 203-222.

Harvey, David. *The Condition of Postmodernity*. Oxford: Blackwell, 1989.

Hassan, Ihab. *The Right Promethean Fire: Imagination, Science, and Cultural Change*. Urbana: University of Illinois Press, 1980.

---. *The Dismemberment of Orpheus: Toward a Postmodern Literature*. New York: Oxford University Press, 1971.

Hayles, Katherine. "Postmodern Parataxis: Embodied Texts, Weightless Information." *American Literary History* 2.3 (Winter 1990): 56-72.

---. "'Who Was Saved': Families, Snitches, and Recuperation in Pynchon's *Vineland*." *Critique: Studies in Contemporary Fiction* 32. 2 (Winter 1990): 77-91.

Heinlein, Robert. *The Puppet Masters*. Garden City: Doubleday, 1951.

Heller, Joseph. *Catch 22*. New York: Dell, 1970.

---. *Something Happened*. New York: Alfred A. Knopf, 1974.

Hertzberg, Hendrik, and David C.K. Mc Clelland. "Paranoia." *Harper's Magazine* June 1974: 51-60.

Hofstadter, Richard. *The Paranoid Style in American Politics*. New York: Alfred A. Knopf, 1967. 3-40.

Hühn, Peter. "The Detective as Reader: Narrativity and Reading Concepts in Detective Fiction." *Modern Fiction Studies* 33.3 (Autumn 1987): 451-466.

Invasion of the Body Snatchers. Dir. Don Siegel. With Kevin McCarthy and Dana Wynter. Allied Artists. 1956.

---. Dir. Philip Kaufman. With Donald Sutherland, Brooke Adams, and Leonard Nimoy. United Artists. 1978.

---. Dir. and Writ. Abel Ferrara. With Meg Tilly, Forest Whittaker, and Terry Kinney. Warner Bros. 1992.

Jameson, Fredric. Rev. of *The Names* by Don DeLillo. *Minnesota Review* 22 (Spring 1984): 117.

---. *Postmodernism or The Cultural Logic of Late Capitalism*. Durham: Duke University Press, 1992.

---. *The Political Unconscious: Narrative as a Socially Symbolic Act*. Ithaca: Cornell University Press, 1981.

---. *The Geopolitical Aesthetic: Cinema and Space in the World System*. Bloomington: University of Indiana Press, 1992.

JFK. Writ. and Dir. Oliver Stone. With Kevin Costner, Tommy Lee Jones, Michael Rooker, and Donald Sutherland. Warner Brothers. 1991.

Johnson, Diane. "Terrorists As Moralists: Don DeLillo." *Terrorists and Novelists*. New York: Alfred A. Knopf, 1982. 105-110.

Johnson, George. *Architects of Fear: Conspiracy Theories and Paranoia in American Politics*. Los Angeles: J.P. Tarcher, and Boston: Houghton Mifflin, 1983.

Johnston, John. ""The Dimensionless Space Between": Narrative Immanence in Joseph McElroy's *Lookout Cartridge*." *The Review of Contemporary Fiction* 10.1 (Spring 1990): 95-111.

---. "Generic Difficulties in the Novels of Don DeLillo." *Critique* 30 (Summer 1989): 261-275.

Karl, Frederick. *American Fictions: 1940-1980*. New York: Harper & Row, 1983. 370-383.

---. "*Women and Men*: More Than A Novel." *The Review of Contemporary Fiction* 10.1 (Spring 1990): 181-198.

King, Noel. "Reading *White Noise*: Floating Remarks." *Critical Quarterly* 33.3 (Autumn 1991): 66-83.

Klinkowitz, Jerome. *Literary Disruptions: The Making of a Post-Contemporary American Fiction*. Urbana: University of Illinois Press, 1980.

Kramer, Kathryn. "Dr. Mc Elroy, Homeopath: What One Goes To Him For." *The Review of Contemporary Fiction* 10.1 (Spring 1990): 79-85.

Kucich, John. "Postmodern Politics: Don DeLillo and the Plight of the White Male Writer." *Michigan Quarterly Review* 27 (Spring 1988): 328-341.

Kuehl, John. *Alternate Worlds: A Study of Postmodern Antirealistic American Fiction*. New York: New York University Press, 1989. 193-199.

Lacan, Jacques. *Écrits: A Selection*. New York/London: Norton, 1977.

Lasch, Christopher. *Haven in a Heartless World: The Family Besieged*. New York: Basic Books, 1977.

Least-Heat Moon, William. *PrairyErth (a deep map)*. Boston: Houghton Mifflin, 1991.

LeClair, Thomas. "Joseph McElroy and the Art of Excess." *Contemporary Literature* 21.1 (Winter 1980): 15-37.

---. "Opening Up Joseph McElroy's *The Letter Left To Me*." *The Review of Contemporary Fiction* 10.1 (Spring 1990): 258-267.

---. "An Interview with Joseph McElroy." *Anything Can Happen: Interviews with Contemporary American Novelists*. Ed. Tom LeClair and Larry McCaffery. Champaign: University of Illinois Press, 1983. 235-251.

---. *In The Loop: Don DeLillo and the Systems Novel*. Urbana: University of Illinois Press, 1987.

Lefebvre, Henri. *The Production of Space*. Oxford: Blackwell, 1991.

Lentricchia, Frank, ed. *Introducing Don DeLillo*. Durham/London: Duke University Press, 1991.

---, ed. *New Essays on* White Noise. Cambridge: Cambridge University Press, 1991.

---. "Introduction." *New Essays on* White Noise. Ed. Frank Lentricchia. Cambridge: Cambridge University Press, 1991. 1-14.

---. "Tales of the Electronic Tribe." *New Essays on* White Noise. Ed. Frank Lentricchia. Cambridge: Cambridge University Press, 1991. 87-113.

---. "Don DeLillo." *Raritan: A Quarterly Review* 8.1 (Spring 1989): 1-29. A shorter version of this article was published as "The American Writer as Bad Citizen." *Introducing Don DeLillo*. Ed. Frank Lentricchia. Durham/London: Duke University Press, 1991. 1-7.

187

---. "*Libra* as Postmodern Critique." *Introducing Don DeLillo.* Ed. Frank Lentricchia. Durham/London: Duke University Press, 1991. 193-216.

Levine, Robert. "Introduction." *Conspiracy and Romance: Studies in Brockden Brown, Cooper, Hawthorne, and Melville.* Cambridge: Cambridge University Press, 1989. 1-14.

Lewis, Sinclair. *It Can't Happen Here.* New York: The Sun Dial Press, 1936.

Lovecraft, Howard Philips. *At the Mountains of Madness and Other Novels.* Sauk City: Arkham House, 1964.

Lyotard, Jean Francois. *The Postmodern Condition: A Report on Knowledge.* Minneapolis: University of Minnesota Press, 1984.

McCaffery, Larry, ed. *Storming the Reality Studio: A Casebook of Cyberpunk and Postmodern Science Fiction.* Durham & London: Duke University Press, 1991.

---. "The Desert of the Real." *Storming the Reality Studio: A Casebook of Cyberpunk and Postmodern Science Fiction.* Ed. Larry McCaffery. Durham & London: Duke University Press, 1991. 1-16.

Mc Clure, John. "Postmodern Romance: Don DeLillo and the Age of Conspiracy." *Introducing Don DeLillo.* Ed. Frank Lentricchia. Durham/London: Duke University Press, 1991. 99-115.

Mc Elroy, Joseph. "Neural Neighborhoods and Other Concrete Abstracts." *TriQuarterly* 34 (Fall 1975): 201-217.

---. "Fiction as a Field of Growth: Science at Heart, Action at a Distance." *American Book Review* 14.1 (April/May 1992): 1/30-31.

---. *A Smuggler's Bible.* New York: Harcourt & Brace, 1966.

---. *Hind's Kidnap: A Pastoral on Familiar Airs.* New York: Harper & Row, 1969.

---. *Ancient History: A Paraphase.* New York: Alfred A. Knopf, 1971.

---. *Lookout Cartridge.* New York: Alfred A. Knopf, 1974.

---. *Plus.* New York: Alfred A. Knopf, 1977.

---. *Women and Men: A Novel.* New York: Alfred A. Knopf, 1987.

---. *The Letter Left to Me.* New York: Alfred A. Knopf, 1988.

McHale, Brian. "Women and Men and Angels: On Joseph Mc Elroy's Fiction." *The Review of Contemporary Fiction* 10.1 (Spring 1990): 227-247.

---. "POSTcyberMODERNpunkISM." *Storming the Reality Studio: A Casebook of Cyberpunk and Postmodern Science Fiction.* Ed. Larry McCaffery. Durham & London: Duke University Press, 1991. 309-323.

Mackey, Lewis. "Paranoia, Pynchon, and Preterition." *Sub-stance* 30 (1981): 16-30.

Mailer, Norman. *Harlot's Ghost.* New York: Random House, 1991.

Mamet, David. *House of Games: A Screenplay*. New York: Grove Press, 1987.

---. *Homicide: A Screenplay*. New York: Grove Press, 1992.

Marquez, Antonio. "Everything is Connected: Paranoia in *Gravity's Rainbow*." *Perspectives on Contemporary Literature* 9 (1983): 92-104.

Mathews, Harry. "We For One: An Introduction to Joseph McElroy's *Women and Men*." *The Review of Contemporary Fiction* 10.1 (Spring 1990): 199-226.

Melville, Herman. "Benito Cereno." *The Piazza Tales*. New York: Dix & Edwards, 1856.

Miller, Alicia. "Power and Perception in *Plus*." *The Review of Contemporary Fiction* 10.1 (Spring 1990): 173-180.

Molesworth, Charles. "Don DeLillo's Perfect Starry Night." *Introducing Don DeLillo*. Ed. Frank Lentricchia. Durham/London: Duke University Press, 1991. 143-157.

Moore, Thomas. *The Style of Connectedness: Gravity's Rainbow and Thomas Pynchon*. Columbia: University of Missouri Press, 1987.

Morgan, Robin. *The Demon Lover: On the Sexuality of Terrorism*. New York/London: Norton, 1989.

Morris, Matthew. "Murdering Words: Language in Action in Don DeLillo's *The Names*." *Contemporary Literature* 30.1 (1989). 113-127.

Morrow, Bradford. "An Interview with Joseph McElroy." *Conjunctions* 10 (1987): 145-164.

Moscovici, Serge. "The Conspiracy Mentality." *Changing Conceptions of Conspiracy*. New York: Springer, 1978. 151-169.

Moskowitz, Bette Ann. "*The Letter Left To Me* by The Letter Left To Me." *Review of Contemporary Fiction* 10.1 (Spring 1990): 272-274.

Nadeau, Robert. "Don DeLillo." *Readings from the New Book On Nature: Physics and Metaphysics in the Modern Novel*. Amherst: University of Massachussetts Press, 1981.

Newman, Kim. *Bad Dreams*. New York: Carroll & Graf, 1991.

Norfolk, Lawrence. *Lempriére's Dictionary*. New York: Crown, 1991.

O'Brien, John, ed. *The Review of Contemporary Fiction* 10.1 (Spring 1990).

O'Donnell, Patrick. "Engendering Paranoia in Contemporary Literature." *boundary 2: An International Journal Of Literature and Culture* 19.1 (Spring 1992): 181-204.

---. "Obvious Paranoia: The Politics of Don DeLillo's *Running Dog*." *The Centennial Review* 34.1 (Winter 1990): 56-72.

Palmer, James. "In a Lonely Place: Paranoia in the Dream Factory." *Literature/Film Quarterly* 13.3 (1985): 200-207.

189

---, and Michael Riley. "America's Conspiracy Syndrome: From Capra to Pakula." *Studies in the Humanities* 8.2 (March 1981): 21-27.

Palmer, Jerry. *Thriller: Genesis and Structure of a Popular Genre*. London: Edward Arnold, 1978.

Pinsker, Sanford. "America's Conspiratorial Imagination." *The Virginia Quarterly Review* 68.4 (Autumn 1992): 605-625.

The Player. Dir. Robert Altmann. Writ. Michael Tolkin. With Tim Robbins, Lyle Lovett, and Greta Scacchi. Fine Line Features. 1992.

Polen, Dana. *Power and Paranoia: History, Narrative, and the American Cinema: 1940-50*. New York: Columbia University Press, 1986.

Porush, David. "The Imp in the Machine: Mc Elroy's *Plus*." *The Soft Machine: Cybernetic Fiction*. New York: Methuen, 1985. 172-196.

Powers, Richard. *Three Farmer On Their Way To A Dance*. New York: William Morrow & Company, 1985.

---. *Prisoner's Dilemma*. New York: William Morrow & Company, 1988.

---. *The Goldbug Variations*. New York: William Morrow & Company, 1991.

---. *Operation Wandering Soul*. New York: William Morrow & Company, 1993.

Pynchon, Thomas. *V*. Philadelphia: Lippincott, 1963.

---. *The Crying of Lot 49*. New York: Bantam, 1967.

---. *Gravity's Rainbow*. New York: Viking, 1973.

---. *Vineland*. Boston: Little, Brown, 1990.

Rabkin, Eric. *The Fantastic in Literature*. Princeton: Princeton University Press, 1976.

Reed, Ishmael. *Mumbo Jumbo*. New York: Atheneum, 1988.

Richardson, Joan. "Metaphor Master." *The Review of Contemporary Fiction* 10.1 (Spring 1990): 156-172.

Russell, Alison. "Deconstructing *The New York Trilogy*: Paul Auster's Anti-Detective Fiction." *Critique: Studies in Contemporary Fiction* 31.2 (Winter 1990): 71-84.

Sanders, Scott. "Pynchon's Paranoid History." *Twentieth Century Literature* 21.2 (May 1975): 177-193.

Said, Edward. *Orientalism*. New York: Pantheon, 1978.

Schaub, Thomas. "What is now Natural: DeLillo's Systems." *Contemporary Literature* 30.1 (1989): 128-132.

Schor, Sandra. "*The Letter Left To Me*." *Review of Contemporary Fiction* 10.1 (Spring 1990): 268-271.

Shea, Robert, and Anthony Wilson. *The Illuminatus Trilogy*. New York: Dell, 1975.

Siemion, Piotr. "Chasing the Cartridge: On Translating McElroy." *Review of Contemporary Fiction* 10.1 (Spring 1990): 133-139.

Simmons, Dan. *Children of Night.* New York: Warner, 1993.

Smith, Paul. "Paranoia." *Discerning the Subject.* Minneapolis: University of Minnesota Press, 1988. 83-99.

Sneakers. Dir. Phil Alden Robinson. Writ. Phil Alden Robinson and Lawrence Lasker. Prod. Robert Redford. With Robert Redford, Sidney Poitier, and Ben Kingsley. Universal. 1992.

Soja, Edward. *Postmodern Geographies: The Reassertion of Space in Critical Social Theory.* London: Verso, 1989.

Stonehill, Brian. "Intimations of Human Divinity in Joseph Mc Elroy's *Lookout Cartridge.*" *Review of Contemporary Fiction* 10.1 (Spring 1990): 127-132.

Swanson, David, Philip J. Bohnert, and Jackson A. Smith. *The Paranoid.* Boston: Little Brown & Company, 1970.

Tabbi, Joseph. ""The Generous Paranoia of Those Who Pursue Themselves": McElroy, Mailer, and *Ancient History.*" *Review of Contemporary Fiction* 10.1 (Spring 1990): 86-94.

---. "'Strung into the Appollonian Dream': Pynchon's Psychology of Engineers." *Novel* (Winter 1992): 160-180.

Tani, Stefano. "The Dismemberment of the Detective." *Diogenes* 120 (Winter 1982): 22-41.

Tanner, Tony. "Towards An Ultimate Topography: The Work of Joseph McElroy." *TriQuarterly* 36 (1976): 214-52.

---. *City of Words: American Fiction 1950-1970.* New York: Harper & Row, 1971.

The Thing. Dir. Howard Hawks. Writ. John Campbell. With Robert Cornthwaite and James Arness. RKO. 1951.

---. Dir. John Carpenter. With Kurt Russell and Wilford Brimley. Universal. 1982.

Valdez Moses, Michael. "Lust Removed from Nature." *New Essays on* White Noise. Ed. Frank Lentricchia. Cambridge: Cambridge University Press, 1991. 63-87.

Wagner, Bruce. *Force Majeure.* New York: Random House, 1991.

Walsh, Robert. "A Wind Rose: Mc Elroy's *Women and Men.*" *Facing Texts: Encounters Between Contemporary Writers and Critics.* Ed. Heide Ziegler. Durham: Duke University Press, 1988. 263-272.

White, Hayden. *The Content of Form: Narrative, Discourse, and Historical Representation.* Baltimore: Johns Hopkins University Press, 1987.

White Hadas, Pamela. "Green Thoughts on Being in Charge: Discovering Joseph McElroy's *Plus*." *The Review of Contemporary Fiction* 10.1 (Spring 1990): 140-155.

Wilcox, Leonard. "Baudrillard, DeLillo's *White Noise*, and the End of Heroic Narrative." *Contemporary Literature* 32.3 (1991): 346-65.

The Wild Palms. Writ. Bruce Wagner. Prod. Oliver Stone. Dir. Kathryn Bigelow, Peter Hewitt, Phil Jouanou, and Keith Gordon. With Kim Catrall, Angie Dickinson, Robert Loggia. ABC Miniseries. April 1993.

Willson, Robert. "DeLillo's *Libra*, Fiction and Pseudo-History?" *Notes on Contemporary Literature* 19.4 (September 1989): 8-9.

Woodward, Bob. *Veil: The Secret Wars of the CIA: 1981-1987*. New York: Simon & Schuster, 1987.

---, and Carl Bernstein. *All the President's Men*. New York: Simon & Schuster, 1974.

Young, James Dean. "A Don DeLillo Checklist." *Critique: Studies in Modern Fiction* 20.1 (1978): 25-26.

Zinman, Toby. "Gone fission: The Holocaustic Wit of Don DeLillo." *Modern Drama* 34 (March 1991): 74-87.

Hartmut Heuermann / Bernd-Peter Lange (eds.)

Contemporaries in Cultural Criticism

Frankfurt/M., Bern, New York, Paris, 1991. 470 pp.
ISBN 3-631-43052-3   HC. DM 98.--*

A sequel to *Classics in Cultural Criticism I* and *II*, this volume extends the synoptic view into the present and thus systematically supplements the first two volumes. The overall conception is analogous to that of the predecessors and, consistent with the general design, the book is again the fruit of a joint labor of English/American and German scholarship. The contemporary critics dealt with encompass Raymond Williams *(Tony Pinkney)*, Leslie Fiedler *(Walter Kühnel)*, E.P. Thompson *(Richard Stinshoff)*, Fredric Jameson *(Ingrid Kerkhoff)*, Daniel Bell *(Heinz Tschachler)*, Susan Sontag *(Gary Grieve-Carlson)*, James Baldwin *(Klaus Ensslen)*, Theodore Roszak *(Thomas R. West)*, Edward Said *(Günter H. Lenz)*, Christopher Lasch *(Rosita Becke)*, Stuart Hall *(Ingrid von Rosenberg)*, Kate Millett *(Blanche Linden-Ward)*, C.L.R. James *(Jens David)*, Adrienne Rich *(Elizabeth Meese)* and Neil Postman *(Peter Ludes)*. The book is prefaced by the editors and again features bibliographies of the works of all critics under discussion.

Peter Lang ≡≡≡ **Europäischer Verlag der Wissenschaften**
Frankfurt a.M. • Berlin • Bern • New York • Paris • Wien
Auslieferung: Verlag Peter Lang AG, Jupiterstr. 15, CH-3000 Bern 15
Telefon (004131) 9411122, Telefax (004131) 9411131
- Preisänderungen vorbehalten - *exklusive Umsatzsteuer